WITHDRAWN
POCKET IN BACK
by
JEFFERSON COUNTY

S0-AXP-426

CATALOGING
of
AUDIOVISUAL MATERIALS
A Manual Based on AACR 2

Nancy B. Olson

Third Edition

Edited by
Sheila S. Intner
and
Edward Swanson

MINNESOTA SCHOLARLY PRESS
DeKalb, Illinois
1992

Published by:
MINNESOTA SCHOLARLY PRESS, INC.
and Media Marketing Group
P.O. Box 611
DeKalb, Illinois 60115

Copyright © 1992 Nancy B. Olson
All rights reserved. No part of this book may be reproduced or transmitted in any form or by any means, electronic or mechanical, including photocopying, recording or by any information storage and retrieval system without written permission from the author, except for the inclusion of brief quotation in a review.

Printed in the United States of America

Excerpts from *Anglo-American Cataloguing Rules*, second edition, 1988 revision, reprinted with permission of the American Library Association.

ISBN 0-933474-48-2

This book was entirely designed and produced on an Apple Macintosh II computer. The pages were output on an Apple LaserWriter printer. Software included Aldus PageMaker and Microsoft Word. Paste-up and layout by Sharon Olson of Apple Blossom Books.

R
025.347

OLSON

111780110
TX

*This book is dedicated with love
to the memory of my parents*

Vivian Kelly Butterfield
1903-1983

Student, Teacher, Farm wife, Mother, Grandmother, Friend

Stuart E. Butterfield
1909-1988

Civil Engineer, Dairy Farmer, Mathematics Teacher
Owner of Soldier Creek Dairy Farm
(registered Guernseys)

ACKNOWLEDGEMENTS

Third Edition

I would like to thank Edward Swanson and Sheila Intner for agreeing to edit this edition of my book. Editing is a time-consuming task, with little thanks from the one whose work is being criticized. I really do appreciate their suggestions, comments, and corrections.

I also must thank my 1991 class at the University of Pittsburgh (where I teach summer school) for using the draft edition and telling me where I needed to write more, or explain better, or fix something. They convinced me that one example was completely wrong; it has now been redone according to the class discussion.

I continue to depend on family members for advice on computers, both hardware and software, and on business matters. Tim is the family computer expert while his wife, Sharon, does all the stages of book production including taking the final product to the printer. I couldn't function without them. The others, Andy and Mel, Susan and her Tim, and Steve, all give me advice on many topics, some of them related to business.

EDITORS' FOREWORD TO THE THIRD EDITION

by

Sheila S. Intner and Edward Swanson

"You've come a long way, baby," aptly describes the evolution of *Cataloging of Audiovisual Materials* from its relatively humble beginnings to this fine Third Edition, larger and better in every way than its two predecessors. Careful examination of the table of contents reveals augmented treatments for audiovisual materials published serially and in multi-part kits, and, generally, longer chapters with more examples and detailed commentaries.

It will be no surprise to readers that the audiovisual media have come a long way, too, since librarians' first encounters with films and sound recordings in the late 1930s and early 1940s. To be sure, maps and objects have been part of U.S. library collections since the 1800s and earlier, when Benjamin Franklin included scientific apparatus among the collections he accumulated for the edification and entertainment of members of his prototype public library in Philadelphia, but the idea of cataloging and processing them in the manner of books had yet to begin to flourish. *COAM 3*'s updated chronology indicates that audiovisual cataloging began to come into its own after World War II, and new developments have spiraled onward in ever faster revolutions to the present time.

Editing *COAM 3* was a great deal easier than editing its predecessor. Readability is greatly enhanced by the layout and printing, thanks to ongoing improvements to the computer hardware and software used in producing *COAM 3*. (Of course, these improvements also fuel responses in cataloging rules to accommodate the innovations, providing the impetus for new editions. Isn't it a harmonious combination of phenomena?) Original data sources are clearer, making the reasons for decisions more understandable. Even editors benefit from such progress, although the benefits for readers are first and foremost in the minds of the publisher.

COAM 3 facilitates a cataloger's ability to produce standard bibliographic records for virtually anything that appears on his or her desk, regardless of its shape or size, moving parts, and likelihood of perpetual succession. This, in itself, is a gigantic step forward, worthy of notice in the many institutions where information is collected in all of its physical manifestations and by the many librarians who wish to promote the use of all their holdings. *COAM 3* goes a long way toward helping librarians link knowledge with the people who seek it.

Sheila S. Intner
Monterey, Massachusetts

Edward Swanson
Saint Paul, Minnesota

PREFACE

Third Edition

This edition contains many new examples, including examples of computer files on CD-ROM, both monographic and serial, and examples of interactive media, both on videodisc and on CD-ROM. Many videorecordings have been added to the motion picture and videorecording chapter, reflecting the increase in that type of media in public, school, academic, and other types of libraries. A chapter on cartographic materials has been added, with assorted examples. The chapter on audiovisual serials has been expanded. All the text has been revised and expanded from the previous edition.

The text uses the rules found in the 1988 revision of the second edition of the *Anglo-American Cataloguing Rules*. All relevant Library of Congress Rule Interpretations are included or cited.

All examples carry subject headings (Sears and LC) and classification numbers (Dewey and LC).

MARC coding and tagging for OCLC input for each example is available in a separate publication, *A Cataloger's Guide to MARC Coding and Tagging for Audiovisual Material*.

I would appreciate comments, corrections, and suggestions for future editions.

Nancy B. Olson
Professor
Memorial Library
Mankato State University
Mankato, MN 56002

CONTENTS

Chapter 1

INTRODUCTION

"... wherever practicable ... "
"... if no part of the item supplies data that can be used ... "
"... exception to this ... "
"... unless one of the following applies ... "
"... prefer a chief source of information ... "
"... if there is no discernible first part ... "
"... only if this can be done without loss of essential information."
"... appearing prominently ... "
"... record the statements in the order that makes the most sense ... "
"If this criterion is not applicable ... "
"Add an explanatory word or short phrase ... "
"If it is not practicable ... "
"In case of doubt ... "

0.9. These rules recognize the necessity for judgement and interpretation by the cataloger. Such judgement and interpretation may be based on the requirements of a particular catalogue or upon the use of the items being catalogued. The need for judgement is indicated in these rules by words and phrases such as *if appropriate, important,* and *if necessary.* Such words and phrases indicate recognition of the fact that uniform legislation for all types and sizes of catalogue is neither possible nor desirable, and encourage the application of individual judgement based on specific local knowledge. This statement in no way contradicts the value of standardization. Apply such judgements consistently within a particular context and record the cataloguing agency's policy.

These and similar phrases from the second edition of the *Anglo-American Cataloguing Rules (AACR 2)* illustrate the necessity for judgment and interpretation by the cataloger when using these rules. There is no substitute for common sense, good judgment, and experience in cataloging, especially in the cataloging of audiovisual material.

Audiovisual material of all types can be cataloged using the *Anglo-American Cataloguing Rules.* This manual will discuss general principles of cataloging audiovisual material and then the details of cataloging each type of audiovisual material. An appendix includes sections on how cataloging rules are changed, audiovisual cataloging at the Library of Congress, and an annotated chronology (1901-1990) concerning audiovisual cataloging developments.

A supplementary publication explains the MARC formats and coding and tagging, and shows all the examples from this manual with MARC coding and tagging for OCLC input.

This manual is designed to be used with the *Anglo-American Cataloguing Rules,* second edition, 1988 revision; the relevant rules are referenced, and parts of the basic rules are quoted, but the complete text of the basic rules and all the additional rules themselves must be studied by the cataloger. This manual also includes rule interpretations from the Library of Congress.

This is a practical manual, not a theoretical one. I explain the way I catalog, and why I do it this way.

Material covered in this manual includes cartographic material (AACR 2 chapter 3), sound recordings (AACR 2 chapter 6), motion pictures and videorecordings (AACR 2 chapter 7), graphic material of all types (AACR 2 chapter 8), computer files (AACR 2 chapter 9), three-dimensional objects and realia (AACR 2 chapter 10), microforms (AACR 2 chapter 11), audiovisual serials (AACR 2 chapter 12), and kits.

WHY CATALOG AUDIOVISUAL MATERIAL?

Administrators and others sometimes ask why audiovisual materials should be cataloged. The report of the Carnegie Commission on Higher Education called *The Fourth Revolution* said, "... nonprint information, illustration, and instructional software components should be maintained as part of a unified informational-instructional resource that is cataloged and stored in ways that facilitate convenient retrieval as needed by students" (New York: McGraw-Hill, 1979, p. 39).

The 1986 Standards for College Libraries recommended: "The library's collections shall comprise all types of recorded information, including print materials in all formats, audiovisual materials, sound recordings, materials used with computers, graphics, and three-dimensional materials" (*College & Research Libraries News*, Mar. 1986, p. 189-200).

The 1990 Standards for Community, Junior, and Technical College Learning Resources Programs state: "The learning resources program shall make available an organized collection of materials and diversified forms of information useful in the educational process, including various forms of print and non-print media, computer software, optical storage technologies, and other formats" (*College & Research Libraries News*, Sept. 1990, p. 757-67).

From the 1987 "Guidelines for Audiovisual Services in Academic Libraries": "The goal [of the Guidelines] is to support the development and administration of an increasingly important component of college and university service" (*College & Research Libraries News*, Oct. 1987, p. 533-36). They address planning, budget, personnel, facilities, equipment and supplies, collection development, acquisition, cataloging, collection maintenance, and service of audiovisual materials.

The cataloging component states:

1. Make audiovisual materials accessible through the same retrieval mechanisms available for other library materials.
2. Catalog audiovisual materials in accordance with current national standards and practices.
3. Provide full subject access in addition to descriptive cataloging.
4. Classify audiovisual materials like other types of materials but assign location or accession designations as determined by organizational and functional considerations.

In 1970, Warren B. Hicks and Alma M. Tillin stated: "The purpose of the catalog is to enable the user to determine easily all types of materials which might be useful in a given situation" (Warren B. Hicks and Alma M. Tillin. *Developing Multi-Media Libraries*. New York: Bowker, 1970, p. 71). These same authors later wrote, "The comprehensive goal of cataloging is to assist library users and staff in the determination and the location of available resources which will best suit their specific needs and best satisfy their particular purpose" (*Managing Multimedia Libraries*. New York: Bowker, 1977, p. 166).

This is the best reason to catalog audiovisual material: assisting patrons.

From another source: "Librarians and media specialists will accept media in all formats and integrate them not only for the benefit of present users but for the even larger number of potential users as well" (Pearce S. Grove, ed. *Nonprint Media in Academic Libraries*. Chicago: American Library Association, 1975, introduction, p. x).

Mary Jane Scherdin discusses curriculum centers, which she defines as facilities including children's literature, textbooks, and curriculum guides for kindergarten through grade twelve, nonprint material and equipment for the campus, and the audiovisual production area. She emphasizes

Because of the additional time and difficulty in cataloging audiovisual and curricular materials, a strong commitment needs to be made. This support is necessary so these materials have the same accessibility as the traditional book collection ("A Marriage That Works: An Approach To Administrative Structure in Curriculum Centers." *College & Research Libraries News*, Mar. 1984, p. 145).

More justification of the decision to catalog all material is provided by Sandra Jones-Warren.

> A strong case can be made for controlling, storing and distributing media in the same institutional unit as other information sources; i.e., the library. The library, in its role as information gatherer and dispenser, is the location where common sense leads the user when seeking knowledge about a subject. As libraries and librarians have already developed systems for the retrieval and circulation of materials to the user, it is relatively easy to expand and modify these systems to include media. Abbreviated and inconsistent subject entries, with insufficient subject coverage, are too often the result when information control is managed by a non-librarian, untrained in the theories and application of information cataloging. The user is shortchanged by an inadequate and elementary system wherein all relevant resources are not readily identified. The user is also inconvenienced by having to hunt in a variety of locations for information available within the institution. Centralization of all information sources within a library is of immeasurable help to the user. It becomes possible to refer to one catalog of available materials and to locate those materials in a central spot, sometimes even side-by-side on the same shelf ("Cooperating to Provide Information." *Media Management Journal*, Fall 1982, p. 8).

In a 1981 survey of public libraries, Sheila S. Intner found that 83% of them now are providing cataloging for nonprint holdings. She believes her study clearly indicates the trend toward "recognition of the responsibility for providing bibliographic access to nonprint materials directly to the public through vehicles similar, if not identical, to those used for print." She also believes:

> Media cataloging is entering a period of great progress with *AACR 2*. The immediate benefits will accrue to public library users, who will have increased access to the rich resources now residing in nonprint media collections. Information seekers of all kinds will also benefit from broad dissemination of media information in an integrated mode, made possible by public library adoption of *AACR 2* for all holdings ("Equality of Cataloging in the Age of *AACR 2*." *American Libraries*, February 1983, p. 103).

DECISIONS TO BE MADE BEFORE CATALOGING

There are many decisions to be made by an institution before the first item of audiovisual material is cataloged. Jean Weihs explains why.

> Many catalogers have related a sad tale, which more or less follows the same story line. Their center has acquired a few items, such as a dozen filmstrips or a few rolls of microfilm. In the context of a large book collection, the cataloging of these items seems unimportant and the idea that these are but the forerunners of a large collection of nonbook materials is not considered. These items are cataloged in a nonstandard way with no attempt made to relate them to the general collection. A few more items appear and they are treated in the same manner. Over the next few years the nonbook collection grows and at one point the staff has to start recataloging it all because the materials cannot be retrieved easily by the catalog record which now exists. The moral of this tale is that you should catalog the first nonbook item with the same care you will devote to the ten thousandth and recognize the possibility that your library may become a media center ("Problems and Prospects in Nonbook Cataloging". In *The Nature and Future of the Catalog*. Phoenix, Ariz.: Oryx Press, 1979, p. 272).

Before a library begins to purchase audiovisual material, decisions should be made concerning the processing, storage, and use of the material. All staff who will be involved in the handling of the material should be involved in the decision-making process. Assume the collection is going to grow. Decisions made on the basis of a few items, without taking into consideration the growth of the collection over many years, lead to the kind of problems Weihs relates.

Intner makes an important point in her book *Access to Media* (Neal-Schuman, 1984, p. 15) when she says "Successfully managing media collections requires that the purpose of the collection and its end uses be clearly identified." Too often a collection has a small beginning and grows without formal direction or purpose.

Cost of audiovisual material

Audiovisual materials are expensive. Average prices for audiovisual material in 1990, based on an unpublished study by David A. Allan, are $512.04 for a color film, $241.07 for a video, $54.33 for a filmstrip with cassette, and $134.67 for a "kit" that contains a filmstrip, cassette, teacher's manual, worksheets, etc. Film prices varied from $225 for a 10-minute film to $975 for a 60-minute film. Video prices (not including feature films) ranged from $70 to $395 (a markdown from $500). These averages were determined by examining a number of distributor's catalogs, determining a median price for each type and length of film/video for each distributor, then averaging those median prices.

Because of their cost, few libraries can afford to have more than a limited number of audiovisual titles as compared with their holdings of books. The high cost and the relatively small number of items in most collections of audiovisual material justify special treatment through subject access so as to provide the broadest possible access to this material.

In making decisions concerning the collection, the librarian organizing the collection of audiovisual material should consider the needs of the users of the collection, the existing practices for the book collection, the budget for material and staff, and the space available.

Throughout this discussion, my general recommendation is to catalog and classify audiovisual material for a library in the same way books are treated in that library.

While the topics that follow are discussed independently, the decisions are interrelated.

Terminology

The terms "audiovisual," "nonprint," and "nonbook" are used in essentially the same way. "Audiovisual" is thought by some to be too school oriented. "Nonprint" and "nonbook" are both negative terms; they imply what the material is not, rather than what it is. "Media" is used by some to represent audiovisual material, by others to represent the entire range of materials including print. Terminology in this area has always been, and continues to be, a major problem. Sound recordings have been called *audiodiscs, phonodiscs* (and *audiodisks* and *phonodisks*), *audiotapes, phonotapes, audiocassettes, phonocassettes, phonograph records*, and *records*. Patrons are confused by the inconsistency of the terminology. Throughout this book, I use the term "audiovisual material" to refer to all material other than books. I also use the terminology of *AACR 2* in referring to the specific types of media.

For definitions of audiovisual material, see *Audiovisual Material Glossary* by Nancy B. Olson (Dublin, Ohio: OCLC Online Computer Library Center, 1988).

Questions to be asked

The following sections include questions to be asked before cataloging begins. Each question needs a decision; most decisions should involve all staff who will be working with the collection.

Use

Will the audiovisual material in the collection circulate, or will its use be restricted? Will certain classes of users be allowed to check out audiovisual materials, while other users cannot do so? Will some types of audiovisual materials circulate, while other types are restricted?

Is the collection intended as a demonstration collection, one that must remain intact at all times?

Will the material be available for interlibrary loan? If the material does circulate or go out on interlibrary loan, for what period? What restrictions, if any, apply? Will equipment be available for check out?

If audiovisual material circulates, equipment for viewing or listening should also circulate.

There will be some damage and loss in the collection whether the material circulates or is used in a supervised or semisupervised setting.

Once the administration and/or public service staff has made decisions about use, decisions can be made on shelving, packaging, and cataloging.

Shelving

Will the collection be housed in open or closed stacks, or will it be split between the two? Will the audiovisual material be intershelved with the books?

Open stacks encourage use by inviting the patron to browse. Closed stacks theoretically make it possible to control use and loss, but take much more staff time to service. In a library with closed stacks, the patron must approach the material through the catalog or through some other finding tool.

The use of closed stacks, with all filmstrips shelved together, all slides together, etc., has been proposed as a space-saving method of shelving. This may be carried to extremes, with all items removed from packages and filmstrips put into drawers with special filmstrips-sized holes, sound recordings put elsewhere, and teacher's guides filed into drawers. This method requires considerable staff time to retrieve all items for circulation and to put all away upon check-in. If the items are shelved in the packages in which they are received, no additional cost of packaging is incurred. Package sizes, even for one type of media, are not uniform. There will be as much difference in size between filmstrip containers (or between containers for any one type of media) as there is between containers of different types of media. There is no uniformity in packaging, nor in the size of material that accompanies the audiovisual component. Wide shelving is available. It will hold most materials.

Intershelving of books and audiovisual material has been tried in some school and public libraries with great success. Weihs recommends it highly, speaking of easy patron access to all materials. In *Accessible Storage of Nonbook Materials* (Phoenix, Ariz.: Oryx Press, 1984) she also writes about informal studies in which all media were intershelved and says that circulation of books, as well as that of nonbook materials, rose as patrons found related material on the same topic shelved together.

In a large library it may be more practical to house the collection, equipment, and trained audiovisual service and reference staff all in one area.

Packaging

Most audiovisual material comes in containers that can easily be marked and shelved. Packaging of all kinds and sizes is available for those materials needing to be packaged or repackaged.

Some objects are too big to shelve; a block can be put on a shelf in place of the object. The block would be labeled with the name and number of the item and directions for finding the item.

Some libraries have separated out each component of a package, putting all filmstrips together in filmstrip cabinets, sound recordings together in cabinets, slides in slide cabinets, and manuals in vertical files. This method, recommended by some in the late 1960s and early 1970s, is compact shelving carried to the extreme. It certainly makes effective use of space, but is very inconvenient and time-consuming for staff and patrons when the original components of a package have to be reassembled for use. The special storage cabinets also are extremely expensive.

Other libraries have repackaged all material in specially designed containers, sometimes printed with the name of the library. These also are expensive. Years ago some audiovisual material was received without packaging or was packaged in flimsy containers. Now most commercially produced material comes in attractive sturdy containers that have useful information printed on them. Throwing away these containers for the sake of uniformity does not make good economic sense. It also causes problems for the cataloger, who frequently needs the container information for descriptive cataloging.

Repackaging should be considered for some material. A set of filmstrips presenting all the concepts covered in a year of fourth grade social studies would be a good candidate for repackaging in a school library. No student or teacher would want the entire set at once. If this set were located in a curriculum center at a university, however, the set might be kept together, since these centers are designed to show those who are learning to teach the kinds of materials available in schools.

Cataloging

Weihs says it best: "Catalog no media, see no media, use no media." (*The Nature and Future of the Catalog*. Phoenix, Ariz.: Oryx Press, 1979, p. 285). It makes no sense to spend money on audiovisual material, then not catalog it. Administrators have been heard to say, "But nobody is using it." How can patrons use what they don't know exists?

Before *AACR 2*, there was no one set of rules for cataloging audiovisual material. Motion pictures and filmstrips and sound recordings could be cataloged using *AACR 1*, but those rules were designed for the use of large research libraries and were more detailed than necessary for school or public or smaller academic libraries. The Canadian Library Association had developed rules for use in school and small public libraries that applied to all audiovisual materials. (See Appendix C for chronology and citations.) In the United States, school librarians developed their own rules, first published by the Division of Audiovisual Instruction of the National Education Association (DAVI); later editions were published by the same group, later known as the Association for Educational Communications and Technology (AECT). State departments of education, school districts, public libraries, church library associations, and individuals published "rules" or "standards" they had developed and/or were using. There was no coordination among any of these groups and no uniformity in the rules developed.

In a survey Carol Truett found that "many school librarians feel no need for the detail found in rules such as the *Anglo-American Catalog[u]ing Code*." She also found that "[school librarians] appear to be more likely to be involved in cataloging [nonprint] materials than print materials, probably due to the fact that commercial processing for nonprint materials is less available than it is for print media ("Is Cataloging a Passe Skill in Today's Technological Society?" *Library Resources & Technical Services*, July/Sept. 1984, p. 272-73).

The following statements provide several important reasons for cataloging audiovisual material, and cataloging that material using a standard set of rules.

> To have a single standard for purposes of cooperation is better than to have several incompatible ones ... the individuals who work as specialists in the newer media—those who feel most comfortable with nonprint—have frequently been unaware of traditional means of bibliographic control because of their different training. Some have even scorned those traditional means as irrelevant, and prefer to reshape the hubcap while reinventing the wheel (Ronald Hagler, "Nonbook Materials." In *The Making of a Code*, ed. Doris Hargrett Clack. Chicago: American Library Association, 1980, p. 74-75).

> A standard bibliographic description based on consistently applied rules and developed from sound principles is the cornerstone to bibliographic networking (JoAnn V. Rogers, *Nonprint Cataloging for Multimedia Collections*. Littleton, Colo.: Libraries Unlimited, 1982, p. 9).

> The purpose of the catalog, as opposed to the shelflist, is to afford ordinary people easy access by multiple access points to the titles in the collections. The purpose of the shelflist, on the other hand, is to provide a record of item-specific information which can be accessed by its location within the collection by trained staff. The call number is, in many libraries, a unique identification mark and thereby an efficient access point as well. The shelflist is intended for specific uses, the catalog for general use (Sheila S. Intner, *Access to Media*. New York: Neal Schuman, 1984, p. 17).

> An online catalog must, if it is to meet needs defined by the user, integrate access to all resource formats in one system (Margaret M. Beckman, "Online Catalogs and Library Users." *Library Journal*, Nov. 1, 1982, p. 2046).

AACR 2 provides general rules for cataloging, as well as specific rules for most types of media. Any item can be cataloged using *AACR 2*. It is a national and international standard and should be used by everyone cataloging audiovisual material. Changes are made through an international body, the Joint Steering Committee for Revision of AACR (JSC) (see Appendix A). The rules of *AACR 2* are clear and are much easier to use than those in *AACR 1*. A concept new with *AACR 2*, levels of cataloging, allows the cataloger to put in as much, or as little, detail as is needed for the patrons of a particular library, while still cataloging within the standard.

Classification

AACR 2 covers only descriptive cataloging, that is, the bibliographic description and the choice and form of access points (main and added entries). The kind of classification scheme used and type of subject headings used are not part of this standard, but are decisions to be made at the local level.

For classification, a library may choose to use a classification number system, accession numbers, or some homemade scheme for audiovisual material.

Locally developed schemes should be avoided. Their use depends upon the person who devised the scheme; when that person is no longer available, the scheme deteriorates. Time also is needed to create and revise the scheme; that time could be better spent using an existing scheme.

Accession numbers have sometimes been recommended. Accession numbers take no training to use. Types of media can be kept together when a "media code" is combined with an accession number, for example the code "MP" for motion picture used with the accession number 243.

Media codes were originally established by the Task Force on Computerized Cataloging and Booking of Educational Media, organized in 1966 by DAVI. These codes were used by AECT in their rules for catalogers. Some of these codes, such as "FS" for filmstrip and "MP" for motion picture, were easy for the patron to decipher. As types of media and number of media codes increased, the codes became more confusing for patrons. The lack of standard terminology added to this confusion (examples: "RD" for recorded disc, "RT" for recorded tape vs. the terms audiotape, phonotape, sound recording tape).

There are problems with the use of media codes and/or accession numbers. A patron cannot browse open shelves by subject if the items are shelved by accession number or by media code and accession number. For a small collection, or a small collection handled by one librarian, accession numbers would seem to be satisfactory. But small collections grow and librarians change jobs. As one who has had to recatalog a collection of 10,000 titles that were given media codes and accession numbers rather than classification numbers (and were shelved by broad subject category!), I can attest to the difficulties caused by lack of planning in the establishing of a collection.

The two major classification systems in use in the United States are the Dewey decimal classification and the Library of Congress classification. Classify the audiovisual material by whatever scheme is used for the other materials in the library and shelve by that classification. Patrons then can browse the audiovisual collection in the same way they browse the book collection.

Subject access

Decisions concerning the type of subject heading system to be used are similar to those that must be made concerning the type of classification scheme to be used. A library must choose whether to use a standard subject heading scheme or to make up one. Locally developed schemes take time to develop and depend on the person(s) who developed the scheme.

The major lists of subject headings in the United States are *Sears List of Subject Headings* and the *Library of Congress Subject Headings*. A library should use the same subject headings for audiovisual material that it uses for books.

PRECIS indexing

At the 1971 international symposium, Subject Retrieval in the Seventies, Derek Austin described a new indexing system in his speech "The PRECIS System for Computer-Generated Indexes and Its Use in the *British National Bibliography*." The description of this system follows:

> PRECIS is a set of working procedures which combines human intellectual effort in subject analysis and indexing with the data processing power of the computer. The indexer is free to select terms and concepts found in the work being indexed. The subject statements, or strings, include a number of terms, each set in context with the others to describe precisely the content of the work. The indexer is also free to decide which terms in a string are to appear as lead terms and identifies these by a machine-readable code. Other codes, called role operators, set the terms in the string into a pattern

prescribed by a grammar resembling that of natural language. A single form of the string, with codes, is input to a machine-held file and from it the computer produces a full set of index entries with the appropriate typography and associated punctuation. "See" and "See also" references are produced in the computer-generated subject index catalogue (Brian Burnham and Audrey Taylor, principal investigators. *PRECIS Indexing: Development of a Working Model for a School Library Cataloguing/ Information Retrieval Network*. Ontario: Ontario Ministry of Education, 1982, p. 4).

The PRECIS system has been applied successfully in a number of countries, including Canada. The National Film Board of Canada in 1981 produced a PRECIS index to 16 mm films. Aurora High School, near Toronto, began a test project in 1972 using PRECIS for a collection of books and audiovisual materials. By 1981, this project had expanded to include seven schools. The project has since ended for lack of funds.

The Library of Congress studied PRECIS in 1977 with the idea of adding these terms to MARC records. The results of the study, as reported in the *Library of Congress Information Bulletin* (March 3, 1978), showed that an online retrieval system using Boolean logic on information in existing fields of the MARC record would give about the same access at less cost.

The Catalog

What kind of catalog will be prepared? Will there be cards, COM (computer output microform), or a list generated by a computer? Will the catalog be online through a bibliographic utility, a local system, or a microcomputer? These are some of the other decisions that must be made before proceeding to process the collection.

Entries for audiovisual material should appear with the entries for books, whether the catalog is a card catalog, an online catalog, or some other form. These entries should look the same, be prepared using the same rules, and contain classification numbers and subject headings established by the same schemes as the entries prepared for books.

Color codes for media cards were once recommended by some. The colors faded. Not enough distinct colors exist for the types of media that can be cataloged. There was no uniformity in card stock from one supplier to the next, nor from one batch of card stock to the next. Computer-produced cards don't come color coded. COM catalogs and computer printouts cannot be color-coded. Online catalogs could display audiovisual titles in colors, but it is better to display all types of media uniformly.

We catalog audiovisual material so patrons will have access to them through the catalog by titles, personal authors, corporate bodies, series, and subjects, and, in our online catalogs, by title term, subject term, general term, and by using Boolean logic. We also provide access by actors, producers, etc., as necessary. Patrons are likely to look in only one catalog when searching for material; therefore the catalog records for audiovisual material should be in the same place as catalog records for books. Patrons using an online catalog expect to find everything in that catalog. We must provide that access.

Processing

Once all the other decisions have been made, decisions must be made about the physical processing of the material. Will every piece in every container be labeled? What about each card in a deck of cards, each page in a loose-leaf notebook, each wooden bead in a box of 1,000 wooden beads (designed for making "sets")? If each item is labeled, those found on the floor or in the wrong containers can be put where they belong.

A workable guideline is to label everything necessary for use of the item. If loose-leaf pages have a running title that matches the item title, they can be matched up with little difficulty. If five beads of the 1,000 in a set are missing, little harm is done.

A list of package contents can be typed on the book pocket for each package and used by the circulation staff as the material is checked in and out and when inventory is taken. In an online system, book cards and pockets may no longer be used. A list of contents should be somewhere on the item, available to the circulation staff. The circulation check-in system should be programmed to alert the circulation staff when items in the package need to be matched against the list.

Placement of card and pocket, date due slip, ownership information, etc., requires a good deal of common sense. There is no one place on any type of audiovisual material where processing staff can expect to put these things. Labeling each item with the call number also requires a bit of ingenuity at times. These things will be discussed in more detail in the cataloging examples.

Theft-detection systems

Magnetic theft-detection systems can destroy some materials by erasing or partially erasing some of the magnetically coded information, although some newer systems use weaker magnetic fields that are not supposed to harm magnetic coding. Do not allow sound recording cassettes, videocassettes, computer software, or any package containing such material to go through such systems. Label these packages with a warning against demagnetization and train all circulation staff to spot the labels.

Selection

There are several books and many articles available on selection of audiovisual material.

A few warnings concerning selection should be included at this point. Watch out for old material that has been packaged in a new container. The box might be attractive and carry a recent copyright date, but the dates on the material inside might be old. For some subject matter this is not important. For material on rapidly changing topics, such as the United States role in space, or showing what girls can be and what boys can be when they grow up, anything more than a few years old should be evaluated. If there are no dates on the material, one can tell approximate age by the clothing and hair styles shown and by such background details as make and model of automobiles.

Some producers repackage material under different titles. In some cases they simply have glued a strip with the new title over the old title on guides. In other cases they have reprinted guides and created new packaging but have not changed title frames of filmstrips. The original material might well be excellent, but it isn't needed under two titles. If the original title is now part of a series, it still should carry the same original title or have some reference to that title in ads and on the package.

Producers also issue the same content in a different format. It is useful to have the same material available commercially as filmstrip and slide. Making motion pictures available in several formats, as well as in several sizes and formats of videorecordings, is a service; frequently users prefer one format to the other, or have equipment for only one format. But converting a set of slides to videocassette has questionable value. Faculty have ordered these videorecordings from ads that exclaim about the wonderful new titles. They might have preferred the slides if they had known that format was also available.

Weeding

Weeding of a collection should be done before any cataloging begins, and it should be performed periodically. Unfortunately, audiovisual material deteriorates even when kept under controlled conditions. Heat, humidity, and dust are major factors in the deterioration of film and of magnetic materials. Film (motion pictures, film loops, film strips, slides, and transparencies) becomes brittle and the colors deteriorate to orange or purple, depending upon the type of film used originally. Magnetic media with a film base (videotape, sound recordings on tape, computer tape, disks) have the film problem of brittleness, coupled with the possibility of the magnetic coating powdering off the film.

Film materials with sprocket holes suffer from wear. Sprocket holes are torn loose, and film surfaces are scratched when used in poorly maintained equipment, or by poorly trained operators. Film and filmstrips are torn, and content is lost when spliced.

Slide mounts become warped and the corners may swell in humid areas, causing the slides to jam in projection equipment.

Sound discs become scratched. Sound discs warp when hot. Dust in the grooves ruins both the playback equipment and the discs.

Periodic inspection during inventory will reveal deterioration. Then one must make the decision to repair, replace, or discard.

Other factors also lead to weeding.

Even though the content of an item may still be current and/or important, when the people seen in a film are wearing outdated clothes and hair styles, and the setting reveals period automobiles, students watching the material will tend to concentrate on the cars and clothes rather than on the content.

The content of the item may no longer be valid or may conflict with current knowledge. It may even give dangerously wrong information. The educational need for the item may be past — the course may no longer be taught; the professor may have retired; the demand for the topic may no longer be high.

The technology may be outmoded. Film loops were an important type of media in the 1960s. We had several self-paced classes using film loops during the 1970s. Eventually we could no longer replace the worn-out film loops, nor could we keep the projectors functioning.

Parts of an item may have been lost, damaged, or stolen. Can they be replaced? Can the rest of the item be used without the missing parts? Is the remaining portion worth keeping?

All these are factors to be considered when evaluating whether or not an item should be added to a collection, and when considering the retention of an item in the collection.

New types of media

We can catalog almost anything following rules given in *AACR 2* chapter 1.

In recent years I have been asked how to catalog holograms, a collection of historical medical instruments, and "parts of people" (a medical library asked this; they wondered about making an added entry for the person from whom the part had been removed).

One kind of disc is an "aroma disc" which plays on a special machine. These, however, are used up when played.

One kind of videocassette contains music but no picture. The physical item is a video, but the content is pure music.

Compact discs may contain music, computer files, or any combination of sound, video, pictures, text, maps, and computer files. These discs are available, or have been announced, in 2½, 3½, 4¾, 8, and 12-inch sizes.

INTERACTIVE MEDIA

Laser technology makes it possible for compact discs or videodiscs to contain copies of motion pictures, still pictures, music, maps, text, spoken material, and computer files. Computer technology allows this material to be indexed, accessed in any order, and played back, displayed, copied, edited, and/or printed out as desired. The interaction of a user with the contents of a disc, using a computer or computer technology, is referred to as "interactivity," and the material as "interactive media" or "interactive video." Programming codes are not standardized within the industry, requiring different codes for different players. Some titles come with their own players, with the entire package being a self-contained hand-held device.

Videodisc producers have devised a system of guidelines that defines five levels of interactivity.

Level-O discs are the equivalent of pre-recorded videocassettes. There is no interaction with the contents.

Level-I discs may be searched by chapters (sections of the disc) or by individual frame. The producer of the disc can program it to stop at selected points during playback. See example 35B, *Singin' in the Rain* (CLV).

Level-II discs require microprocessor-equipped players. Discs may be pre-programmed by the producer, or may be programmed by the user who is "interacting" with the material on the disc. Programming may include continuous loops, or timed loops, of some of the program material. See example 35C, *Singin' in the Rain* (CAV).

Level-III discs require an external computer that becomes a programmable controller for the videodisc or compact disc player. The discs contain no pre-programmed codes; all is done in an interactive fashion. There are many systems available now to take advantage of this technology. See example 67, *Beethoven's Symphony no. 9*.

Level-IV discs contain computer files in addition to the audiovisual information. This level, only recently added, is being developed.

Terminology

Interactive systems are also referred to in the current literature as hypermedia, multimedia, or full motion media. There is no standard terminology at present.

Background

There are two types of laser videodiscs, CLV (constant linear velocity) and CAV (constant angular velocity). Both use analog signals, not digital. Development of digital interactive systems is underway by Philips, using the standard compact disc format.

CLV discs allow 60 minutes of playing time per side, but while some can be searched by individual frame, the image displayed is not as high quality as that displayed by a CAV disc. The CLV discs are not suitable for interactive purposes.

CAV discs contain up to 54,000 frames per side, or 30 minutes of playing time. Each frame uses one track, and the player can be programmed to select one frame for display as a still image for any length of time. These are the videodiscs used in current interactive systems.

An earlier type of videodisc (CED) used a stylus for playback rather than a laser. This type is no longer produced.

Examples

Lions of the African Night, a 60-minute film by the National Geographic Society, is an example of a level-O videodisc. It is played continuously.

The National Gallery of Art has produced a videodisc including a 22-minute segment on the history of the National Gallery, a 27-minute tour of the gallery, and 3353 frames that show 1645 items in the collection, each with a frame containing information about the artist and the work. This level-I disc uses random access, slow motion, freeze frames, and chapter-search as interactive features. A computer program, available recently from Voyager, is designed to be used with this videodisc to provide interactive features.

An example of a level-III package is *The '88 Vote*, produced by ABC News Interactive, and distributed by Optical Data Corp. It includes a two-sided videodisc, a HyperCard stack (for use on a Macintosh computer), printed curriculum guides, and support material. The video includes footage from the 1988 presidential campaign including portions of debates and press conferences. One audio channel contains the live sound, the other commentary by an ABC correspondent. Text is displayed on the computer screen through HyperCard. Users can create their own documentaries from this product. Other titles from ABC News include *In the Holy Land* and *The Great Quake of '89*.

Interactive systems have been designed for the IBM PC or PS/2, the Commodore Amiga, and the Apple Macintosh and the Apple IIGS.

Cataloging

Levels O, I, and II are cataloged as videorecordings. The purchaser receives a videodisc and perhaps some written material. The only hardware needed is the videodisc player with monitor, cables, etc. The level II disc needs a special player. Sony and Pioneer discs are not interchangeable.

The levels III and IV discs usually come with computer files on their own carriers and need a computer connected to the videodisc player, unless they come with a special player or device. The computer files include data as well as programs. There will be discussion about the cataloging of these levels at the national and international level during the next few years.

Cataloging in the future

Joyce made an interesting observation:

> The recent nature of [technological] change has confused the relation between information and the medium in which it is carried. Whether an artifact is a book, microfilm, handwritten or typed document, or newer technological product, it is distinguished from the information it contains. For example, a videodisc can carry both graphic images, text, and music. As one medium develops the capacity to carry different kinds of information, such as the case of machine-readable records, there is increasing emphasis on cataloging the information, not necessarily the medium carrying it (William L. Joyce. "Rare books, Manuscripts, and Other Special Collections Materials, Integration or Separation?" *College & Research Libraries*, Nov. 1984, p. 444).

The dividing line between types of media is becoming less distinct as new media are developed and as new uses are found for older forms of media.

CIP for AV

Cataloging-in-Publication (CIP) copy has been provided for books for more than twenty years through a cooperative program between book publishers and the Library of Congress. The Library does preliminary cataloging from copies of title pages and "front matter" provided by the publishers; the publishers then print a copy of this preliminary cataloging on the verso of the title page of the book as it is published.

A survey found that many users want the CIP program expanded to include coverage of audiovisual material. An experimental program was announced in fall 1984 to provide CIP for computer files. This is the first use of CIP for material not in book form.

Chapter 2

CATALOGING AUDIOVISUAL MATERIAL

"Cataloging should be fun. And challenging. And useful."

Sanford Berman. *The Joy of Cataloging*
(Phoenix, Ariz.: Oryx Press, 1981, p. xi).

This chapter will explain the general rules for cataloging that apply to all types of media. Specific rules for individual types of media will be explained in the chapters that follow.

Cataloging under *AACR 2* begins with preparation of the bibliographic description, and then proceeds to the choice of access points. No thought is given to those entries until the description is finished. The process is best explained by Michael Gorman:

> One of the fundamental concepts of *AACR 2* is that the cataloging process is viewed as one in which the cataloger establishes a standard description of the physical object (the book, videorecording, map, etc.), using clues derived from that physical object, and then establishes the access points (headings and uniform titles), which not only provide access to the standard description but relate that description to the work of which it is a manifestation. The descriptive process is concerned with the object in hand ... This formula for all international descriptive cataloging was a direct result of the policy decision that was made for *AACR 2*: all library materials would receive equal and consistent treatment in its descriptive rules ("*AACR 2*, Main Themes." Doris Hargrett Clack, ed. *The Making of a Code*. Chicago: American Library Association, 1980, p. 42).

Most inconsistencies between chapters in the 1978 edition of *AACR 2* have been resolved in the 1988 revision. With few exceptions, the chapters are uniform.

Rule interpretations are prepared by the Library of Congress for the guidance of its own catalogers. These useful interpretations are printed in the quarterly *Cataloging Service Bulletin* (*CSB*) for our information. Most libraries choose to follow the Library of Congress in these interpretations.

Materials Needed for Cataloging

- *Anglo-American Cataloguing Rules,* second edition, 1988 revision. (Chicago, Ill.: American Library Association, 1988).

   Chapter 1 contains the general rules used for descriptive cataloging of all material; chapters 2-12 are for specific types of material, chapter 13 for analytics, chapter 21 for choice of main and added entries, chapters 22-25 for form of personal name, geographic name, corporate name, and uniform title headings, and chapter 26 for references.

- *Cataloging Service Bulletin.* (Washington, D.C.: Library of Congress, Collections Services, 1979-).

   This quarterly bulletin is the earliest source of the rule interpretations that are prepared by the Library of Congress. Cumulated rule interpretations are available from the Library of Congress and from Oberlin College, Ohio.

• *Cataloging Service Bulletin Index.* (Lake Crystal, Minn.: Soldier Creek Press, 1979-).

  This is an annual cumulative index to LC's bulletin.

• Online Audiovisual Catalogers. *Newsletter.* (Tucson, Ariz., 1981-).

  This quarterly publication of Online Audiovisual Catalogers is available only through membership. While designed for those cataloging online through one of the bibliographic utilities, the *Newsletter* contains as much material on cataloging as on coding and tagging bibliographic records.

  Other books and manuals that apply to specific materials are listed at the beginning each of the following chapters.

Areas of the Bibliographic Record

The bibliographic description is divided into eight areas as follows:

    Area 1. Title and statement of responsibility area
    Area 2. Edition area
    Area 3. Material (or type of publication) specific details area (chapters 3, 5, 9, and 12 only)
    Area 4. Publication, distribution, etc., area
    Area 5. Physical description area
    Area 6. Series area
    Area 7. Notes area
    Area 8. Standard number and terms of availability area

Most areas are subdivided into elements.

In chapters 1-12 the rule numbers for the chapter begin with the chapter number and a period. Following the period is the area number, followed by an alphanumeric subdivision. Rule numbers containing ".7" are always rules for notes, just as "area 5" or rules containing ".5" always refer to the physical description area regardless of the chapter or type of material involved.

Punctuation of the Bibliographic Record

Areas 2-8 are preceded by a period-space-dash-space (. —) unless the area begins a new paragraph. When typed, this appears as period-space-hyphen-hyphen-space.

> **LCRI 1.0C.** For the ending of either the paragraph that precedes the physical description area or the paragraph that precedes the first note of the note area use a period unless a closing parenthesis or bracket is present. In the latter case, let the parenthesis or bracket be the ending punctuation without period following. As an exception, also of long-standing practice, if the publication distribution, etc., area ends in an "open" date, so that the last mark is a hyphen or some blank space (designated, for monographs, by angle brackets) for an entirely missing date, do not add the period.
>
> Ending punctuation refers to one of the following when it is the very last mark: period, question mark, exclamation point, closing parenthesis or bracket, and double quotation mark.
>
> For punctuation at the endings of notes, see LCRI 1.7A1. (*CSB* 50)

> **LCRI 1.7A1.** Start a new paragraph for each note; end each paragraph with a period or other mark of punctuation. If the mark of final punctuation is a closing bracket or parenthesis, however, add a period. (*CSB* 44)

LC follows the practice stated here. Note that the examples in this text , as a matter of style, do not show ending periods for notes. Note also that closing brackets or parentheses are followed by as period in a note, but *not* elsewhere. Punctuation also is prescribed within each area to separate elements within that area. Note the punctuation that accompanies the area or element is that *preceding* the area or element.

Levels of Detail in the Description

A new concept is presented in *AACR 2*, that of levels of detail. This feature enables libraries that want brief records or brief cataloging to follow the standards but include only the minimum information prescribed for first level cataloging as specified in rule l.0Dl. Those libraries wanting all possible information would use the third level as given in rule l.0D3. Most libraries probably would prepare bibliographic records with some intermediate amount of detail as permitted in rule 1.0D2.

While level one is a minimum, and level two is also given as a minimum, many libraries might want to catalog somewhere between levels one and two or between levels two and three. This is permitted (unless one is part of a cooperative project in which all are required to maintain at least level two cataloging). Levels one and three might be viewed as the two ends of a continuum with permissible descriptive cataloging falling somewhere between those two ends.

Users of audiovisual material have some special needs that must be met by catalogers.

> The same general principles that guide the degree of descriptive cataloging determined for books apply to the cataloging of nonbook materials. However, because of the physical format of these materials and the variety of storage facilities, it may be difficult to examine them. Therefore, the description on the card should be precise and definite, and full enough to inform the searcher that this may be the material he desires. Conversely, the description should not be so complete and lengthy as to be confusing (Warren B. Hicks and Alma M. Tillin. *Developing Multi-Media Libraries*. New York: Bowker, 1970, p. 71).

> The nature of most nonbook materials makes immediate access and inspection difficult, so the description provided should be sufficiently complete to identify the work, to distinguish it from all other versions of the same work, and to guide the user in the selection of any equipment which may be necessary to utilize the material (Alma M. Tillin and William J. Quinley. *Standards for Cataloging Nonprint Materials*. Washington, D.C.: Association for Educational Communications and Technology, 1976, p. 19).

In the following examples of the three levels, note the difference in the amount of information included. These bibliographic records are for three similar kits produced by the Minnesota Historical Society. It would be possible to prepare more notes to add to the level three record. These examples are presented without added entries to save space here. The main entry in each case would be title. A later section of this chapter discusses choice of main and added entries. These examples also show cataloging of kits, which is mentioned in *AACR 2* only in rule 1.10. The three ways of handling the physical description area for kits are shown in these examples. For each level, the areas required are named first, then the example showing the use of that level is given. There is no standard for the form in which information is presented. If the descriptive cataloging is prepared on cards, there is no *AACR 2* requirement as to indentions or lines left blank on the catalog card. Note the capitalization, punctuation, and spacing shown in these examples. This is capitalization, punctuation, and spacing as prescribed in *AACR 2*.

Examples throughout this text are in Courier type because it shows spacing exactly as it should be. The body of the text uses a proportional type face and spacing.

Level one

> Title proper / first statement of responsibility if different from main entry heading in form or number or if there is no main entry heading. — Edition statement. — Material (or type of publication) specific details (if applicable). — First publisher, etc., date of publication, etc. — Extent of item. — Note(s). — Standard number.

Level one example (using 1.10C2c)

```
     The Immigrant experience / produced by the Education
Division, Minnesota Historical Society. -- The Society,
c1979.
          various pieces.
     A Minnesota history resource unit including narrated
filmstrips, posters, and reproductions of original materi-
als.
```

Level two

> Title proper [general material designation] = parallel title : other title information / first statement of responsibility ; each subsequent statement of responsibility. — Edition statement / first statement of responsibility relating to the edition. — Material (or type of publication) specific details (if applicable). — First place of publication, etc. : first publisher, etc., date of publication, etc. — Extent of item : other physical details ; dimensions. — (Title proper of series / statement of responsibility relating to series, ISSN of series ; numbering within the series. Title of subseries, ISSN of subseries ; numbering within subseries). — Note(s). — Standard number.

Level two example (using 1.10C2a)

```
The Ojibwe [kit] : a history resource unit / produced by the
     Ojibwe Curriculum Committee in cooperation with the
     American Indian Studies Department, University of Minne-
     sota, and the Educational Services Division, Minnesota
     Historical Society. -- St. Paul, Minn. : The Society,
     c1973.
          8 filmstrips, 4 sound discs, 18 charts and posters, 34
     identical elementary booklets, 1 secondary booklet, 1
     teacher's guide ; in container 34 x 34 x 34 cm.
          Issued also with 34 identical copies of secondary
     booklet and 1 copy of elementary booklet.
          Filmstrip titles: Life through the seasons -- Legends
     and songs of the people -- To be one of the people --
     Adawagan, fur trade : a meeting of the Ojibwe and the
     White Man -- The story of a treaty : 1837 -- The battle
     at Sugar Point -- The melting pot myth -- The Anishinabe
     : 1930-1970.
```

Level three

For this level, all elements from the rules that are applicable to the item being described are included.

Level three example (using 1.10C2b)

```
Minnesota politics and government [kit] : a history resource
   unit / produced by the Educational Services Division,
   Minnesota Historical Society. -- St. Paul, Minn. : The
   Society, c1976.
      8 filmstrips : col. ; 35 mm.
      5 sound discs : analog, 33 1/3 rpm ; 12 in.
      1 game (player's manual, cards) ; in portfolio 28 x 14
cm.
      8 reproductions : b&w ; 15 x 28-64 x 46 cm.
      17 cartoons : b&w ; 28 x 22 cm.
      9 biography banners : col. ; 56 x 22 cm.
      4 issue cards : b&w ; 28 x 22 cm.
      1 student guide, intermediate (30 p.) : ill. ; 28 cm.
      35 identical student guides, secondary (64 p.) : ill.
; 28 cm.
      1 teacher's guide (32 p.) ; 28 cm.
      In container 34 x 34 x 34 cm.
      Issued also with 35 identical intermediate student
guides and 1 secondary student guide.
      Filmstrips: The beginnings of a state, 1660-1865 (83
fr.) -- The years of Republican control and the Populist
revolt, 1865-1895 (92 fr.) -- Progressives, patriots, and
ethnic loyalties, 1892-1918 (104 fr.) -- Minnesota's
third-party experiment, 1919-1938 (76 fr.) -- Minnesotans
in state and national politics, 1945-1972 (64 fr.) -- The
voters, who are they? (93 fr.) -- Making changes (88 fr.)
-- Government response to people's needs (82 fr.).
      Intermediate student guide title: People serving
people.
      Secondary student guide title: Minnesota, political
maverick.
      Four sound discs narrate filmstrips.
      Title of remaining sound disc: Voices of Minnesota
politicians. Includes voices of Floyd B. Olson, Harold E.
Stassen, Luther Youngdahl, Orville L. Freeman, Elmer L.
Andersen, Walter Judd, Eugenie M. Anderson, Hubert H.
Humphrey, Eugene McCarthy.
      Biography banners: Cushman K. Davis, Magnus Johnson,
John Lind, Anna Dickie Olesen, Victor Leon Power, Jane
Grey Swisshelm, Clara Hamson Ueland, Andrew John
Volstead, J. Frank Wheaton.
      Reproductions from Winona times (May 15, 1858), Minne-
apolis journal (Sept. 14, 1917), Minneapolis tribune
(Nov. 5, 1930; July 15, 1948; Mar. 20, 1963), St. Paul
pioneer press (Nov. 9, 1938).
```

Unpublished Material

   Treat an unpublished audiovisual item of any type in the same way one would a manuscript or unpublished thesis. Include the date as the only item in the publication, distribution, etc., area.

   The OnLine Audiovisual Catalogers are preparing a manual on the cataloging of unpublished material.

What is it?

The first, and frequently most difficult, decision in the cataloging of audiovisual material is to decide what the item is.

The chapters of *AACR 2* are: (those with * are discussed in this manual):

1.* General rules for description
2. Books, pamphlets, and printed sheets
3.* Cartographic materials
4. Manuscripts
5. Music
6.* Sound recordings
7.* Motion pictures and videorecordings
8.* Graphic materials
9.* Computer files
10.* Three-dimensional artefacts and realia
11.* Microforms
12.* Serials
13.* Analysis
21.* Choice of access points
22. Headings for persons
23. Geographic names
24. Headings for corporate bodies
25. Uniform titles
26. References

Chapters 2-11 of part I of *AACR 2* cover specific kinds of media. We first must decide what an item is to know which chapter to use for cataloging that item. Some things are no problem. A filmstrip is described using chapter 8. A set of slides also is described using chapter 8. A videodisc is cataloged by the rules in chapter 7. A recorded lecture is cataloged by the rules in chapter 6. But what about activity cards; transparencies and teacher's guide and exercise sheets bound together as a book with perforated pages; a box of materials for a semester unit on social studies (teacher's guide, classroom set of student manuals, test booklets, answer key, progress chart, posters, activity cards, etc.); a filmstrip with a sound cassette containing narration for the filmstrip; a set of four filmstrips with two sound discs containing the narration; a set of four filmstrips with two sound discs containing the narration and a third sound disc with other material; a microfiche that is all reproductions of art work? Is a book with a sound cassette of someone reading the book cataloged as a book with accompanying sound, or as a sound recording with accompanying text, or is it two separate items? What do we do with sets of duplicating masters, or spirit masters, or reproduction masters? What about a set of playing cards; a set of flannel-backed shapes for use with a flannel board; a calendar? What do we do with manipulative aids?

These are some of the problems. One must carefully study the introductory section of each chapter of *AACR 2*. This introductory section explains the scope of the chapter and lists the materials to be cataloged using that chapter.

We should look at the item as a whole rather than concentrate on one aspect of it. If one has a replica of a cylinder seal impression, the replica then mounted on plastic, one could be confused by reasoning that an impression of a cylinder seal is a manuscript, a reproduction of a manuscript is a book, etc. When we look at the item as a whole, we see it is a model to exact scale of the cylinder seal impression.

When cataloging an item that does not fit neatly into one chapter of *AACR 2*, decide by elimination which chapter to use. In other words, eliminate all chapters that obviously do not relate to the item and see which chapter is left.

Dominant Medium

When there are two or more kinds of media in the package, one must first decide if one type is dominant. A filmstrip with recorded narration would be cataloged as a filmstrip with accompanying sound. The filmstrip would be considered to be the dominant medium. The addition of a teacher's guide does not change the decision.

This does not mean, however, that every filmstrip-cassette or filmstrip-disc package has the filmstrip as the dominant medium. There are sets in which the filmstrip (or slides) illustrate the discussion of music that is contained on the sound recording. In these cases the sound recording is the dominant medium, and the film material is treated as accompanying material.

There are also sets in which the filmstrip is to be viewed separately and the sound is related, but is not narration, nor is it to be used simultaneously with the filmstrip. In this case, the package that has two or more items of media, none of which is dominant, is treated as a kit.

We cannot make rules such as "a filmstrip with a sound cassette is always cataloged by rules of chapter 8." Each package must be examined individually. In the set *Music 300, An Introduction to Form in Music*, 60 slides "present immediate visual association with the [musical] forms illustrated on the recordings." In this set the sound recording is the dominant medium, and the visual material is the accompanying material.

When no one part is dominant, the set may be called a kit. Kits are cataloged according to rule 1.10 and are defined in rules 1.10A-1.10C and in a footnote on page 20 of *AACR 2*. Their cataloging is discussed in chapter 11 in this manual.

Sources of Information

Chief source of information

Each chapter in part I of *AACR 2* specifies the chief source of information for the type of material covered by that chapter. We are directed to "prefer information found in that chief source to information found elsewhere."

> **LCRI 1.0A.** When more than one title proper appears in the item, choose as the title proper the title that appears in the chief source specified in the particular rule for chief source in the appropriate chapter. (*CSB* 11)
> **1.0H1a.** In cataloguing an item comprising different works and with no chief source of information pertaining to the whole item, treat the chief sources of information as if they were a single source ....

Prescribed sources of information

A table in each chapter of *AACR 2* specifies the prescribed sources of information for each area of the bibliographic description.

Title and Statement of Responsibility Area

The title and statement of responsibility area is composed of the following elements:
  title proper
  general material designation
  parallel title
  other title information
  statement of responsibility.

Title proper

> **1.1B1.** Transcribe the title proper exactly as to wording, order, and spelling, but not necessarily as to punctuation and capitalization ....
> **1.1B7.** ... If no title can be found in any source, devise a brief descriptive title ... enclose [it] in square brackets.

A title supplied by the cataloger is always given in square brackets, and a note is made stating that the title is supplied by the cataloger.

Titles always have been a problem with audiovisual material. There may be several forms of a title on an item, or even completely different titles on the same item. By first specifying a chief source of information for each type of material, the designers of *AACR 2* helped ensure the uniformity of bibliographic records. When we catalog a sound disc, for example, we are told the chief source of information is the disc label(s). We take the title proper from those label(s). If the sound disc has one title on the label, a different title on the front of the sleeve, another title on the spine, and yet another on the back of the sleeve, we no longer are confused. We use the label information for the title proper, and make notes of all the other titles. We make access points for all the variant titles if the differences are significant, and thus the patron can find the bibliographic record for the sound disc by whatever title happens to be remembered.

There still will be problems when one cataloger has an incomplete package and does not know it is incomplete; the chief source might be missing, leading to differences in the bibliographic description. There also will be problems when a machine is required to view the chief source of information and the cataloger does not have access to such a machine.

Information preceding the title

Another title problem has been encountered with increasing frequency. This is the problem of information appearing before the "real" title.

Examples: Godfrey the Safety Gopher presents the 1983 Minnesota Department of Public
        Safety Film Library, starring films on ... (from the cover of their film catalog);
    Walt Disney Productions present Escape to Witch Mountain (from the title
        frames of a motion picture);
    Xerox Films presents Multiplication Rock (from the container of a set of
        filmstrips with sound);
    Fred Flintstone presents All-time favorite children's stories and songs (from the
        label of sound disc);
    Mattel Electronics presents Blackjack & poker (from the title frame of a video
        game);
    Selznick International, in association with Metro-Goldwyn-Mayer, has the honor
        to present its Technicolor production of Margaret Mitchell's story of the Old
        South, Gone with the wind (from the title frames of a videorecording)

More examples:
    Richard Burton as Winston Churchill in The Gathering Storm (from the opening
        frames of television production);
    Ed Asner as Lou Grant (opening of TV series);
    Mary Martin in The sound of music (sound disc label);
    Peter Sellers is Inspector Jacques Clouseau in The return of the Pink Panther
        (from title frames of motion picture);
    George Minter presents Alastair Sim as Scrooge in Charles Dickens' A Christ-
        mas carol (title frames of videorecording)

More examples:
    Neil Simon's California suite (title frames of motion picture);
    Reader's digest Popular songs that will live forever (title page of song book);
    All the words to all the songs in Reader's digest Popular songs that will live
        forever songbook (title page of separately published book of words for the
        songs).

And more examples:
    Alexander H. Cohen // proudly presents // Angela Lansbury // Dear world
        (sound disc label, lines marked);
    Columbia Pictures and Rastar Pictures present // Barbra Streisand // James Caan
        // A Ray Stark Production of a Herbert Ross Film // Funny lady (title frames
        of motion picture);

> The Theatre Guild presents Oklahoma! a musical play based on the play Green grow the lilacs by Lynn Riggs (score).

Relevant rules:

> **1.1A2.** ... Transcribe the data as found, however, if case endings are affected, if the grammatical construction of the data would be disturbed, or if one element is inseparably linked to another.
>
> **1.1B1.** Transcribe the title proper exactly as to wording, order, and spelling ....
>
> **1.1B2.** If the title proper includes a statement of responsibility or the name of a publisher, distributor, etc., and the statement or name is an integral part of the title proper (i.e., connected by a case ending or other grammatical construction), transcribe it as part of the title proper.
>
> **1.1E1.** Transcribe all other title information appearing in the chief source of information ....
>
> **1.1E2.** Transcribe other title information in the order indicated by the sequence on, or the layout of, the chief source of information.
>
> **1.1F1.** Transcribe statements of responsibility appearing prominently in the item in the form in which they appear there ....
>
> **1.1F3.** If a statement of responsibility precedes the title proper in the chief source of information, transpose it to its required position unless it is an integral part of the title proper.

A special rule interpretation has been written for motion pictures and videorecordings.

> **LCRI 7.1B1.** When credits for performer, author, director, producer, "presenter," etc., precede or follow the title in the chief source, in general do not consider them as part of the title proper, even though the language used integrates the credits with the title. This does not apply to the following cases:
>
> 1) the credit is *within* the title, rather than preceding or following it;
>
> > CBS special report
> > IBM puppet shows
>
> 2) the credit is actually a fanciful statement aping a credit;
>
> > Little Roquefort in Good mousekeeping
>
> 3) the credit is represented by a possessive immediately preceding the remainder of the title.
>
> > Neil Simon's Seems like old times

(*CSB* 13)

Ben Tucker, Chief, Office for Descriptive Cataloging Policy, Library of Congress, comments on this LC rule interpretation as follows: "The rule interpretation is deliberately limited to chapter 7 ... For any materials other than those covered by chapter 7, do not apply our rule interpretation for 7.1B1." (*Music Cataloging Bulletin*, 15 (6), 4)

We transcribe the information exactly as shown on the title page or title page substitute (chief source of information), even if it seems odd. In a national or international cooperative environment, we must be consistent in our cataloging. If the chief source has certain words on it and we transcribe them all, someone else using our record for cataloging or interlibrary loan will know it is the same item. This becomes even more important when foreign languages are involved. If I am trying to match an object in hand to a bibliographic record on OCLC, if the words match exactly, in the same order, I know it is most likely the same item. When words are omitted and/or rearranged, I cannot be sure I have the same item.

A uniform title can be used for the actual title and a title added entry can be made for "real" title to provide the access patrons need.

> **25.2A.** Use a uniform title for an entry for a particular item if:

>> 4. the title of the work is obscured by the wording of the title proper (e.g., because of introductory words or statements of responsibility present in the title).

The title proper for each of the preceding problems would be as follows:

```
Godfrey the Safety Gopher presents the 1983 Minnesota Depart-
ment of Public Safety Film Library
    (cataloging of a film catalog)

Escape to Witch Mountain [motion picture]

Xerox Films presents Multiplication rock [filmstrip]

Fred Flintstone presents All-time favorite children's stories
and songs [sound recording]

Mattel Electronics presents Blackjack & poker [computer file]

Gone with the wind [videorecording]

The Gathering storm [videorecording]

Lou Grant [videorecording]

Mary Martin in The sound of music [sound recording]

The Return of the Pink Panther [videorecording]

Charles Dickens' A Christmas carol [videorecording]

Neil Simon's California suite [motion picture]

Reader's digest Popular songs that will live forever [music]

All the words to all the songs in Reader's digest Popular songs
that will live forever songbook [text]

Dear world [sound recording]

Funny lady [motion picture]

The Theatre Guild presents Oklahoma! [music]
```

Incomplete titles

Another title problem is one of abbreviated words in titles. Titles often are abbreviated on labels of sound cassettes of speeches from conferences. Because of lengthy titles and small labels, words are abbreviated (sometimes oddly) or omitted. As in all audiovisual cataloging, common sense is needed.

Sound cassette label:

> Acid Precipita.: Ecolo/Societal Effects, Pt. 1 American Association for the Advancement of Science 1981 Annual Convention January 3-8, Toronto.

Suggested title proper: `Acid precipita[tion]`

(Verna Urbanski. "Incomplete Titles on Conference Proceedings." Online Audiovisual Catalogers. *Newsletter.* 2 (Mar. 1982), 8).

Dependent titles

Another kind of title problem is commonly found on videorecording series and on series of film loops. This problem occurs when the titles found on individual items are not meaningful by themselves such as:

> Introduction
> Operation
> The studio.

The preceding titles depend on the series title for meaning:

```
Communicating about computers to the educator.  No. 1, Introduction.
The jointer.  Part 4, Operation.
Interactive techniques for teleconferencing.  Program 3, The studio.
```

If a part title depends on the main title for clarity, the title proper should consist of

> Main title. Part number, Dependent title

If, however, the part title is a complete, understandable, sensible title by itself, it is used as the title proper, and the rest of the information is used as series title and series number.

If one were cataloging an entire set at once, one would look at all the titles and, if any one of them were dependent, would catalog all the set as dependent titles. All titles in the set should be treated the same way. See LCRI 25.6A (*CSB* 11) for further comments on this type of title.

Title added entries should be made for each part title that could be thought of as a title.

General material designation

In each bibliographic record there are two elements that contain terms identifying the medium of the item being described. The first is called the general material designation (GMD). Its use is optional, but if it is used, it usually appears immediately after the title proper in area 1, the title and statement of responsibility area. The second is called the specific material designation (SMD) and appears as part of the extent of item in area 5, the physical description area.

Those preparing *AACR 2* could not reach agreement on a single list of terms to be used as general material designations. Therefore there are two lists appearing in rule 1.1C1. One list is to be used by North American agencies, the other list by British agencies. The list we are to use, with corresponding *AACR 2* chapters, is as follows:

Chapter 1	kit (rule 1.10)
Chapter 2	text
	braille
Chapter 3	map
	globe
Chapter 4	manuscript
Chapter 5	music

Chapter 6	sound recording
Chapter 7	motion picture
	videorecording
Chapter 8	art original
	art reproduction
	chart
	filmstrip
	flash card
	picture
	slide
	technical drawing
	transparency
Chapter 9	computer file
Chapter 10	art original
	art reproduction
	diorama
	game
	microscope slide
	model
	realia
	toy
Ch. 11	microform

The terms *braille, large print,* or *tactile* may be added to the above terms as appropriate.

Note that the use of a general material designation is optional. Some of these terms may not be really useful in conveying information to the patron; it might be better to choose to omit them. The specific material designation names the item exactly, and that information is always present in the bibliographic record.

Parallel titles

> **1.1D1.** Transcribe parallel titles in the order indicated by their sequence on, or by the layout of, the chief source of information.

Other title information

> **1.1E1.** Transcribe all other title information appearing in the chief source of information ....

Because this element is restricted to information appearing on the chief source of information, other title information appearing elsewhere on the item would be mentioned in a note if important.

Statement of responsibility

> **1.1F1.** Transcribe statements of responsibility appearing prominently in the item in the form in which they appear there. If a statement of responsibility is taken from a source other than the chief source of information, enclose it in square brackets.
> **1.1F2.** If no statement of responsibility appears prominently in the item, neither construct one nor extract one from the content of the item ... Do not include in the title and statement of responsibility area statements of responsibility that do not appear prominently in the item. If such a statement is necessary, give it in a note.
> **0.8.** The word *prominently* ... means that a statement to which it applies must be a formal statement found in one of the prescribed sources of information for areas 1 and 2 for the class of material to which the item being catalogued belongs.

The LC rule interpretation for rule 1.lF repeats some of these directives in order to emphasize certain points, e.g., the utility of the note area for recording statements that have to be rejected for the title and statement of responsibility area, or the fact that it will easily happen that the title and statement of responsibility area lacks a statement of responsibility. Ben Tucker, in a letter to the author (10 Mar. 1985), discusses basic issues in bibliographic description and offers some further clarification. The name of the area designates two elements, the first of which, "title," is essential, a *sine qua non* for the record. The second element, "statement of responsibility," is like another area, the "edition area," in that it is transcribed only when present in the source. For such elements as these, one must emphasize the character of *description* in the record: it describes what is there, not what is not there. When under the rules no formal, prominent statement is found, then the cataloger must not manufacture such a statement, at least for inclusion in the title and statement of responsibility area. When it comes to the note area, where *description* is not the issue, but *information* is, anything is permissible: either picking up non-prominent statements or manufacturing them from information available.

An LCRI for 1.7 (*CSB* 11) tells us that at-head-of-title information can be transposed to the statement of responsibility when appropriate. When the information does not seem appropriate for this area, it goes in a note.

Name in copyright statement

If a person is named only in a copyright statement, a note may be made for that information.

Example: Copyright by E. Averett.

This person may be chosen as main entry, if appropriate under the rules in chapter 21, even though not named in the statement of responsibility.

An example of this would be a computer program for which a copyright statement, "program copyright 1982 by John Jones," is found on the package. No other information lists an author, and there is nothing in the package in addition to the computer disk. However, if the package also contained a large manual, we probably would not use Jones as main entry unless we found he also was the author of the manual.

If the information about the author is found in very small print, whether in the copyright statement, the introduction, or elsewhere, it probably can not be considered to appear prominently, so would be recorded in the note area if at all. Sometimes the name of an author will only appear in a copyright statement. This information may be given in a note, and the name may be chosen as main entry. Be careful, however, to distinguish between a copyright statement that applies only to a single piece of material and one that applies to the entire audiovisual package.

Information that appears on the chief source of information with the statement of responsibility, such as a person's title, faculty rank, or place of employment, is not recorded. This information has traditionally been ignored when it appears on the title page (rule 1.1F7), and is to be ignored when cataloging audiovisual material. The LCRI for 1.1F7 is only to be used when a corporate body for which an access point is needed appears only in conjunction with the author's name on the title page.

Edition Area

1.2B1. Transcribe the edition statement as found on the item ....

1.2B3. In case of doubt about whether a statement is an edition statement, take the presence of such words as *edition, issue, version* (or their equivalents in other languages) as evidence that such a statement is an edition statement, and transcribe it as such.

LCRI 1.2B3. Whenever an item contains a phrase that calls attention to changes from a previous issue of the item, treat that phrase as an edition statement even if it does not otherwise look like one. (*CSB* 27)

The concept of edition is one that catalogers of audiovisual material did not often encounter in the past. Most items were produced or published once, and never reprinted, revised, or issued in new editions. This is still the case with many types of audiovisual material. Now, however, we are encountering various types of edition statements, especially for two types of material: computer files and videorecordings.

Computer files are issued for different types of computers and are updated and/or revised repeatedly. We are advised (rule 9.5B2) to consider the words *edition, issue, version, release, level,* and *update* as evidence of an edition.

Motion pictures and videocassette releases of feature films and children's films lead to edition-related problems. The original motion picture might have been reprinted and released later on 16 mm, 8 mm, and super 8mm film. The video release may be in VHS and Beta, as well as on videodisc. Are these editions or versions? Are they cataloged as new works? And what about the colorized version, the "fully-restored version", and the 25th or 50th anniversary editions? And what do we do with remakes of old films, using the same title as the original?

Examples of cataloging of some of these items will be found later in this book. See the videorecording examples *A Star is Born, New York, New York,* and the 50th anniversary edition of the game *Monopoly.*

To carry this to absurd lengths, the General Mills cereal, *Lucky Charms,* came out in 1987 with what was clearly labeled on the front of the box as the "Swirled Whale Edition." Al Sicherman reported this in the *Minneapolis Star and Tribune* with the comment: "Great galloping Gutenberg! Editions of breakfast cereals—where have we gone wrong?" (*Minneapolis Star and Tribune,* Jan. 25, 1987, p. 8 Fx)

Figure 1

Publication, Distribution, Etc., Area

A letter from Richard Thaxter includes the following information on publication:

Publication is defined in the copyright law (Title 17, United States Code, section 101) as follows:

"Publication" is the distribution of copies or phonorecords of a work to the public by sale or other transfer of ownership, or by rental, lease, or lending. The offering to distribute copies or phonorecords to a group of persons for purposes of further distribution, public performance, or public display, constitutes publication. A public performance or display of a work does not of itself constitute publication (Verna Urbanski. "Publication Defined." Online Audiovisual Catalogers. *Newsletter*, 3 (Sept. 1983), 20).

Place of publication

1.4C1. Transcribe the place of publication, etc., in the form and the grammatical case in which it appears.

1.4C3. ... Supply the name of the country, state, province, etc. ... if it does not appear in the source of information but is considered necessary for identification.

Name of publisher, distributor, etc.

1.4D1. Give the name of the publisher, distributor, etc., following the place(s) to which it relates.

1.4D2. Give the name of a publisher, distributor, etc., in the shortest form in which it can be understood and identified internationally.

Date of publication, distribution, etc.

1.4F1. ... Give the date of the first publication of the edition to which the item belongs.

Multiple dates, a frequent problem, are discussed in the December 1981 Online Audiovisual Catalogers *Newsletter* (p.6) in which Sara Clarkson shares her letter to LC and the response by Ben Tucker. The following summarizes that discussion.

Each item in a package of material may carry a different date with the container having yet another date. Use the latest date and make a note with all the dates, or saying the dates vary from "year" to "year." It is important in cases where the individual dates are old and the container date is new to warn patrons they are getting repackaged old material.

Assume we are cataloging a filmstrip, sound cassette, and teacher's guide. The filmstrip has the date c1977. The sound cassette has no date. The guide has the date c1979. There is no date on the container. We would be cataloging the material under chapter 8 rules; we would be cataloging the package as a filmstrip, with the sound cassette and the guide treated as accompanying material. (Note we first must decide what we are cataloging, then go to the appropriate chapter to see what the chief source of information would be for this material.) Let us assume all pieces of material in the container carried the same title. In this case, the filmstrip itself is the chief source of information, rather than the container. But our filmstrip carries a copyright date that is obviously earlier than the publication date for the package. (The filmstrip was produced in 1977; sound may have been added later, or the filmstrip and sound may have been done in 1977 with the guide added in 1979, or rewritten in 1979.)

Look again at the rule above. It does not say copyright date, but publication date. So we use [1979] in the date element of the publication, distribution, etc. area, and in a note say the date on the filmstrip is c1977.

In a note taken from OCLC record no. 7262059 (a pre-*AACR 2* record, but still appropriate):

```
Dates vary: on title frame, c1975; stamped on slide
margin, c1978; guide, c1977; carousel label, c1978; cas-
sette, side A, c1977; side B, c1979.
```

Physical Description Area

Extent of item

Rule 1.5B1 directs us to record the number of physical units of the item being described and the specific material designation. Mulitple copies of material are to be treated as follows:

```
12 identical charts
10 identical sets of 60 slides
```

1.5B3. Specify the number of components as instructed in the [separate] chapters.
1.5B4. If the material being described has a playing time, give the playing time as follows:

a)　If the playing time is stated on the item, give [it] as stated.

```
1 sound disc (42 min.)
1 film loop (4 min., 14 sec.)
4 sound discs (2 hr., 24 min.)
```

b)　If the playing time is ... readily ascertainable, give it.

```
1 film reel (20 min.)
```

c)　... Give an approximate time.

```
1 videocassette (ca. 60 min.)
```

d)　[Multipart items.]

```
4 sound cassettes (12 min. each)
3 sound discs (90 min.)
6 film loops (ca. 4 min. each)
```

There has been some confusion between the terms cartridge and cassette. Both items have material (film or tape) permanently enclosed in a container; in the cassette the material goes from one reel to another, then back again, in the cartridge the material is a continuous loop on one reel. The containers may hold film, videorecording tape, sound recording tape, or computer tape.

Other physical details

1.5C1. Give physical data, (other than extent or dimensions), about an item as instructed in the [separate] chapters.

Dimensions

1.5D1. Give the dimensions of an item as instructed in the [separate] chapters.

Container

> **1.5D2.** *Optionally,* if the item is in a container, name the container and give its dimensions *either* after the dimensions of the item *or* as the only dimensions.

Examples: `various pieces ; in shelf unit with handles 98 x 140 x 90`
`cm.`
  `28 art reproductions : col. ; 31 x 52 cm. in portfolio 28 x`
`32 cm.`
  `6 sound discs : analog, 33 1/3 rpm, stereo. ; 12 in. in 2`
`containers.`
  `6 filmstrips : col. ; 35 mm. + 6 sound cassettes + 1`
`teacher's guide + 30 identical workbooks in box 30 x 30 x 28`
`cm.`

Accompanying material

Rule 1.5E1 lists four ways of recording information about accompanying material:

> a) record the details of the accompanying material in a separate entry
> b) record the details of the accompanying material in a multilevel description [this option
>   is not used by the Library of Congress]
> c) record the details of the accompanying material in a note
> d) record the name of accompanying material at the end of the physical description.

When method (d) is used, the name of the accompanying material is preceded by a space-plus sign-space; multiple items are each preceded by a space-plus sign-space.

> "If the item has any kind of a title on it (teacher's guide, user's manual, program description, student notes, etc.) use that term in the accompanying material statement. If there is no such term or phrase, use a general term (guide, manual, script, etc.) as appropriate." (Ben R. Tucker, letter to author, 21 Feb. 1985)

Examples: `+ 1 teacher's guide`
       `+ 1 set of teacher's notes`
       `+ 1 set of program instructions + 1 user's guide`
       `+ 1 booklet`
       `+ 3 guides`
          (3 different guides)
       `+ 3 identical guides`

Series Area

1.6B1. If an item is issued in a series, transcribe the title proper of the series ...
1.6J1. ... If an item belongs to two or more series and/or ... series and subseries, give separate series statements and enclose each statement in parentheses ...

Notes Area

All notes are optional. However, there are times when certain notes are required, e.g., to justify an access point. Those used must be used in the order specified by the general chapter and by the specific chapters. Not all notes are permitted in all chapters. Any note may be moved to the first position if it is considered the most important note.

Types of notes:

1.7B1.   Nature, scope, or artistic form
1.7B2.   Language of the item and/or translation or adaptation
1.7B3.   Source of title proper
1.7B4.   Variations in title
1.7B5.   Parallel titles and other title information
1.7B6.   Statements of responsibility
1.7B7.   Edition and history
1.7B8.   Material (or type of publication) specific details
1.7B9.   Publication, distribution, etc.
1.7B10. Physical description
1.7B11. Accompanying materials and supplements
1.7B12. Series
1.7B13. Dissertations
1.7B14. Audience
1.7B15. Reference to published descriptions
1.7B16. Other formats
1.7B17. Summary
1.7B18. Contents
1.7B19. Numbers borne by the item
1.7B20. Copy being described, library's holdings, and restrictions on use
1.7B21. "With" notes
1.7B22. Combined notes related to the original

Punctuation in notes

If a note has the same information normally found in a bibliographic record (e.g., title proper and statement of responsibility), give the information in the same order as when constructing a bibliographic record. Use the same punctuation, except substitute a period for the period-space-dash-space used to separate areas.

Punctuation within notes seems inconsistent. In response to a letter questioning punctuation, especially the occasional lack of a space to the left of a semicolon:

Since notes can include both normal punctuation and ISBD punctuation, the primary distinction to be made is between an ISBD mark and a normal mark. This is done by regarding the ISBD punctuation in the areas that precede the notes. Most of the ISBD marks are the same as normal marks, with the addition of a single space fore and aft. Thus,

1. When a colon is used in a note, it has spaces on either side only when it divides a title from other title information, or separates a place from a publisher:

```
Based on: Nocturnes : a girl's own story.
    Reprint. Originally published: New York : Scribner's,
1984.
```

2. When a semicolon is used in a note, it has a space on either side only when it separates statements of responsibility, multiple places of publication, and when it separates series from numbers:

```
First published as: The tale of a mouse / Judy Appel ;
drawings by J. Firmin.
```

3. The slash is used in a note with a space on either side only when it introduces a statement of responsibility (see previous example).

We have found this policy relatively easy to implement, although I admit that one can see records in which the space has also crept in before the "normal" marks (Ben R. Tucker, letter to the author, 23 Feb. 1984).

Remember that notes require ending punctuation, not shown in these examples. See the section "Punctuation of the Bibliographic Record" earlier in this chapter for LCRI 1.7A1.

Explanation of notes

Each of the notes will be explained in the following section and examples of their use given.

1.7A5. ... When appropriate, combine two or more notes to make one note.

Example: Radio drama, recorded from a broadcast of the program Lux
      radio theatre, Nov. 11, 1937, starring Brian Aherne and Marion
      Davies

1.7B1. Nature, scope, or artistic form

To be used to name or explain the form of the item as necessary.

Examples: Database management program
       Radio drama

1.7B2. Language of the item and/or translation or adaptation

To be used to name the language or languages of the item cataloged if not obvious from other information given.

Examples: Guide in German
       Sound accompaniment in French; script in French and English
       Closed-captioned for the hearing impaired

1.7B3. Source of title proper

To be used if the title proper is taken from other than the chief source of information.

Examples: Title from container
       Title supplied by cataloger
       Title from title screen

1.7B4. Variations in title

To be used to note any title appearing on the item that differs significantly from the title proper.

Example: Title on cartridge and container: Trisecting a straight line with
      triangles
      (*Title proper:* Trisecting a line with triangles)

1.7B5. Parallel titles and other title information

To be used for parallel titles and important other title information not recorded in the title and statement of responsibility area.

Example: Subtitle on guide: Wildlife management in Northern Minnesota

1.7B6. Statements of responsibility

To be used to record important information not recorded in the statement of responsibility area.

Examples: `Consultant: Carrol J. Schwartz`
`Software copyright by E. Averett`
`Read by Eileen Heckart, Claudia McNeil, and Mildred`
`Natwick ; edited by Sharon Donovan`

A cataloging decision made at the Library of Congress, published in the *Music Cataloging Bulletin,* June 1989 (p. 4), instructs us to use the same punctuation in performer notes as would be used in the statement of responsibility. The semicolon is set off by a space on each side. This punctuation is followed throughout the other chapters for credits notes.

1.7B7. Edition and history

To be used for information about earlier editions or the history of the item being cataloged.

Examples: `Earlier ed. called: Step by step`
`Adapted from the motion picture of the same title`

1.7B8. Material specific details

Only used for chapters 3, 5, 9, and 12 material.

1.7B9. Publication, distribution, etc.

To be used for important information not recorded in the publication, distribution, etc., area.

Example: `Not available for distribution in the United States`

1.7B10. Physical description

To be used for any important information not given in area 5, the physical description area.

Examples: `HO scale`
`Gameboards on back of poster`
`Compact disc`
`VHS`

1.7B11. Accompanying materials and supplements

To be used for any important information not given in the accompanying material part of area 5.

Examples: `Teacher's guide includes bibliography, exercises,`
`worksheets, glossary, time line`
`Program notes by Stanley Crouch inserted in container`

1.7B12. Series

To be used for any important information not recorded in the series area.

Example: `Originally issued in the series: Vocabulary skills`

1.7B13. Dissertations

To be used for the standard dissertation note when applicable.

Example: `Thesis (M.A.)--Indiana University, 1968`

1.7B14. Audience

To be used to record the intended audience of a work. Use this note only if the information is stated on the item. Do not attempt to judge the audience for an item.

Examples: `Intended audience: For children 3 to 8 years old`
`Rated R`

1.7B15. Reference to published descriptions

To be used to refer to published descriptions of the material.

Example: `Described in: Albrecht Dürer : the complete engravings. Artline,`
`1987`

1.7B16. Other formats

To be used to list other formats in which the work is available. The Library of Congress lists all formats commercially available in this note.

Examples: `Prints of each negative are available from the Library of Congress`
`Also available as slides (b&w or col.), and as photographic prints`
`Issued also on videodisc`

1.7B17. Summary

To be used for a brief objective summary of the content of the item. This may be the most important information we can provide to the user through our cataloging.

> **LCRI 2.7B17.** Guidelines when creating subject notes:
> 1. Make a concise statement, mentioning only major points of the contents. Phrases, rather than sentences, may be used when clarity and good taste permit.
> 2. Include objective statements only, avoiding any explicit or implicit evaluation of the contents from any point of view. If it is the contents of the work that show a bias, which it is important for the subject note to bring out, word the note carefully so that it is clear the author's bias, not the cataloger's, is the one being related.
> 3. Depending on the particular contents of a work note that it is important to bring out such information as
>   a. coverage of a time period or of a geographic area;
>   b. educational level or slant of the material;
>   c. obvious purpose of the contents;
>   d. genre of the contents;
>   e. any other major information considered important.
>
> (*CSB* 24)

Example: `Summary: Describes and compares television journalism and`
`press photography using examples of Minneapolis and St. Paul`
`news items`

1.7B18. Contents

To be used for a formal or informal listing of the contents of the item.

Example: `Contents: Red shouldered hawk -- Red-tailed hawk -- American`
`kestrel -- Chuck-will's widow -- Great horned owl`

An LCRI (*CSB* 49) tells us not to capitalize "v." or "pt." at the beginning of a contents note.

1.7B19. Numbers borne by the item

To be used to list any important number appearing on the item other than those to be recorded in area 8. For material cataloged using *AACR 2* chapter 6, this note is given as the first note in the bibliographic record. The note may be quoted.

Examples: `"S 1967"`
`EMI: ALP 1056-1058`

1.7B20. Copy being described, library's holdings, and restrictions on use

To be used for any notes applicable only to the particular copy of the item being described. Also used for local library restrictions on the material being described, or for information of use only to patrons of the local library.

Example: `Use restricted to Sociology 454 class`

1.7B21. "With" notes

For two or more works that have been issued together without a collective title, create one bibliographic record, or catalog them separately, connecting them through "with" notes.

Examples: `With: Letter game -- Spelling zoo`
`With: Unsteady sun / J.M. Mitchell`

1.7B22. Combined notes relating to the original

Example: `Reprint. Originally published: London : Rutledge Press, 1938`

Standard Number and Terms of Availability Area

There are no special standard numbers to correspond to the ISSN or ISBN for any of the types of audiovisual material. Sometimes the material will carry an ISBN or an ISSN; if so, record it in area 8.

Inconsistencies in the Rules

There are still some inconsistencies in the cataloging rules from chapter to chapter. Many problems were resolved in the 1988 revision, but some still exist. The more uniform the rules are, the better our cataloging can be.

Stereo

The term "stereo" is included in area 5 for sound recordings, but is not permitted in area 5 for videorecordings or for any other type of media. Music videos, some feature films, and some computer files are recorded in stereo.

Colored wood

A colored wooden map would be described in *AACR 2* chapter 3 as "col. wood" but a colored wooden map cut into a puzzle would be described in chapter 10 as "wood, col." This is not a big problem, but it is another application of the rules that is not uniform.

Summary note

The summary note is not permitted in *AACR 2* chapters 3 or 12. We can "borrow" it from chapter 1, but it would be useful to have it included in all chapters.

Order of information in credits notes

By tradition, credits in bibliographic records for music follow the pattern

```
Credits: Name(s), function ; name(s), function.
```

For other materials the credits note is

```
Credits: Function, name(s) ; function, name(s).
```


COMPLETING THE CATALOGING PROCESS

After finishing the descriptive cataloging, the access points are chosen and their forms determined. Then subject headings and classification numbers are added.

Main Entry

There is not necessarily any correlation between statement of responsibility and main entry. One does not automatically use whatever information appears in the statement of responsibility as the main entry, neither is one restricted to the information appearing in the statement of responsibility.

An interesting program, *Chapter 21, AACR 2, and Choice of Access Points for Nonbook Materials, or, How Did We Get From There To Here?*, was held during the 1984 American Library Association conference. This program, sponsored by Online Audiovisual Catalogers, featured speakers Jean Weihs and Michael Gorman. In his remarks, Gorman noted the concept of main entry is too frequently a time-consuming snag in cataloging. He noted that no practical reason exists to maintain main entry, and stated that the decision not to drop main entry in the development of *AACR 2* was purely political and was not decided on a philosophical level, that, as always, the dilemma for cataloging is the conflict between the philosophical concept of authorship versus the practical approach to access.

Personal main entry

21.1A2. Enter a work by one or more persons under the heading for the personal author, the principal personal author, or the probable personal author.

Personal author. The person chiefly responsible for the creation of the intellectual or artistic content of a work.

Corporate main entry

21.1B2. Enter a work emanating from one or more corporate bodies under the heading for the appropriate corporate body if it falls into one or more of the following categories: [Consider a work to emanate from a corporate body if it is issued by that body *or* has been caused to be issued by that body *or* if it originated with that body.]

a) those of an administrative nature dealing with the corporate body itself, or its internal policies, procedures, finances, and/or operations, or its officers, staff, and/or membership, or its resources;

b) some legal, governmental, and religious works of the following types: laws, decrees of the chief executive that have the force of law, administrative regulations, constitutions, court rules, treaties, etc., court decisions, legislative hearings, religious laws, liturgical works;

c) those that record the collective thought of the body (e.g., reports of commissions, committees, etc. ...);

d) those that report the collective activity of a conference, of an expedition, or of an event falling within the definition of a corporate body, provided that the conference, expedition, or event is prominently named in the item being catalogued;

e) those that result from the collective activity of a performing group as a whole where the responsibility of the group goes beyond that of mere performance, execution, etc. ... ;

f) cartographic materials emanating from a corporate body other than a body that is merely responsible for their publication or distribution.

These rules are much more restrictive than past rules. There will be few corporate main entries for audiovisual materials.

The videorecording *Getting The Word Out*, is about products and services of Follett Library Book Company, a library book jobber. The title frames say "by Follett Library Book Company". It is published and distributed by Follett. This videorecording would be entered under the corporate body; it follows rule 21.1Ba above. It "emanates" from the corporate body. The videorecording provides a general description of the company and is used for public relations purposes.

Title main entry

21.1C1. Enter a work under its title proper, or, when appropriate, uniform title, if:

1. the personal authorship is unknown or diffuse, and the work does not emanate from a corporate body, or
2. it is a collection or a work produced under editorial direction, or
3. it emanates from a corporate body but does not fall into any of the categories given in 21.1B2 and is not of personal authorship, or
4. it is accepted as sacred scripture by a religious group.

Title main entry is used often for audiovisual materials.

The concept of authorship

Martha Yee discusses the question of authorship of audiovisual materials:

Non-textual materials have strong visual and aural components which are frequently non-verbal. Their creation usually involves carrying out multiple functions, and these functions may be carried out by different people and corporate bodies. Thus, the making of a map may involve the gathering of data by one person or group of persons and the encapsulation of the data in map form by another or others; one person or group may be responsible for the geographic aspect of a map, and another for the subject aspect. The making of a slide set may involve the taking of photographs, the compiling of appropriate pictures, the writing of an accompanying text, the writing or performing of accompanying music, etc. Visual materials can involve the maker of a picture, and the subject of a picture, which may itself be the intellectual or artistic work of another or others. Films, for example, are the products of the art of photography, and can be used to display all the other arts, including dance, music, drama, sculpture, etc., or they can display a person presenting his or her intellectual work in any subject area. Sound recordings, motion pictures and videorecordings frequently display the performance by one person or persons of the work of another or others. Traditional cataloging codes dealt predominantly with the monograph, originally a text written by a single person, and still usually a text created by the exercise of a single function, that of writing. Thus traditionally authorship has consisted to a large degree of the creation of or the taking of responsibility for that single function. When one considers the number of functions that are performed in creating nonbook materials, it can be seen that it is no easy matter to integrate rules to deal with these complex forms of authorship into a code originally designed to deal with authorship of monographs (Martha M. Yee. "Integration of Nonbook Materials in *AACR 2*" *Cataloging & Classification Quarterly*, 3 (summer 1983), 4).

Adaptations

Adaptations have been the focus of many cataloging questions. A sound recording of someone reading a book is not an adaptation, but a dramatized book is an adaptation.

A filmstrip showing each page of a book, accompanied by a sound recording of someone reading the book, is an adaptation. Much more is involved here than a simple reading of the book. At least one company (Weston Woods) has some of the pictures re-done to put them in the proper format for the filmstrip dimensions. They also compose music for the production.

These adaptations would be entered under the heading appropriate to the adaptation, not to the original work. An added entry would be needed for the heading for the original work, and for the illustrator in the case of children's picture books, so the user of a catalog would find bibliographic records for the book and bibliographic records for the reading of the book and bibliographic records for the filmstrip of the book all together.

Added Entries

LCRI 21.29. Give added entries in the following order:

1. Personal name;
2. Personal name/title;
3. Corporate name;
4. Corporate name/title;
5. Uniform title;
6. Title traced as Title-period;
7. Title traced as Title-colon, followed by a title;
8. Series.

(*CSB* 12)

For arrangement within any one of these groupings, generally follow the order in which the justifying data appears in the bibliographic description. If such a criterion is not applicable, use judgment.

> **21.29C.** … make an added entry under the heading for a person or a corporate body or under a title if some catalogue users might suppose that the description of an item would be found under that heading or title rather than under the heading or title chosen for the main entry.
> **21.239D.** If, in the context of a given catalogue, an added entry is required under a heading or title other than those prescribed in 21.30, make it.

LCRI 21.29, 21.30. In making added entries for audiovisual materials, follow the general rules in 21.29, and apply, in addition to those in 21.30, the following guidelines:

1) Make added entries for all openly named persons or corporate bodies who have contributed to the creation of the item, with the following exceptions:

a) Do not make added entries for persons (producers, directors, writers, etc.) if there is a production company, unit, etc., for which an added entry is made, unless their contributions are determined significant, e.g., the animator of an animated film; the producer/director of a student film, the director of a theatrical film; the filmmaker or developer of a graphic item attributed as author on the data sheet and/ or prominently named on the accompanying material ("a film by").

In the absence of a production company, unit, etc., make added entries for those persons who are listed as producers, directors, and writers. Make additional added entries for other persons only if their contributions are determined significant.

b) If a person, filmmaker, developer of a graphic item, etc., is the main entry heading, do not make added entries for other persons who have contributed to the production, unless the production is known to be the joint responsibility of collaboration of the persons or the contributions are determined significant.

2) Make added entry headings for all corporate bodies named in the publication, distribution, etc., area.

3) Make added entries for all featured players, performers, and narrators with the following exceptions:

a) If, for a motion picture or videorecording, the main entry is under the heading for a performing group (in accordance with 21.1B2e), do not make added entries under the headings for persons performing as members of that group. If a person's name, however, appears in conjunction with, preceding or following the name of the group, do not consider him or her to be a member of that group.

b) If there are many players (actors, actresses, etc.), make added entries under the headings for those that are given prominence in the chief source of information. If that cannot be used as a criterion, make added entries under the headings for each if there are no more than three.

4) Similarly, make added entries under the headings for persons in a production who are interviewers or interviewees, delivering lectures, addresses, etc., or discussing their lives, ideas, work, etc., and who are not chosen as the main entry heading.

(*CSB* 45)

A comment on the preceding LCRI: "These LC policies are mainly a matter of practicality and economics. I would encourage other libraries to make more (or fewer) added entries according to their needs" (Richard Thaxter, letter to author, 10 Mar. 1985).

An extensive LCRI explains how to construct added entries for works:

LCRI 21.30M   Analytical entries

Added Entries for Works

Added entries for works reflect the type of main entry heading of the work being cataloged in the tracing as follows:

Type of main entry	*Type of added entry*
Personal or corporate name	Name heading/uniform title
Title	Uniform title
Uniform title	Uniform title

The phrase "added entries for works" in these instructions is intended to encompass all the various types of added entries listed above.

Added entries for works are of two types: analytical and simple. They are made on the basis of various rules, some of which prescribe an analytical added entry in explicit terms, others of which do not. Whenever the added entry is made to furnish an access point to the substance of a work contained in the item being cataloged, it should be an analytical added entry (e.g., 21.7B1, 21.13B1, 21.19A1). If the added entry serves only to provide an approach to the item being cataloged through a related work, however, and the text of this work is not present in the item being cataloged, then a simple added entry for the work is appropriate (e.g., 21.12B1, 21.28B1, 21.30G1).

The relationship that is expressed between works by means of an added entry, either analytical or simple, is limited to a single access point, namely, that of the main entry. An added entry in the form of the main entry heading for a work provides the sole access to the work; do not trace in addition any added entries for that work's title (when main entry is under a name heading), joint author, editor, compiler, translator, etc.

Analytical Added Entries

Formulate analytical added entries as follows:

Type of analytical a.e.	*Components*
Name heading/title	Heading in catalog entry form plus uniform title
Title	Uniform title
Uniform title	Uniform title

In addition, following the uniform title, provide the language (if appropriate) and the publication date of the item being cataloged. In making analytical added entries, note expecially the following details:

1. Reduce the publication date to a simple four digit form that most nearly represents the publication date (of the first volume or part if more than one) given in the publication, distribution, etc., area. Convert a hyphen to a zero.

2. Do not abbreviate the names of languages.

3. Do not enclose uniform titles within brackets.

4. Do not give in the tracing a title found in the item being cataloged that is different from the uniform title.

Simple Added Entries

Formulate simple added entries as follows:

Type of simple added entry	*Components*
Name heading/title	Heading in catalog entry form plus uniform title
Title	Uniform title
Uniform title	Uniform title

Note that subject entries for works are formulated in the same manner as simple added entries (*CSB* 45).

These guidelines call for all headings to be in uniform title format. Different forms of titles would be handled by cross-references, or by an authority system. For those of us working in less-than-ideal worlds, we need to make added entries for the title in other forms, as well as the uniform title form.

Added entries are made for persons and corporate bodies capable of authorship. Puppets and cartoon characters would not qualify for added entry. However 21.29D and 21.30H do permit us to make added entries for important access points under certain conditions. Ben R. Tucker tells me subject headings must be used as access points for cartoon characters.

Uniform title

Some motion pictures and/or videorecordings may need uniform title main entry when "the title of the work is obscured by the wording of the title proper" or when there are two or more works with the same title in your catalog.

LCRI 25.5B. Conflict resolution

Radio and Television Programs

Add the qualifier "(Radio program)" or "(Television program)" to the title of a radio or television program whenever the program is needed in a secondary entry and the title is the same as a Library of Congress subject heading or the title has been used as the title of another work. (It does not matter if the other work is entered under title or under a name heading.) This same uniform title for the radio or television program must be used in all entries for the particular work. (Existing records in which the radio or television program has been used as a main or added entry must be adjusted.)

Motion Pictures

If a motion picture is entered under a title proper that is the same as the title proper of another motion picture (or other work), do not assign a uniform title to either to distinguish them, even if there are multiple editions of either work. However, if a motion picture is needed in a secondary entry and the title of the motion picture is the same as a Library of Congress subject heading or the title is the same as the title of another work, add the qualifier "(Motion picture)" to the title of the motion picture. This same uniform title must be used in all entries for the particular work. Existing records in which the motion picture is used as a main or secondary entry must be adjusted (*CSB* 46).

These are *qualifiers* added in parentheses, *not* GMDs. See example 27, *A Star is Born,* for further explanation and illustration.

GMD in added entries

The Library of Congress does not take the GMD into consideration in filing, so it does not use the GMD's in added entries, including title added entries. The Library also does not use the GMD in uniform titles. If a conflict occurs when filing, a qualifier is added to the entry. That qualifier may use the words of a GMD, but will be in parentheses rather than in square brackets.

Form of Access Points

Form of the access point is governed by chapters 22-25. These rules guide the cataloger in determining whether, for example, a person's middle initial or birth date may be used in a heading, in what form a corporate body is to be given, and what, if any, qualifiers need to be added to the heading.

Rules in these chapters also can help us decide the form of access points for names such as the following, whether they are used as main or added entries or as subject headings, as appropriate:

Kermit, the Frog (Puppet)
Piggy, Miss (Puppet)
Big Bird
Kangaroo, Captain
Rogers, Mister
Grandpere (Puppet)

Subject Headings

Hans Wellisch, at an international symposium held in 1971, said:

> Some catalog studies make it seem as if the subject approach to documents were not very widespread among library users and that most of them look for authors and titles and turn to subject enquiries only when other attempts to locate books fail. But such results tend rather to emphasize the fact that subject retrieval in present day dictionary catalogs is both difficult and frustrating (Hans Wellisch. "Subject Retrieval in the Seventies — Methods, Problems, Prospects." In *Subject Retrieval in the Seventies, New Directions*. Westport, Conn.: Greenwood Press, 1972, p. 4).

David Haykin pointed out some of the problems of subject catalogs and subject cataloging. He said:

> [The subject catalog] suffers from several limitations, some accidental, others inherent in its nature and structure. Whatever rules or principles were applied in choosing or devising headings in the past, it is clear that they were often based on no more than the limited personal experience of the cataloger. One of the most serious weaknesses of the headings now found in our catalogs is that the terms chosen are not derived from precise knowledge of the approach used by many readers of different backgrounds ... Even if the cataloger were to determine conclusively the mental processes of the reader and to choose the terms, structure, and arrangement of headings which most closely correspond to the reader's approach, he would still have to take account of linguistic problems ... A semantic problem with which catalogers must struggle constantly is that of imperfect synonyms. Scientific terms are, generally speaking, quite precise in their meanings; in other fields of knowledge and in the use of popular terms, which may be preferred to scientific terms in certain instances, meanings are inexact, the same term being used in different senses by different categories of readers or in different regions, just as different terms are applied to the same thing (David Judson Haykin, *Library of Congress Subject Headings*. Washington, D.C.: U.S. GPO, 1951, p. 4).

Lois Mai Chan also speaks of the difficulties with subject cataloging:

> The frequent criticisms of the subject catalog for being too specific or too general reflect the conflicting demands on the catalog. Modern writers recognize in general two methods of subject representation : summarization and exhaustive (or depth) indexing. The former aims at displaying the overall subject content of biobliographic entitites (books, journals, etc.), while the latter attempts to bring out the content of smaller units of information (e.g., chapters in books, articles in journals, etc.) within bibliographic entities. Many users are content to have the subject catalog fulfill the function of summarization, and leave exhaustive or depth indexing to bibliographies and indexes (Lois Mai Chan, *Library of Congress Subject Headings*. Littleton, Colo.: Libraries Unlimited, 1978, p. 19).

Karen Markey states:

> A bleak picture has been presented regarding the experiences of traditional subject catalog searchers when matching their vocabulary with that of the catalog (Karen Markey, *Subject Searching in Library Catalogs*. Dublin, Ohio: OCLC, 1984, p. 56).

Haykin also listed the fundamental concepts of subject headings. These are summarized as follows:

> 1. *The reader as focus.* The reader is the focus in all cataloging principles and practice.
> 2. *Unity.* A subject catalog must bring together under one heading all the books which deal principally or exclusively with the subject, whatever the terms applied to it by the authors of the books and whatever the varying terms applied to it at different times.
> 3. *Usage.* The heading chosen must represent common usage or, at any rate, the usage of the class of reader for whom the material on the subject within which the heading falls is intended.
> 4. *English vs. foreign terms.* Foreign terms should be used only when the concept is foreign to Anglo-American experience and no satisfactory term for it exists, and when the foreign term is precise, whereas the English one is not.
> 5. *Specificity.* The heading should be as specific as the topic it is intended to cover. As a corollary, the heading should not be broader than the topic; rather than use a broader heading, the cataloger should use two specific headings which will approximately cover it (Haykin, *Library of Congress Subject Headings*, p. 7-11).

Lucienne Maillet explains some of the complications involved in choosing subject headings:

> The process of determining subject headings for input into the library's catalog is a complex intellectual operation which is primarily guided by the cataloging policies of the institution. The process involves some subjective judgement which is influenced by the cataloger's background, the individual's understanding of the subject matter, the objectives of the catalog, the needs of the users, and the effectiveness of communication between the author or producer and the cataloger (Lucienne Maillet, *Subject Control of Film and Video*. Chicago, Ill.: American Library Association, 1991, p. 32).

Subject access for each item of audiovisual material should be considered carefully. Narrow topics will need narrow subject headings as explained above under point 5, Specificity. General topics will need general subject headings. Motion pictures and other materials that cover a range of topics may need many subject headings to bring out all significant aspects of their content.

Every aspect of a topic treated in an item of audiovisual material needs to be considered for subject access, since the item may represent the only audiovisual treatment in the collection on that topic.

When cataloging material to be added to an audiovisual collection that is small in comparison to the library's book collection, consider adding more subject headings to allow access by general term as well as the most specific ones. However, keep in mind the cautions expressed by Sheila S. Intner:

> While it is within the scope of the local library's indexing policies to add descriptors if they are useful, indexers should not lose sight of the standards that govern indexing for all types of library cataloging. The advantages of access to a smaller bibliographic unit that results from doing deeper indexing may have to be balanced against its cost as well as the disadvantages of finding that the special treatments afforded some materials make it difficult to interfile the records into one integrated catalog, or the disappointment of clients upon discovering that the whole film or video is not about the expected topic (Sheila S. Intner and William E. Studwell, *Subject Access to Films and Videos*. Lake Crystal, Minn.: Soldier Creek Press, in press, p. 2).

The patron wanting information on Indian pottery might not look under the specific heading MARTINEZ, MARIA MONTOYA, but might look under POTTERY, or INDIANS OF NORTH AMERICA—POTTERY. The motion picture *Hands of Maria* should have all of these subject headings.

Locally-devised subject headings

Current topics do present a problem when it comes to selecting subject headings. If I can't find an appropriate subject heading in *Library of Congress Subject Headings* or its supplements, I go to *Reader's Guide to Periodical Literature* to see what term it uses and then use that term. Because I catalog online through OCLC, I can assign a special code (690) to that term so others seeing the record on OCLC will know the subject heading shown is a locally assigned subject heading.

Another problem is presented by very specific topics such as represented in a filmstrip on drawing curves or one on adding two-digit numbers. Sometimes there is a subject heading in *LCSH* for the specific topic. If there is something similar, I make up a subject heading, patterning it after an existing similar heading. If there is nothing similar, I make up the heading as best I can.

Purpose of subject headings

Occasionally there is confusion about the purpose of subject headings. Their traditional purpose is to represent the subject matter of the item, not the form or purpose of the item. A filmstrip on coal mining would have a subject heading reflecting the content, COAL MINES AND MINING, but would not have the subject heading FILMSTRIPS.

Form subdivisions

There is some question about the use of subject heading subdivisions for the medium. If these were used for the example above in a library with a card catalog, the subject card for POTTERY—MOTION PICTURES would not be interfiled with POTTERY, but would follow it in a separate sequence. There would also be separate sequences for POTTERY—SLIDES and POTTERY—FILMSTRIPS. If format subdivisions are given to subject headings for audiovisual material, the patron will not find all information on a subject together. Patrons are not likely to look through more than one alphabetic sequence in a catalog. They will, if necessary, look through POTTERY with main entries from A to Z, but are not likely to continue past POTTERY—BIBLIOGRAPHY and through all the other subdivisions to find POTTERY—VIDEORECORDINGS.

Sometimes it is necessary to use subject headings for form of medium in order to provide otherwise inaccessible information to patrons. An example would be the assigning of the subject headings SIMULATION GAMES IN EDUCATION or MANAGEMENT GAMES, as appropriate, to actual games, as well as to materials about these types of games. There is no other way for patrons to find these types of games unless they know game titles. This same reasoning could lead to assigning format headings for all materials, and this has been done by libraries. I am somewhat uncomfortable with this alternate use of subject headings, but Jean Weihs, in a speech at the Institute on NonBook Materials held in Washington, D.C., October 11-14, 1984, said she sees nothing wrong with this practice.

In an online catalog, access by form is available through coded fixed fields. Specific words in a subject subdivision are not needed.

Order of subject headings

The order in which LC subject headings are to be listed on the bibliographic record is given in *Subject Cataloging Manual: Subject Headings* (Washington, D.C.: Library of Congress, 1991, p. H80).

> Assign subject headings in the order of descending significance, i.e. according to the importance of each subject heading for the assignment of the class number:
> a. Tracing 1 should represent the actual class number assigned to the particular work.
> b. In case two headings are required to represent the complete class number, these two headings should be listed as Tracings 1 and 2.
> c. Important headings that narrowly miss representing the class number (such as a special approach to the major topic) should be listed next.
> d. Headings added to designate topics touched on only marginally in the work should be assigned last.

Classification

Library of Congress classification

In a discussion of the Library of Congress classification, Phyllis Richmond makes the following comments:

> ... making and, to a lesser degree, assigning classification, as with any subject approach to knowledge, can be a highly subjective matter. Here, perhaps, more than in any other area of intellectual endeavor, one man's meat is another's poison. Librarians probably all agree that like materials should be shelved together, but they do not agree on what is like because they approach the subject with different backgrounds and viewpoints. For libraries, the important thing is less that the fields of knowledge should be distinguished precisely in some glorious, universally accepted, ideal, logical classification than that the material put into storage should be found again quickly (Phyllis A. Richmond. "General Advantages and Disadvantages of Using the Library of Congress Classification." In *The Use of the Library of Congress Classification*. Chicago, Ill.: American Library Association, 1968, p. 210).

We should keep her practical approach in mind; the important thing is "that the material put into storage should be found again quickly."

A classification number is chosen to reflect the general subject content of the item. If a class number is not listed in *LCSH* with the chosen subject heading, or if I do not immediately know what schedule or part of a schedule to go to, I use the *Cumulative Subject Index to the MARC Data Base, 1968-1978* (Arlington, VA.: Carrollton Press, 1978) or the *Combined Indexes to the Library of Congress Classification Schedules* (Washington, D.C.: U.S. Historical Documents Institute, 1975) to find class numbers for topics. I have also done term searches of the REMARC database to find class numbers and subject headings for new topics. Subject searching of the OCLC database, through the EPIC service, should be helpful.

Work numbers

After the classification number is assigned to a work, something must be added to that classification number to determine the item's position when shelved relative to other items bearing the same class number. A common method is to assign a work number based on the main entry using the following directions (from *CSB* 3):

> Library of Congress call numbers consist, in general, of two principal elements: class number and book number, to which are added, as required, symbols designating a particular work.

Library of Congress book numbers are composed of the initial letter of the main entry heading, followed by Arabic numerals representing the succeeding letters on the following basis:

1. After initial vowels:

for the second letter:	b	d	l,m	n	p	r	s,t	u-y
use number:	2	3	4	5	6	7	8	9

2. After the initial letter S:

for the second letter:	a	ch	e	h,i	m-p	t	u
use number:	2	3	4	5	6	7-8	9

3. After the initial letters Qu:

for the third letter:	a	e	i	o	r	y
use number:	3	4	5	6	7	9

for names beginning Qa-Qt use 2-29

4. After other initial consonants

for the second letter:	a	e	i	o	r	u	y
use number:	3	4	5	6	7	8	9

5. When an additional number is preferred

for the third letter:	a-d	e-h	i-l	m	n-q	r-t	u-w	x-z
use number:	2	3	4	5	6	7	8	9

Since the tables provide only a general framework for the assignment of numbers, the symbol for a particular name or work is constant only within a single class. Each entry must be added to the existing entries in the shelflist in such a way as to preserve alphabetic order in accordance with Library of Congress filing rules.

A problem can arise when working with a series all having the same main entry, or with title main entries that vary only in the last word or words, as in the following example:

> The Metal turning lathe. Group 3, Basic operations. Part 1, Facing.
> The Metal turning lathe. Group 3, Basic operations. Part 2, Straight outside diameter turning.
> The Metal turning lathe. Group 3, Basic operations. Part 3, Straight inside turning or boring.
> The Metal turning lathe. Group 3, Basic operations. Part 4, Simple taper turning with the lathe compound.

All these film loops would have the same classification number. A simple way to distinguish between them would be to construct book marks as follows: .M4 for the first word in the main entry after "The", Metal; then add the group number and part number, resulting in unique book marks: .M431 (or .M43 if one follows LC convention not to use numbers ending in "1"), .M432, .M433, .M434, etc. This series of book marks allows us to put the film loops in order on the shelf by group and part number, rather than arranging them alphabetically by the individual part title, an order that would not be as desirable.

For the following series all of which use the same classification number and which have no numeric designation, we could assign the book marks to produce the following alphabetical arrangement:

> .M43 Metalworking tools, adjustable, open-end, and socket wrenches
> .M44 Metalworking tools, files
> .M45 Metalworking tools, hacksaw
> .M46 Metalworking tools, pliers etc.

Subject cataloging, or subject analysis, includes both subject headings and classification. Neither of these processes is controlled or determined by the *Anglo-American Cataloguing Rules*. A library is free to choose whatever type of subject headings and/or classification it wants to use.

The following Library of Congress guidelines, from *Cataloging Service Bulletin* 48, are LC's own guidelines for subject headings and classification of films. They also include some MARC coding and tagging instructions.

Guidelines for Subject Cataloging of Visual Materials

For convenience, the words film and films are used throughout these guidelines to refer to any type of visual material, including motion pictures, filmstrips, video recordings, and slides.
1. *Target audience.* Films are assigned one of the following MARC codes for target audience:
    a Age 0-5 (preschool through kindergarten)
    b Age 6-8 (primary)
    c Age 9-15 (intermediate through junior high)
    d Age 16-19 (senior high)

e   Adult
f   Special audiences
g   General

Films coded "a," "b," or "c" are treated as juvenile films. For classification purposes only, fiction films coded "d" are also treated as juvenile. The target audience of films coded "f" must be determined from the title, summary, or intended audience note (521 field). Films coded "e" or "g" are treated as adult films.

2. *Subject headings*

a. *Topical films.* Since, for all practical purposes, it is impossible to browse a film collection, greater detail in subject cataloging treatment is required for films than is normally provided for books. In addition to the normal rules governing the assignment of subject headings, the below listed special rules are observed when assigning topical subject headings to non-fiction films:

1. A subject entry is made for all important topics mentioned in the summary statement. If a specific topic is emphasized in order to illustrate a more general concept, subject headings are assigned for both the specific and the general topics. Form subdivisions are assigned only to the extent that such subdivisions are applicable both to print and audiovisual media. The form subdivision **—Pictorial works** is *not* used.

520 field: Describes the highlights of Colombia, including the production of coffee.
Subject entries: Colombia—Description and travel
                     Coffee—Colombia

520 field: Surveys the industries of India, with special emphasis on the steel industry
Subject entries: India—Industries
                     Steel industry and trade—India

520 field: Documents the intellectual expansion in medieval Germany, as illustrated by the Nuremberg chronicle
Subject entries: Schedel, Hartmann, 1140-1514. Liber chronicarum
                     Germany—Intellectual life—History

2. When a topic is discussed in conjunction with a particular place, a subject entry is made, insofar as possible, under both the topic and place.

520 field: Describes the oases of the Sahara
Subject entries: Oases—Sahara
                     Sahara—Description and travel

520 field: Interviews with medical personnel and participants in a drug abuse treatment program in New York City
Subject entries: Drug abuse—New York (N.Y.)
                     New York (N.Y.)—Social conditions

3. When a film treats a particular person as illustrative of a profession or activity, a heading is assigned for both the person and the field of endeavor. Such films are not, as a general rule, treated as biographies.

520 field: A day in the life of prizefighter Muhammad Ali as he trains for a championship bout
Subject entries: Ali, Muhammad, 1942-
                     Boxing

520 field: How modern dance exponent Martha Graham functions as an artist and choreographer

> *Subject entries:* Graham, Martha
>   Modern dance
>   Choreography

4. *Commercials.* A heading is assigned for the generic name of the product being advertised. A heading is also assigned for the particular advertising medium, if it is identified.

> *520 field:* Television commercial for Bayer aspirin
> *Subject entries:* Aspirin
>   Television advertising

b. *Fiction films.* The following headings are assigned, as appropriate, to individual fiction films:

1. Topical headings with the subdivision —**Drama** (or, in the case of juvenile fiction films, the subdivision —**Juvenile films**). Headings of this type are assigned to the same extent that such headings are assigned to individual dramas in book form (cf. *Subject Catalgoing Manual: Subject Headings,* H 1780, p. 2, sec. 4).

2. Form headings that express either genre (e.g., **Comedy films, Western films**) or technique (e.g., **Silent films, Experimental films**).

3. The form heading **Feature films** or **Short films. Feature films** is assigned to fiction films with a running time of 60 minutes or more. **Short films** is assigned to those with a running time of less than 60 minutes.

Note that headings (1) and/or (2) are assigned only as appropriate for the particular film being cataloged, but that heading (3) is required for *all* fiction films. When more than one of these headings are assigned to a particular film, they are assigned in the order listed above.

c. *Films for the hearing impaired.* Either **Films for the hearing impaired** or **Video recordings for the hearing impaired** is assigned to all films produced with captions or sign language for viewing by the hearing impaired.

3. *LC classification number*

a. *Specificity of class numbers.* Films are assigned the most specific class numbers available in the LC classification schedules, including Cutter numbers for topics, places, or persons, if they are printed in the schedule. Cutter numbers are not included for places or individuals if the caption in the schedule reads, for example, "By region or country, A-Z," or "Individual, A-Z" and printed Cutters are not present. Shelflisting subarrangements are not provided. New topical class numbers are not established for films. If a number for the specific topic of the film has not been established, the next broader class number is assigned.

b. *Adult belles lettres.* To critical films about an individual literary author, the appropriate literary author number is assigned from the relevant subclass of the P schedule. Literary author numbers are also assigned to films of an author reading his or her work. If a specific Cutter number has not yet been established for the author, a class number is assigned with an incomplete Cutter, e.g., [PR6052.B].

Adult fiction films. The following guidelines are observed in classifying individual adult fiction films (i.e., those coded "e" or "g," as well as those that are coded "f" and that are determined to have an adult targeted audience):

1. All individual adult fiction films, except for comedy, experimental, and animated films, are classed in PN1997, provided that their primary purpose is entertainment. Films that are dramatizations of literary works are classed in literary author numbers only if their intention is clearly to teach about or criticize the author or the author's style or to provide opportunity for discussion, rather than simply to entertain. Certain series, such as *The Novel* or *The Short Story*, fall into this category.

2. Comedy films are classed in PN1995.9.C55; experimental films in PN1995.9.E96. These numbers are assigned to a film only when it is explicitly described as a comedy or experimental film in the 520 field.

3. Adult animated fiction films are classed in PN1997.5.

c. *Foreign language teaching films.* Films intended for use in teaching foreign languages are classed in the P schedules with the language being taught, rather than in the class for the special topic of the film. As a corollary, the heading [...] **language—Films for [...] speakers** is assigned as the first heading, and any special topics are brought out by assigning additional headings.

4. *Juvenile films.* Films are assigned a MARC code for targeted audience as described above. Films with the codes "a," "b," or "c" are treated as juvenile films. Films coded "f" are also treated as juvenile if it is clear from the title, summary, or intended audience note (521 field) that the film is juvenile in nature. For classification purposes only, fiction films coded "d" are treated as juvenile. Films coded "e" or "g" are not treated as juvenile. The guidelines below are observed when treating a film as juvenile.

a. *Subject headings.* The free-floating form subdivison —**Juvenile films** is used after all topical subject headings assigned. Children's literature catalogers assign bracketed juvenile headings as required

b. *Classification.* Topical juvenile films are classed with the appropriate topic in classes A-Z, using the number for juvenile works if one is provided under the topic. All juvenile fiction films (i.e., those coded "a," "b," "c," or "d"), whether animated or live action, are classed in PZ5-90.

c. *Special categories of juvenile films*

1. *Folk tales.* When possible, a subject entry is made under the name of an individual hero or figure around whom a series of tales or legends have been told, e.g., **Bunyan, Paul (Legendary character)—Juvenile films.** An entry is also made for the form, even in the case of individual tales, e.g., **Tales—United States—Juvenile films** and **Folklore—United States—Juvenile films**, and for the category, i.e., **Children's films.**

2. *Juvenile reading films.* A subject entry is made to bring out the topic, if the film is topical, and to bring out the form. The heading **Reading (Primary, [Elementary etc.])— Juvenile films** is generally used to bring out the form. The heading **Readers** or **Primers** is *not* used. Such films are classed in the numbers for readers in the subclasses of the P schedule.

520 field: A reading readiness film for primary grades on the subject of rain
Subject entries: Rain and rainfall—Juvenile films
                Reading readiness—Juvenile films
                Reading (Primary)—Juvenile films
050 field: [PE1127]

Motion picture and video examples in this manual have been assigned subject headings, including genre headings, as outlined in the above guidelines. For LC classification, the breakdown at PN1995.9 has been used rather than the more general PN1997 in which films are alphabetized by title. The above policy is that used at LC for their cataloging of films from data sheets, none of which go into their collections. A general classification number serves as guidance for eventual users of LC catalog copy. In actual use, the subject/genre breakdown at PN1995.9 has worked well at the library for which I catalog. An online browse through the shelflist shows films of the same type classed together.

Subject headings for examples in this manual

All examples include LC subject headings. Some examples also include Sears subject headings. The Sears headings are enclosed in square brackets.

Classification numbers for examples in this manual

Both LC classification numbers and Dewey numbers are given with each example in this manual. Most examples have Dewey numbers from the 20th edition of DDC. I'm not a regular Dewey user, so feel free to disagree with me on any of these choices.

"In" Analytics and Other Methods of Analysis

One of the many problems in cataloging audiovisual materials is deciding what to do when a boxful of material might be cataloged as a unit, but one or more parts of it seem important enough to be cataloged separately.

Chapter 13 of *AACR 2* includes rules for cataloging such material. It describes analytics of monographic series and multipart monographs, treatment in the note area of such material, analytical added entries, "In" analytics, and multilevel description. The Library of Congress is not using multilevel description; however, we are free to use any of the methods described in this chapter.

In chapter 3 of this manual, example 6 shows the cataloging of a map in a book as an "In" analytic. An example in chapter 4 of this manual, *The Funeral of Sir Winston Churchill*, shows the cataloging of a sound recording as an "In" analytic.

If we have a large package of material we wish to catalog as a kit, and that package contains a motion picture that was designed as part of the kit but could be used separately, we can catalog the kit as a whole, and, in addition, make a separate bibliographic record for the motion picture as an "In" analytic.

Sets of material

Frequently we receive boxes of material containing several titles that could be cataloged individually or could be cataloged as a unit. Either treatment is correct. These items can be treated as one unit, or the individual titles can be cataloged separately as a monographic series. The decision on treatment is a matter of the cataloger's judgment and library policy. The examples in chapter 6, *Word Processing* and *Careers*, show two ways to handle this type of material, as does the example *Cat Skeleton* in chapter 8.

If the separate titles would have similar, or identical, summaries, and would all have the same subject headings and same added entries, the whole package should be cataloged as a unit, with added entries made for each title. If, however, each title should have its own distinctly different summary, and each would have different subject headings, each should be cataloged with its own bibliographic record.

A set that could be cataloged as a whole with a contents note taking the place of a summary, is a set of filmstrips, part of a series on elementary mathematics, called *Addition and Subtraction of Fractional Numbers With Any Denominator*.

Individual titles are:

Review and Extension,
Union of Two Sets and Addition of Two Numbers,
Separation of Sets and Subtraction of Numbers,
Fractional Numbers and Some Basic Properties,
Addition and Subtraction of Fractional Numbers with the Same Denominator.

A set of filmstrips that clearly needs individual cataloging is the set titled *Continental Europe in Revolution (1789-1890)*. In this set, the individual summaries would provide information important to the user, and each title would have different subject headings.

Individual titles are:

> Prelude to the French Revolution (1789),
> The French Revolution (1789-1795),
> Napoleon and the Empire (1795-1815),
> The Metternich Era (1815-1848),
> The Revolution in ideas (1840-1860),
> The Unification of Italy (1848-1870),
> The Rise of Germany (1860-1890).

These filmstrips would have very different summaries and many different subject headings. They should be treated as a monographic series. It is not necessary to repackage items when cataloging them separately. The set comes in a sturdy box and can be left in the box. The series area on the bibliographic record for each separate title will carry the information about the title of the set, and the series added entry will direct the user to the set, as will the individual bibliographic records. The titles can be cataloged individually, but the set can remain packaged as a unit, or one can choose to repackage these individually.

The arithmetic example would get the same classification number whether the titles would be cataloged individually or as a set. The European history item would not. If one wanted these items each to be shelved with the appropriate number for the country and time period, one could choose to repackage them individually as they were cataloged. They could be classified individually at that time.

Some advice

Here I'd like to offer some advice to catalogers. The rules and their changes may be bewildering, and you may have difficulty in deciding what is *right*. While we want our cataloging to be done correctly, the more important word of those two (*done* and *correctly*) is "done." We catalog materials to provide a service to our users, to describe the material so they know enough about it to decide if it is what they might want to use, and to provide access by enough words, terms, phrases, and names so the user can find it. But we must complete the cataloging before that description or access or the item itself is available to the user.

Don't worry about your cataloging. Do it step by step, beginning with the information on the item designated as the chief source of information. Decide on the title proper. Then decide on the GMD. Then decide if there is other title information. And so on. Concentrate on one little decision at a time, and, if one presents a problem, skip over it and go on to the next. Look up rules and rule interpretations as needed. Make a decision, then go on to the next. Once a decision is made, don't go back to it. Get the cataloging *done*.

Another secret. The fewer bits of information there are on an item to be cataloged, the easier the cataloging is. You might have to supply a few bits of information to complete the cataloging, but you don't have to deal with multiple forms of title, excess publishers and distributors, or other confusing words strewn over a container. Try it.

Card Format

Card format is used in the examples. There is no standard format for layout of catalog cards; those using cards may choose whatever format they wish.

```
Main entry (personal, corporate, conference, or uniform
title)
     Title proper [GMD] : other title information / statement
of responsibility. -- Edition information. -- Place of pub-
lication : Name of publisher, distributor, etc., Date of
publication.
     Extent of item : color or other information ; size. --
(Series ; series number)

     Notes ...............................and continutation
of notes.
     Each note begins a separate paragraph.

     1. Subject heading.  I. Added entry.


Title main entry with title proper [GMD] : other title informa-
     tion / statement of responsibility. -- Edition information.
     -- Place of publication : Name of publisher, distributor,
     etc., Date of publication.
     Extent of item : color or other information ; size. --
(Series ; series number)

     Notes .................................................and
continutation of notes.
     Each note beings a separate paragraph.

     1. Subject heading.  I. Added entry.
```

MARC Coding and Tagging

All the examples in this book can be found with MARC codes and tags for OCLC's PRISM service in the publication *Catalogers' Guide to MARC Coding & Tagging for AV Materials*, by Nancy B. Olson. (DeKalb, Ill.: Minnesota Scholarly Press, 1992).

Chapter 3

CARTOGRAPHIC MATERIALS

AACR 2 Chapter 3

This chapter covers cartographic materials of all kinds. For items that have cartographic content, but whose physical form would be covered by another chapter (for example, map puzzles), rules for both relevant chapters are used together. For more detailed information, users are referred to: *Cartographic Materials: A Manual of Interpretation for AACR 2,* prepared by the Anglo-American Cataloguing Committee for Cartographic Material, Hugo L. P. Stibbe, general editor (Chicago, Ill. : American Library Association, 1982). This AACCM manual is out of date in some respects, but still contains much helpful information. Another publication that may be helpful is *Map Cataloging Manual*, prepared by Geography and Map Division, Library of Congress (Washington, D.C.: Cataloging Distribution Service, Library of Congress, 1991).

Special Rules for Cataloging Cartographic Materials

In this section the special rules for cataloging cartographic materials will be discussed. Parts of some of the rules are given; the user is referred to *AACR 2* for the complete text and examples.

Chief Source of Information

The chief source of information is the cartographic item itself. If there are multiple parts, all the parts are considered as one.

Title and Statement of Responsibility Area

Rule 3.1E2 directs us to supply, in brackets, a word or phrase indicating the geographic area covered by the map if the title proper with any other title information does not indicate this geographic area.

```
The National Road [GMD] : [eastern United States]
```

Mathematical Data Area

Area 3 is used in this chapter for statement of scale, statement of projection, and statement of coordinates and equinox.

Statement of scale

The scale is given as a representative fraction expressed as a ratio. Other expressions may be added.

```
Scale 1:1,550,000
Scale 1:71,000. 1 cm. = ca. 0.7 km. 1 in. = ca. 1.1 mi.
```

If the scale found on the item is not given in this form, calculate it from the information given.

Example of calculations

>   On the item: `1 inch = 58.4 miles.`

We need to find the number of inches in 58.4 miles. There are 63,360 inches in 1 mile (5,280 ft. x 12 in./ft.). 63,360 in./mi. x 58.4 mi. = 3,700,224 inches. Round to 3,700,000.

>   `Scale [ca. 1:3,700,000]`

The fraction is given in brackets because it is calculated; it did not appear on the chief source in this form.

Statement of projection

The projection statement, and phrases associated with it, are given following the scale statement.

>   `; Lambert conformal conic proj., standard parallels 47° 55´ and`
>   `59° 35´`
>   `; transverse Mercator proj.`
>   `; Albers conical equal-area proj., standard parallels 29° 30´`
>   `and 45° 30´`

Statement of coordinates and equinox

Coordinates are given in degrees, minutes, and seconds. Longitude (up and down) is given first, then latitude (width). The four coordinates are given in order: westernmost extent of area — easternmost extent of area/northernmost extent of area — southernmost extent of area.

>   `(W 97° --W 89° /N 49° 30´´--N 46°)`
>   `(W 145° 0--W 102° /N 67° --N 46°)`
>   `(W 140° 00´00´´--W 138° 30´00´/N 45° 00´00´´--N 42° 30´00´´)`

Physical Description Area

Extent of item

Terms that may be used as specific material designations include:

>   atlas
>   diagram
>   globe
>   map
>   map section
>   profile
>   relief model
>   remote-sensing image
>   view

Terms may be borrowed from other chapters if needed.

>   `1 puzzle`

One map may be printed in segments, or several sheets. Several maps may be printed on one sheet. The rule give very detailed directions on giving extent of maps.

```
1 map on 3 sheets
3 maps on 1 sheet
```

Other physical details

Details specified here include:

> number of maps in an atlas
> color
> material (if other than paper)
> mounting

Dimensions

The size of a map is given as height, then width, in centimeters, rounded to the next whole centimeter (68.4 cm. is rounded up to 69 cm.).

If the map has a border, the border is *not* included in the dimensions. If there is a *neat line* (a narrow line enclosing and touching the actual map) measurements are made within the neat line.

```
1 map : col. ; 69 x 103 cm.
```

If a part of the map extends through the neat line into the border, that extension is included in the measurement. If there is no border, the entire map is measured, and the words "on sheet" are used.

```
1 map : col. ; on sheet 58 x 89 cm.
```

The *AACR 2* rules give direction for handling the many complications of describing and measuring maps. The AACCCM manual illustrates some of these possibilities with diagrams. Measuring folded maps also is explained.

Notes Area

Notes permitted in this chapter are:

3.7B1. Nature and scope of the item
3.7B2. Language
3.7B3. Source of title proper
3.7B4. Variations in title
3.7B5. Parallel titles and other title information
3.7B6. Statements of responsibility
3.7B7. Edition and history
3.7B8. Mathematical and other cartographic data
3.7B9. Publication, distribution, etc.
3.7B10. Physical description
3.7B11. Accompanying material
3.7B12. Series
3.7B13. Dissertation
3.7B14. Audience
3.7B16. Other formats
3.7B18. Contents
3.7B19. Numbers
3.7B20. Copy being described, library's holdings, and restrictions on use
3.7B21. "With" notes

Explanation of notes

Each of the notes will be explained in the following section and examples of their use given.

1.7A5. ... When appropriate, combine two or more notes to make one note.

3.7B1. *Nature and scope of the item*

To be used to make notes on the nature or scope of a cartographic item, unless that information is obvious from the rest of the bibliographic description. Also used to note unusual features of the item.
There is no summary note used in this chapter. Explanatory description must go in this note.

> *Examples:* ` Locates covered bridges existing in Ohio in 1972`
> ` "Contour interval 10 feet"`
> ` Relief shown by contours, hachures, and spot heights`

3.7B2. *Language*

To be used to name the language or languages of the item if not obvious from the description.

> *Example:* ` Text in English and French`

3.7B3. *Source of title proper*

To be used if the title proper is taken from other than the chief source of information.

> *Example:* ` Title supplied by cataloger`

3.7B4. *Variations in title*

To be used to note any title appearing on the item that differs significantly from the title proper.

> *Example:* ` Panel title: New York, New Jersey, Pennsylvania`
> (*Title proper:* The Northeast)

3.7B5. *Parallel titles and other title information*

To be used for parallel titles and important other title information not recorded in area 1.

> *Example:* ` Panel title: I [love] NY.  The word "love" is represented by a`
> ` heart`

3.7B6. *Statements of responsibility*

To be used to record information not given in area 1.

> *Example:* ` "Produced for and funded by the United States Department of Educa-`
> ` tion, Office of Special Education and Rehabilitative Service"`

3.7B7. *Edition and history*

To be used for information about earlier editions or about the history of the item.

Example: Supplement to The national geographic magazine, v. 153, no. 1 (Jan. 1978).

3.7B8. *Mathematical and other cartographic data*

To be used for important information not already given in area 3.

Example: Scale of most counties ca. 1:210,000

3.7B9. *Publication, distribution, etc.*

To be used for important information not recorded in area 4.

Example: Base map by Jeppesen & Co., 1964, "revised 5-68"

3.7B10. *Physical description*

To be used for important information not recorded in area 5, especially if the details may affect the use of the item.

Example: Raised outlines for buildings, raised dotted lines for streets, street names and building symbols in braille and large print

3.7B11. *Accompanying material*

To be used for details not given in area 5 concerning the accompanying material.

Example: Sheet of additions, deletions, and corrections dated "1972, revised 1984"

3.7B12. *Series*

To be used for additional series information.

Example: Some maps also part of series: Maps of Asia

3.7B13. *Dissertations*

To be used for the standard dissertation note when needed.

Example: Thesis (Ph. D.)--University of Wisconsin, 1990

3.7B14. *Audience*

To be used to state the intended audience of an item, *if* the information is stated on the item.

Example: Intended audience: Students in grades K-3

3.7B16. *Other formats*

To be used to name other formats the item has been published in.

Example: Also issued in microfiche

3.7B18. Contents

To be used to describe contents of a collection. To be used to list contents of an item, including insets, illustrations, and information on the verso of an item.

Examples: `On verso: Glittering cities, lonely wild lands`
`Includes inset maps: W. Washington County -- N. Perry County`
`-- Cent. Preble County`

3.7B19. Numbers

To be used to record important numbers on the item other than ISBN or ISSN.

Example: `"[Roll] 226--[frame] 14 44916 HAP 85"`

3.7B20. Copy being described, library's holdings, and restrictions on use

To be used for local information.

Example: `Library copy lacks acompanying brochure`

3.7B21. "With" notes

To be used for "with" notes.

Example: `With: Lands of the dinosaur`

I'm not an experienced map cataloger, although for the past two years I have cataloged the items for which we could not find copy on OCLC. When working in an unfamiliar format, or with unfamiliar materials, it always helps to begin with items that have good OCLC copy, then progress to those that have copy needing minor editing, then to those needing major editing, and finally to those that need original input. Thus we learn from others who are cataloging this material, even though we might never meet any of them. In the examples that follow, I have attempted to use all the rules as well as the suggestions from the AACCCM manual listed at the beginning of this chapter. If you see something that is not correct, please let me know.

Map classification numbers have more parts to them than other classification numbers in the LC system. The map class numbers shown in these examples are *not* complete. They contain only that part of the number that goes in subfield ǂa of the 090 in the MARC format; the cutter number for main entry (subfield ǂb) is not included. Map classification numbers frequently have three cutter numbers, the third, given after the situation date, being for the main entry.

Example 1: Geologic Map

This first map is one I needed to catalog last fall. It had all the pertinent information clearly given, and was prepared by the U.S. Geological Survey.

It has latitude and longitude clearly marked in each corner. This information is to be transcribed in a prescribed order and format as part of area 3.

The scale is given on the map, so does not have to be calculated.

Rules for notes are, in order, 3.7B1, 3.7B18.

From the bottom of the map

GEOLOGIC MAP OF THE VICINITY OF THE OUTLET OF GLACIAL LAKE AGASSIZ, NORTH DAKOTA, SOUTH DAKOTA, AND MINNESOTA

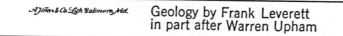

Geology by Frank Leverett
in part after Warren Upham

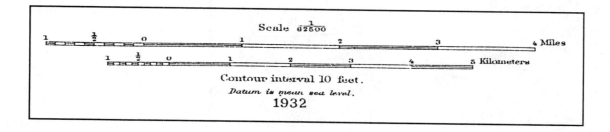

Scale $\frac{1}{62500}$

Contour interval 10 feet.

Datum is mean sea level.

1932

From the upper left hand corner of the map

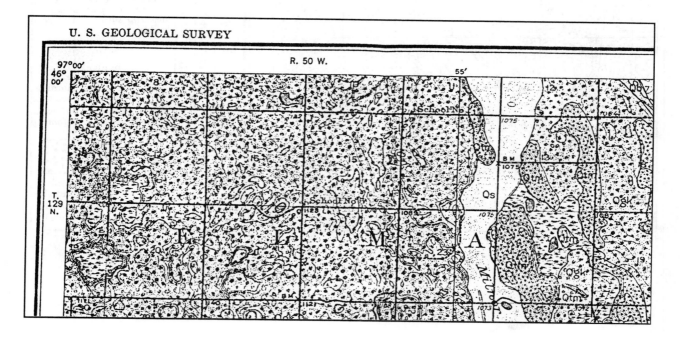

Example 1: Geologic Map

From the upper right hand corner of the map

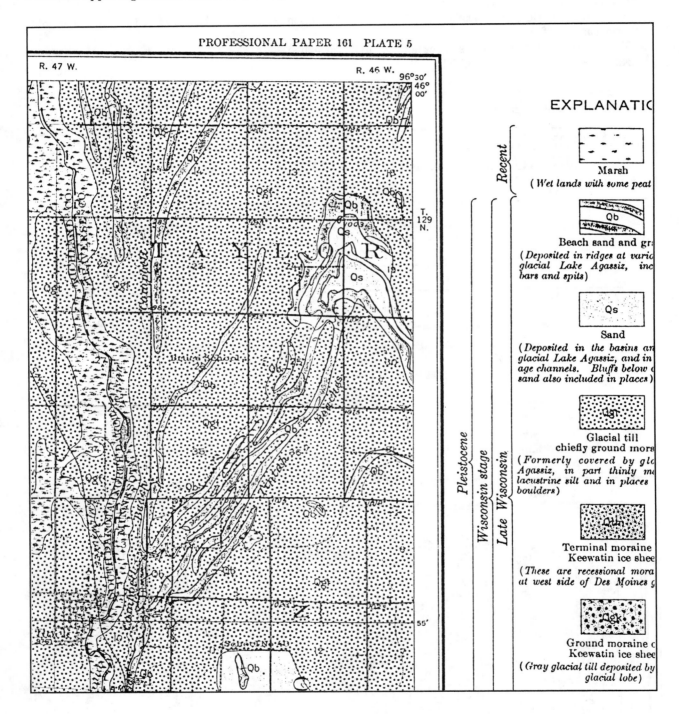

Example 1: Geologic Map

```
G         Geological Survey (U.S.)
4141          Geologic map of the vicinity of the outlet of
.C5       glacial Lake Agassiz, North Dakota, South Dakota,
1932      and Minnesota [map] / U.S. Geological Survey ;
          geology by Frank Leverett in part after Warren
912.776   Upham. -- Scale 1:62,500. (W 97°--W 96°30´/N
          46°00´--N 45°30´). -- Baltimore, Md. : A. Hoen,
          1932.
              1 map : col. ; 89 x 63 cm. -- (Professional paper ;
          161, plate 5)

          Relief shown by contour lines, hachures; contour
          interval 10 ft.
          Includes index, explanation.

              1. Geology--Minnesota--Maps.  2. Glacial lakes--Maps.
          3. Agassiz, Lake--Maps.  I. Leverett, Frank, 1859-1943.
          II. Upham, Warren, 1850-1934.  III. Series: Geological
          Survey professional paper ; 161, plate 5.
```

Example 2: Map Showing Lines of Transportation

This next map is one that has hung in my house since 1976. There was no classification number that exactly represented the area covered; this railroad line crossed the border between Colorado and New Mexico nine times in the relatively short distance between Chama and Antonito. A steam train makes the run daily during the summer.

The place of publication is transcribed from the map. If the state name had been spelled out, we would abbreviate it to "Colo." as given in *AACR 2* Appendix B.

Rules for notes are, in order, 3.7B1, 3.7B18.

Full view of map

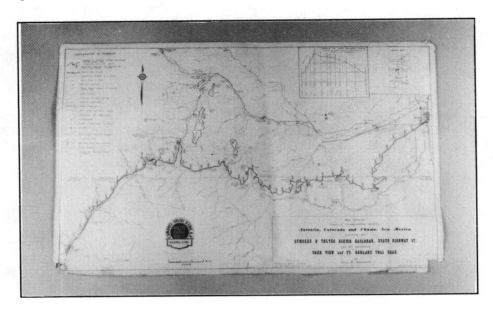

Bottom right hand corner of map

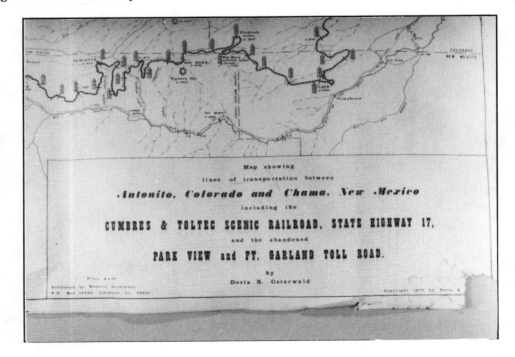

Example 2: Map Showing Lines of Transportation

Facsimile of information at bottom of map title area

Map showing
lines of transportation between
Antonito, Colorado and Chama, New Mexico
including the
CUMBRES & TOLTEC SCENIC RAILROAD, STATE HIGHWAY 17,
and the abandoned
PARK VIEW and FT. GARLAND TOLL ROAD.

Price: $1.50
Published by Western Guideways
P.O. Box 15532, Lakewood, Co., 80215

by
Doris B. Osterwald

Copyright 1975 by Doris B. [torn corner]

```
G          Osterwald, Doris B.
4311           Map showing lines of transportation between
.P3        Antonito, Colorado, and Chama, New Mexico [map] :
1975       including the Cumbres & Toltec Scenic Railroad,
           State Highway 17, and the abandoned Park View and
912.788    Ft. Garland toll road / by Doris B. Osterwald. --
           Scale [ca. 1:63,630]. -- Lakewood, Co. : Western
           Guideways, c1975.
               1 map ; 52 x 84 cm.

           Relief shown by hachures and spot heights.
           Includes index map and "Profile of C&TS railroad
           track."

               1. Colorado--Road maps.  2. New Mexico--Road maps.  3.
           Cumbres and Toltec Scenic Railroad--Maps.  I. Title.
```

Example 3: City of Lake Crystal

This map is of the town where I (and Soldier Creek Press) live. As you can see, there are very few words of cataloging information printed on the map. The resulting catalog record is very brief, and uses lots of brackets. Because the person or corporate body responsible for making the map is unknown, title main entry is used.

The note uses rule 3.7B7.

Map of Lake Crystal, Minnesota

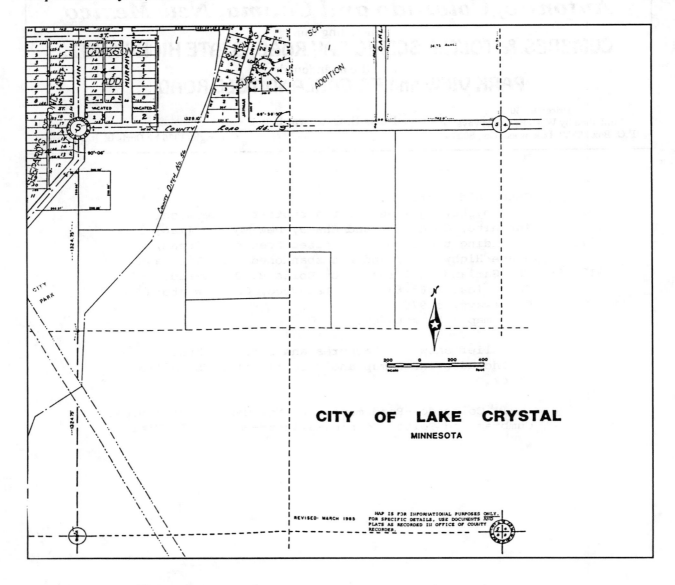

```
G           City of Lake Crystal, Minnesota [map]. -- Rev.
4144           -- Scale [ca. 1:7,200]. -- [Minnesota? :
.L34A1      s.n.], 1985.
1985           1 map ; on sheet 43 x 56 cm.

912         "Revised March 1985."
.77621

            1. Lake Crystal (Minn.)--Maps.
```

Example 4: Mankato, Minnesota

This is a photo taken from space of the town in which I work at Mankato State University. It has no information on it except a line of numbers and letters. The shipping container gave me some information. The main entry is as found in the online authority file in OCLC.

If you've never had opportunity to examine one of these photos, you would find it hard to believe the details that can be identified.

In the class number shown below G4144 means Minnesota cities, M3 is for the specific city Mankato, A3 is for an aerial photo, and 1986 the "situation" date, the date corresponding to the image recorded on the map.

Rules for notes are 3.7B3, 3.7B9, 3.7B19.

Map of Mankato, Minnesota

```
G          Earth Resources Observation Systems.
4144          [Mankato, Minnesota, area satellite image]
.M3A3      [map]. -- Scale [ca. 1:85,000]. -- [Sioux Falls,
1986       S.D. : U.S. Geological Survey, EROS Data Center,
           1989]
912           1 remote-sensing image ; 23 x 23 cm.
.77621
              Title supplied by cataloger.
              Sheet dated 8-8-86.
              "[Roll] 228-[frame] 14 449416 HAP 85."

              1. Mankato (Minn.)--Photographs from space.   I.
           Title.
```

Example 5: Ohio Covered Bridges

This map came with a sheet of additions, deletions, and corrections that showed how many covered bridges no longer existed twelve years after the map had been made. Happily, some had been moved to safe locations.

The sheet of information is treated as accompanying material. The title of the sheet included the ampersand, so it is used in area 5.

Rules for notes are 3.7B1, 3.7B9, 3.7B11, 3.7B18, 3.7B18.

Map of Ohio covered bridges

Example 5: Ohio Covered Bridges

```
G          Ohio covered bridges [map]. -- Scale
4081           indeterminable. -- Columbus, Ohio : Ohio
.P24           Historical Society, 1972.
1972             1 map : col. ; 42 x 37 on sheet 43 x 55 cm. +
               1 sheet of additions, deletions & corrections.
912.771
                   Locates covered bridges existing in Ohio in 1972.
                   "Published ... with the cooperation and assistance
               of the Ohio Covered Bridge Committee."
                   Sheet of additions, deletions, and corrections
               dated "1972, revised 1984."
                   Includes inset maps: W. Washington County -- N.
               Perry County -- Cent. Preble County.
                   Sketches of truss designs and list of covered
               bridges on verso.

                   1. Covered bridges--Ohio--Maps.  I. Ohio Historical
               Society.  II. Ohio Covered Bridge Committee.
```

Example 6: The National Road

    This is an example of an *In* analytic. The map is the centerfold of a pamphlet on the National Road. The publication is a reprint of a 1940 pamphlet; the reprint date is not given.

    Other title information is added in brackets as directed by rule 3.1E2.

    In the LC classification number, 1940 is used as the situation date, as that is the date of the situation represented in the map. If the class number were completed, the date of publication to be added after the cutter number for main entry would be 1980.

    The note uses rule number 3.7B15.

    In the National Road Museum in Ohio is a marvelous diorama showing the construction of the road through the wilderness. I found myself thinking about cataloging the diorama for an *AACR 2* chapter 10 example.

Reprinted booklet uses original title page.

THE
NATIONAL
ROAD

in song and story

Compiled by
Workers of the Writers' Program
of the Work Projects Administration
in the State of Ohio

———————

Published by
The Ohio Historical Society
Columbus, Ohio 43211

Copyright, 1940

Example 6: The National Road

Map of The National Roap

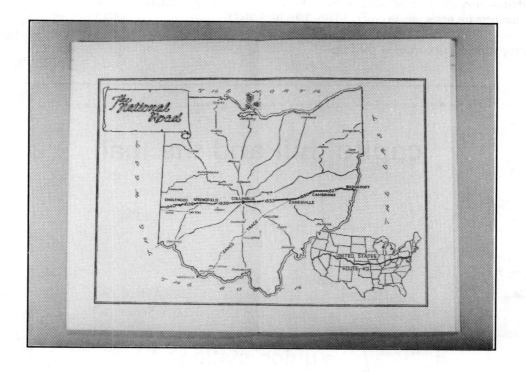

```
G          The National Road [map] : [eastern United States].
4081            -- Scale indeterminable.
.P2              1 map ; 17 x 24 cm.
1940

                 Inset: Map of United States Route 40.
912.771         In The National Road in song and story.
                -- Columbus Ohio : Ohio Historical Society,
           [198-].

                 1. National Road--Maps.
```

Example 7: Capitol Hill

This next item is a plastic map with raised lines and braille for the blind and visually handicapped, and print for the sighted. Information about the publisher is found in the accompanying brochure.

Rule numbers for notes are, in order, 3.7B6, 3.7B10, 3.7B11.

From the top right hand corner of the map

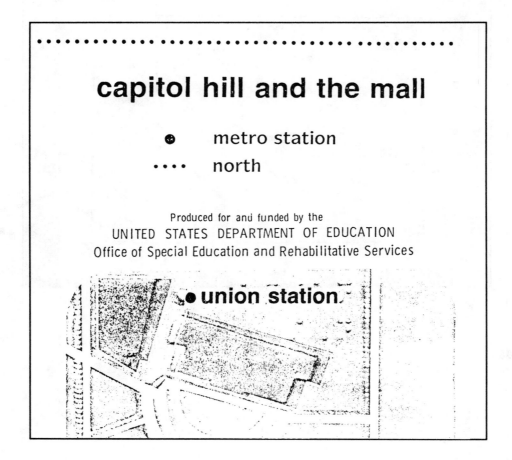

From the bottom left hand corner of the map

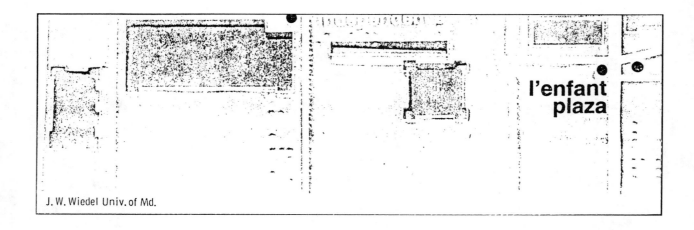

Example 7: Capitol Hill

Map of Capitol Hill and The Mall

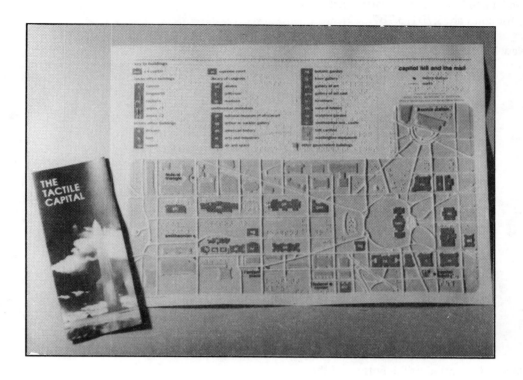

```
G          Weidel, Joseph W.
3851          Capitol Hill and the Mall [map] : [Washington,
.A7        D.C.] / J.W. Wiedel. -- Scale indeterminable. --
1988       [Ellicott City, Md. : Schuyler Fonaroff Associates,
           1988].
912.753    1 map (print, braille, and tactile) : col.,
           plastic ; 35 x 48 cm. + 1 brochure.

              "Produced for and funded by the United States Depart-
           ment of Education, Office of Special Education and Reha-
           bilitative Service."
              Raised outlines for buildings, raised dotted lines for
           streets; street names and building symbols in braille and
           large print.
              Brochure, "The tactile capital," describes exhibit,
           photographs, maps, and model of the Tactile Capital
           project for the blind, visually impaired, and others with
           disabilities.

              1. Washington (D.C.)--Maps for the blind.  2. Washing-
           ton (D.C.)--Maps for the visually handicapped.  3. Public
           buildings--Washington (D.C.)--Maps.  I. United States.
           Office of Special Education and Rehabilitative Service.
           II. Title.
```

Example 8: New Mexico in 3-D

This plastic relief map represents distance on the ground with one scale and distance above sea level with another scale. Area 3 includes both scale statements.
Rules for notes are 3.7B1, 3.7B7.

Map of New Mexico in 3-D

Facsimile of information at the bottom of the map

© 1964 Jeppesen & Co., Denver, Colo., U.S.A.

All Rights Reserved

Revised 5-68

NEW MEXICO IN 3-D

Printed 1975
Vertical Scale 1/16" = Approx. 1000'
Horizontal Scale 1" = Approx. 25 Miles

Produced by Kistler Graphics, Inc.
Denver, Colorado U.S.A.

```
G          Kistler Graphics, inc.
4321           New Mexico in 3-D [map] / produced by Kistler
.C18       Graphics. -- Scale [ca. 1:1,584,000]. 1 in. to ca.
1975       25 miles. Vertical scale [ca. 1:192,000] -- Denver,
           Colo. : Kistler, 1975.
912.789        1 relief model : col., plastic ; 42 x 38 cm.

               Relief shown by raised areas, spot heights.
           Base map by Jeppesen & Co., 1964, "revised 5-68."

               1. New Mexico--Relief models.  I. Jeppesen and Com-
           pany.  II. Title.
```

Example 9: Minnesota Outdoor Atlas

This atlas uses several different scales for the county and state maps in it. They are treated as shown.
There is no publisher named on the atlas, only the distribution statement as given in the cataloging.
Rules for notes are, in order, 3.7B8, 3.8B.

Minnesota outdoor atlas

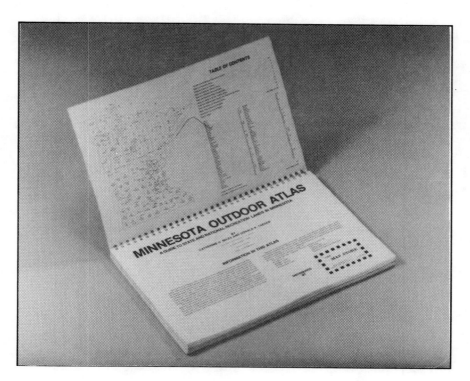

```
G         Miles, Catherine H.
1426          Minnesota outdoor atlas : a guide to state and
.E63      national recreation lands in Minnesota / by
          Catherine H. Miles and Donald P. Yaeger ; two-color
912.776   photographs by D. Yaeger. -- Scales vary. --
          [Minnesota : s.n.] ; West St. Paul, Minn. :
          Distributed by The Map Store, c1979.
              1 atlas (232 p.) : ill. (some col.), col. maps ; 44
          cm.

              Scale of most counties ca. 1:210,000.
              ISBN 0-932880-00-2.

              1. Outdoor recreation--Minnesota--Maps.  2. Minnesota
          --Public lands--Maps.  I. Yaeger, Donald P.  II. Title.
```

Example 10: Atlas of Crawford County, Iowa

This old atlas has lots of "other title information." It shows who owned each farm at the time each map was made.

Title page and table of contents for the Atlas of Crawford County, Iowa

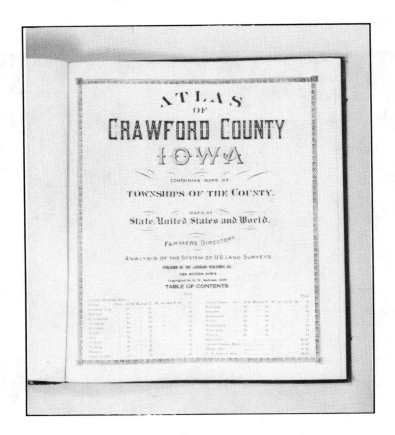

```
G          Anderson Publishing Co.
1453          Atlas of Crawford County, Iowa : containing
.C9        maps of townships of the county, maps of state,
           United States, and world, farmers directory,
912        analysis of the system of U.S. land surveys. --
.77745     Scales vary. -- Des Moines, Iowa : Anderson Pub.
           Co., c1920.
              1 atlas : col. maps ; 46 cm.

              1. Crawford County (Iowa)--Maps.  2. Real property--
           Iowa--Crawford County--Maps.  I. Title.
```

Example 11: Replogle Stereo Relief Globe

This globe has the words "stereo relief" in a box, one over the other, between the words "Replogle" and "Globe." I decided the title proper was as shown below.

No date was given on the globe following the copyright symbol.

The note is based on rule 3.7B1.

Globe

Legend on globe

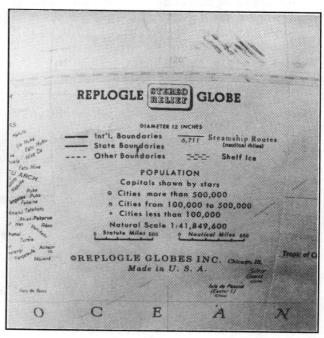

```
G        Replogle Globes, Inc.
3171         Replogle stereo relief globe [globe] -- Scale
.C18      1:41,849,600. -- Chicago, Ill. : Replogle
1970      Globes, [197-]
             1 globe : col, on metal stand ; 12 in. in diam.
912

          Relief shown by raised areas.

          1. Globes.  I. Title.
```

Example 12: Map of United States

    This jigsaw puzzle is a map of the United States, with each piece cut out separately. The pieces are not labeled on the front or on the back, which makes it much harder to reassemble. The names of the states are printed on the wooden base into which the puzzle assembles, but the state outlines are not drawn on the base. It is more challenging to assemble than one would expect.

    Although this is a map, the physical form of the item is a puzzle, so it is cataloged by rules of *AACR 2* chapter 10, with reference to chapter 3 as needed.

    It is interesting that, in area 5, a wooden map cataloged by rules of *AACR 2* chapter 3 would be described as "col., wood" while in *AACR 2* chapter 10, a puzzle is described as "wood, col."

    Rules for notes are, in order, 10.7B1, 3.7B8, 10.7B10, 10.7B14.

Wooden map of the United States

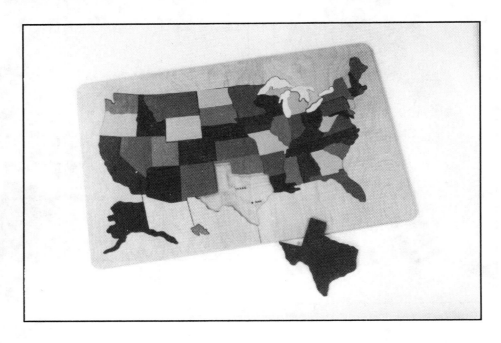

Example 12: Map of United States

Facsimile of the wrapper label

Designed exclusively for
Nashco
by
© David B. Tibbetts 1983

NASHCO PRODUCTS INC.
SCRANTON, PA 18504

GP-102
MAP OF UNITED STATES
16" x 24"
55 PIECES

The name of each state and its
capital appears under each piece.

All puzzles are hand cut and hand colored
with lead-free non-toxic paint.

Not recommended for children under 3 years of age.

```
G          Map of United States [game] / designed exclusively
3701          for Nashco by David B. Tibbetts. -- Scranton, PA
.F1           : Nashco Products, 1963.
                 1 puzzle (55 pieces) : wood, col. ; 41 x 60
912.73     cm.

              Wooden tray with depressed area into which state
           and Great Lakes pieces are to be assembled; name of
           each state and its capital, and each lake, is on tray
           in correct location; pieces not labeled.
              Scale not given.
              "All puzzles are hand cut and hand colored with
           leadfree, non-toxic paint."
              "Not recommended for children under 3 years of
           age."

              1. United States--Maps.  2. Puzzles.  I. Tibbetts,
           David B.  II. Nashco Products, Inc.
```

Example 13: Global Pursuit

This game is a favorite in my family. One must answer questions about explorations, physical geography, economic geography, and political geography, then correctly assemble five-sided map cards into a flat map (and with four sets of these five-sided cards, one can assemble a continuous flat map with four of each continent, ocean, etc.). It's tricky, and challenging, and fun. It can also be embarrassing when you realize you don't know where the map piece in your hand fits onto the world.

Yes, my library does have a copy of this, and it does circulate.

I included it in this chapter because it is map-related. It is cataloged using *AACR 2* chapter 10, with the map notes based on *AACR 2* chapter 3.

Rules for notes are, in order, 10.7B1, 10.7B10, 3.7B11, 10.7B17, 10.7B18.

Game box and pieces

Example 13: Global Pursuit

GV
1485

795.43

Global pursuit [game] / National Geographic. --
   Washington, D.C. : National Geographic Society,
   c1987.
     1 game (various pieces) ; in box 26 x 42 x 8
cm.

"A fun-filled geography game for the whole family."
Map cards are five-sided; each set forms a complete
dodecahedron; include political map, physical map, map
of natural resources, and map of explorations.
Map: The world / produced by the Cartographic
Division, National Geographic Society. Scale
1:67,200,000 ; Van der Grinten proj. Washington, D.C.
: The Society, c1987. 1 map : col., plastic ; 46 x 61
cm. "Prepared specially for National Geographic's
Global pursuit game." Insets: Language groups -- Reli-
gions (both Eckert equal-area proj.) -- Antarctica --
Arctic Ocean.
Summary: Player must answer questions correctly and
assemble map pieces to earn points. For 2-6 players or
teams.
Includes 6 decks trivia cards, 4 sets map cards,
12-sided die, plastic tokens, manual, and wall map.

1. Geographical recreations. I. National Geographic Society (U.S.) II. Title: National Geographic
Global pursuit.

Example 14: Globe Coffee Set

This is an example of what is referred to in *Baseline* (published by the American Library Association Map and Geography Round Table) as a "cartifact," a cartographic-related artifact. It is cataloged using *AACR 2* chapter 10. Rules for notes are 10.7B1, 10.7B3, 10.7B10, 10.7B10.

Pot and cups

```
TX        [Globe coffee set][realia]. -- [United States] :
817           Nescafé,  [198-]
.C6              1 coffee pot, 2 cups : glass ; 16, 7 cm.
              high.
641.877
                  Globe-shaped cups and coffee pot, distributed by
              Nescafé as premiums.
                  Title supplied by cataloger.
                  Continents and latitude and longitude lines etched
              on glass surface. Latitude lines used as indication of
              capacity of coffee pot; marked "Two, four, six."
                  Molded on underside of cups: "Taste your way,
              Nescafé."

                  1. Coffee brewing--Equipment and supplies.  I.
              Nescafé (Firm).
```

Chapter 4

SOUND RECORDINGS

AACR 2 Chapter 6

This chapter shows cataloging of sound recordings. Most examples are non-musical. For cataloging music, catalogers are referred to: *Cataloging Music: A Manual for Use with AACR 2* by Richard P. Smiraglia. 2d ed. (Lake Crystal, Minn.: Soldier Creek Press, 1986).

Special Rules for Cataloging Sound Recordings

In this section the special rules for cataloging sound recordings will be discussed. Parts of some of the rules are given; the user is referred to *AACR 2* for the complete text and examples. All of the Library of Congress rule interpretations (LCRIs) for the material in general, and for non-music items, are included.

Chief Source of Information

The chief source of information for the common types of sound recordings is the information on the label or labels; two labels (sides one and two) are treated as a single chief source.

Rule 6.01B1 allows the use of the container as chief source if it gives a collective title and the labels do not.

Title and Statement of Responsibility Area

LCRI 6.1B1. If the chief source shows the name of an author or the name of a performer before the titles of the individual works and there is doubt whether the publisher, etc., intended the name to be a collective title proper or a statement of responsibility, treat the name as the title proper. *Exception:* If the works listed are musical compositions and the name is that of the composer of the works, treat the name as a statement of responsibility in cases of doubt.

If the chief source being followed is the label of a sound recording and the decision is to treat the name as a title proper but one name appears on the label of one side and another name on the second side, transcribe the two names as individual titles (separated by a period-space). (*CSB* 44)

6.1F1. Transcribe statements of responsibility relating to writers of spoken words, composers of performed music, and collectors of field material for sound recordings ... If the participation ... goes beyond that of performance, execution, or interpretation of a work (as is commonly the case with popular, rock and jazz music), give such a statement as a statement of responsibility. If, however, the participation is confined to performance, execution, or interpretation (as commonly the case with "serious" or classical music and recorded speech), give the statement in the note area.

LCRI 6.1F1. The rule allows performers who do more than perform to be named in the statement of responsibility. Accept only the most obvious cases as qualifying for the statement of responsibility. (*CSB* 11)

Publication, Distribution, etc. Area

The May 1982 issue of *Music Cataloging Bulletin* included the question, "What will be the authority for place of publication for sound recordings if none is given on the label or container?" The answer from the Library of Congress was that LC will use only what appears on the item. If no city is given and there is a country, this will be used. "S.l." can be used if a probable country cannot be given.

A date may be preceded by the letter "p." The symbol ℗ indicates the copyright date of recorded sound. The date is transcribed preceded by the letter "p" instead of "c."

```
p1989
```

If several dates appear on an item, the latest may be used to infer date of publication. An inferred date is bracketed.

Physical Description Area

Extent of item

Rule 6.5B1 lists the terms that may be used as specific material designations:

    sound cartridge,
    sound cassette,
    sound disc,
    sound tape reel,
    sound track film.

If none of these terms is appropriate, we are to give the specific name of the item. See sound page, sound sheet, and sound disc card examples in this chapter.

The item shown in Figure 2 has a strip of magnetic tape applied to IBM tab card stock; the strip of magnetic tape is a sound recording. The item could be called a "sound tape card.".

Figure 2

Another unusual type of media is sound recorded on a videocassette. These are available in VHS and in Beta formats and are supposed to provide high quality sound. Such an item would be cataloged as a sound recording, because that is what it really is. The physical description would use "sound videocassette" for specific material designation. A note would be needed to explain no pictures are involved, though a TV set is needed (or a digital pulse code modulator). A note suggested by Verna Urbanski (Online Audiovisual Catalogers. *Newsletter*, 10 (Mar. 1990), 32) is

```
Recorded on a VHS videocassette for playback on a VCR with
pulse code modulator or CRT.
```

Playing time

New rules in chapter 1 provide four possibilities for recording playing time. If the playing time is stated on the item, we are to give the playing time as stated. It is not to be rounded up or down. If the playing time is not stated, but is readily ascertainable, we are to give it. As an option, if no playing time is stated or readily ascertainable, we may give an approximate time, using "ca."

```
(ca. 5 min.)
```

When one is cataloging a multipart item, the playing time is treated as above, with the addition of the word "each", or a total time may be given.

```
(15 min. each)
(ca. 15 min. each)
```

LCRI 6.5B2. When the total playing time of a sound recording is not stated on the item but the durations of its parts (sides, individual works, etc.) are, if desired add the stated durations together and record the total, rounding off to the next minute if the total exceeds 5 minutes.

Precede a statement of duration by "ca." only if the statement is given on the item in terms of an approximation. Do not add "ca." to a duration arrived at by adding partial durations or by rounding off seconds.

If no durations are stated on the item or if the durations of some but not all the parts of a work are stated, do not give a statement of duration. Do not approximate durations from the number of sides of a disc, type of cassette, etc. (*CSB* 33)

Other physical details

Each sound recording must be identified as "analog" or "digital." If it says digital anywhere on the item, use "digital." If the term digital does not appear on the item, use "analog."

Playing speed is not given if standard for the item. It is not given for sound cassettes and compact discs. Playing speed is to be given for sound discs and for tape reels.

Groove characteristics are specified only if not standard for the type of disc.

Number of tracks are not given if standard for the item.

The terms "mono.", "stereo.", and "quad." are used only when the information is on the item. If the item says "hi-fi," record "stereo."

Dimensions

Dimensions of cartridges and cassettes are to be given only if they are other than the standard dimensions.

Notes Area

Notes permitted in this chapter are:

6.7B1. Nature or artistic form and medium of performance
6.7B2. Language
6.7B3. Source of title proper
6.7B4. Variations in title
6.7B5. Parallel titles and other title information
6.7B6. Statements of responsibility
6.7B7. Edition and history
6.7B9. Publication, distribution, etc.

6.7B10. Physical description
6.7B11. Accompanying material
6.7B12. Series
6.7B13. Dissertations
6.7B14. Audience
6.7B16. Other formats
6.7B17. Summary
6.7B18. Contents
6.7B19. Publisher's numbers
6.7B20. Copy being described, library's holdings, and restrictions on use
6.7B21. "With" notes

Explanation of notes

Each of the notes will be explained in the following section and examples of their use given.

1.7A5. ... When appropriate, combine two or more notes to make one note.

Example: `Radio programs from Dec. 29, 1946, and July 27, 1947,`
`that "journey into the realm of the strange and the`
`terrifying"`

6.7B1. Nature or artistic form and medium of performance

To be used to name or explain the form of the item as necessary.

Example: `Radio program`

6.7B2. Language

To be used to name the language or languages of the spoken or sung content of the item cataloged if not obvious from other information given.

Example: `Narration in Spanish, guide in Spanish and English`

6.7B3. Source of title proper

To be used if the title proper is taken from other than the chief source of information.

Examples: `Title from container`
`Title supplied by cataloger`

6.7B4. Variations in title

To be used to note any title appearing on the item that differs significantly from the title proper.

Example: `Title on container: Folklore in the church`
                (*Title proper*: Church folklore)

6.7B5. Parallel titles and other title information

To be used for parallel titles and important other title information not recorded in the title and statement of responsibility area.

Example: Subtitle on guide: An elder wise man describes his
life & poetry
(*Title proper*: Robert Frost & his world)

6.7B6. *Statements of responsibility*

To be used to record important information not recorded in the statement of responsibility area.

> **LCRI 6.7B6** In giving the names of players in nonmusic sound recordings, caption the note Cast. Add the roles or parts of players if deemed appropriate, in parentheses after the name (cf. 7.7B6). (*CSB* 13)

Examples: Narrator: David Brinkley
Interviewer: Edwin Newman

6.7B7. *Edition and history*

To be used for information about earlier editions, or to record the history of the item being cataloged.

Example: Recorded in Los Angeles, Jan. 8, 1972

6.7B9. *Publication, distribution, etc.*

To be used for important information not recorded in the publication, distribution, etc. area.

Example: Imprint on label: Learning Plans, Inc., Tuscon, Arizona

6.7B10. *Physical description*

To be used for any important information not given in area 5, the physical description area.

> **LCRI 6.7B10.** Give a note on the presence of container(s) only when the number of containers is not clear from the rest of the description. (*MCB* Mar. 1981)

Examples: In two volumes
Compact disc
Durations: 16 min., 7 sec. ; 12 min., 32 sec.

6.7B11. *Accompanying material*

To be used for any important information not given in the accompanying material part of area 5.

Example: Notes by Sharon Donovan on container

6.7B12. *Series*

To be used for any important information not recorded in the series area.

Example: Also issued as part of series: Man and molecule

6.7B13. *Dissertations*

To be used for the standard dissertation note when applicable.

Example: Thesis (M.A.)--University of Minnesota, 1964

6.7B14. Audience

To be used to record the intended audience of a work. Use this note only if the information is stated on the item. Do not attempt to judge the audience for an item.

Example: `Audience: Kindergarten to grade 3`

6.7B16. Other formats available

To be used to list other formats in which the work is available. The Library of Congress lists all formats commercially available in this note.

Example: `Issued also on sound tape reel`

6.7B17. Summary

To be used for a brief objective summary of the content of the item.

Example: `Summary: Interviews with Jewish immigrants and with immigrants from China, Ireland, Italy, Mexico, Poland, Cuba, Germany, Greece, Hungary, Japan, Finland, Norway, Denmark, and Sweden, who arrived in America between 1902 and 1968`

6.7B18. Contents

To be used for a formal or informal listing of the contents of the item.

Example: `Contents: General introduction (2 min.) -- Street gang (9 min., 43 sec.) -- Antiwar demonstration (5 min., 16 sec.) -- Viet Nam veterans (5 min., 46 sec.) -- Frank Garcia (5 min., 30 sec.) -- Rachel Ortiz (14 min., 30 sec.)`

6.7B19. Publishers' numbers

To be used to list any important number appearing on the item other than those to be recorded in area 8.

> **LCRI 6.7B19.** The label name and number note will be the first note on the bibliographic record. (*CSB* 14)

Cataloging Service Bulletin 14 gives details of transcription of spaces, punctuation marks, etc., of this number.

> "The label name is to be the same as the information given in the publication, distribution, etc. area" (Glenn Patton, letter to the author, 27 Dec. 1984).

Example: `CBS: CK 37574`

6.7B20. Copy being described, library's holdings, and restrictions on use

To be used for any notes applicable only to the particular copy of the item being described. Also used for local library restrictions on the material being described, or for information of use only to patrons of the local library.

Example: `Use restricted to those enrolled in Law Enforcement 534`

6.7B21. "With" notes

To be used for "with" notes.

Example: With: The fusion torch / B.J. Eastlund

Cataloging Conference Proceedings

Conference proceedings on sound cassettes can be especially difficult to catalog. In addition to the abbreviated titles often found on the labels (mentioned in chapter 2), there may be problems in determining the names of the speakers, titles of the speeches, and information about the conference itself. Too often the speaker is introduced with "The following speaker needs no introduction." Or "Tom will now tell us about his latest research findings."

When I have a group of conference proceedings to be cataloged, and I cannot find any bibliographic records in OCLC for the titles as given on the labels, I contact the faculty member who ordered or donated the tapes. That person might have a conference program with all the information I need. If not, the faculty member probably will be able to tell me the name of the association that was meeting, or something about the conference. If it is an annual conference of an association or a meeting sponsored by an association, the association's newsletter probably has the information I need.

As I listen to the tapes, I search for any clue as to the actual title and subject matter of each speech, the name of the person speaking or reading a paper (sometimes not the intended speaker), the date of the presentation, site of the meeting, etc. By listening to all the introductions, closings, and speeches themselves, I can sometimes get all the information needed for cataloging. Some speaker might accidentally mention the name of the city or something about the national news of the day that enables me to determine the date. Or a speaker might thank his "esteemed colleague Joe Jones, who has collaborated with me on this research for ten years now." A search of OCLC on the colleague's name could pull up a research paper written by him and our speaker "Tom" on the topic being presented at the conference.

Main Entry for Sound Recordings

There are special, and lengthy, rules and rule interpretations for main entry of sound recordings. Rule 21.23D splits recordings into those "in which the participation of the performer(s) goes beyond that of performance, execution, or interpretation" and those in which it does not.

Excerpts from some of these rules:

21.23A1. Enter a sound recording of one work under the heading appropriate to that work....

21.23B1. Enter a sound recording of two or more works all by the same person(s) or body (bodies) under the heading appropriate to those works....

21.23C1. If a sound recording containing works by different persons or bodies has a collective title, enter it under the heading for the person or body represented as principal performer.

If there are two or three persons or bodies represented as principal performers, enter under the heading for the first named....

If there are four or more persons or bodies represented as principal performers, or if there is no principal performer, enter under title.

Rule 21.23D1a, for a sound recording of popular, rock, or jazz music that contains works by different persons or bodies with no collective title, directs us to enter under principal performer.

If there are two or three principal performers of the popular, rock, or jazz music, we enter under the heading for the first named performer.

If there are four or more performers, and no principal performer, we enter under the heading for the first work.

Rule 21.23D1b, for classical or "serious" music, directs us to enter works with no collective title under the heading appropriate to the first work.

Example 15: Macbeth

This example shows the usefulness of the uniform title. All versions of Macbeth are brought together with the uniform title, regardless of the wording or spelling or language of the chief source of information.

The place of publication is given as shown because it is found in that form on the record label, the chief source of information.

A quoted note is treated as shown in the third note. The source of the quote is given unless the quote is taken from the chief source of information.

Rules for notes are, in order, 6.7B19 (moved into first position), 6.7B6, 6.7B7.

Record jacket, disc, and text

Label from disc, side one

Example 15: Macbeth

```
PR          Shakespeare, William, 1564-1616.
2823            [Macbeth. Selections]
            Great scenes from Macbeth [sound recording] /
            Shakespeare. -- New York, N.Y. : Caedmon, [1963]
                1 sound disc : analog, 33 1/3 rpm ; 12 in. + 1
822.33      booklet (24 p. ; 28 cm.)

                Caedmon: TC 1167.
                Anthony Quayle, Gwen Ffrangcon Davies, Stanley
            Holloway, and cast ; directed by Howard Sackler.
                "From American Shakespeare 7th annual festival
            award winning series"--Album cover.

                1. English drama--Early modern and Elizabethan,
            1500-1600.  I. Davies, Gwen Ffrangcon.  II.
            Holloway, Stanley.  III. Quayle, Anthony, 1913-
            IV. Sackler, Howard.  V. Title.  VI. Title:
            Macbeth.
```

Example 16: Loyalties

The question mark is transcribed as part of other title information.

The statement "A Contact Record" is included as quoted information in a 6.7B7 note.

Both summary and contents notes are used in this example. The title alone is not descriptive, and the contents note gives little indication of the real purpose of the record.

Note the manufacturer's name and record number appear as the first note despite being shown in *AACR 2* chapter 6 as one of the last notes. This follows a Library of Congress rule interpretation to bring this important information to a position of some prominence on a catalog card.

A title added entry is used for the other title information, because some patrons might remember this as the title. A title added entry is also made for the title proper and title added entry together, because some patrons might consider the entire statement to be the title.

Rules for notes are, in order, 6.7B19, 6.7B7, 6.7B11, 6.7B17, 6.7B18.

Cover of record jacket   **Back of record jacket**

Example 16: Loyalties

Side 1 of label

```
BJ      Loyalties [sound recording] : whose side are you
1533       on? / produced by Sheila Turner and Robert Mack
.L8        -- [New York] : Scholastic Magazines, c1970.
              1 sound disc (ca. 44 min.) : analog, 33 1/3
179.9      rpm, stereo. ; 12 in.

              Scholastic Magazines: FS 12004.
              "A Contact record."
              Notes on container.
              Summary: People talking about experiences,
           ideas, and problems in their own lives involving
           their loyalties.
              Contents: General introduction (2 min.) --
           Street gang (9 min., 43 sec.) -- Antiwar demon-
           stration (5 min., 16 sec.) -- Viet Nam veterans
           (5 min., 46 sec.) -- Frank Garcia (5 min., 30
           sec.) -- Rachel Ortiz (14 min., 30 sec.).

              1. Loyalty.  [1. Loyalty--Case studies.]  I.
           Turner, Sheila.  II. Mack, Robert.  III. Title:
           Loyalties, whose side are you on?  IV. Title:
           Whose side are you on?  V. Scholastic magazines,
           Inc.
```

Example 17: Great American Women's Speeches

The four record labels are the chief source of information for these sound discs.

Date is given with a "p" because it appears that way on the item.

The approximate total time is used in the physical description area; the exact times are given in the contents note.

Main entry for this item has varied as rules changed. The original LC copy (72-750999) had this bibliographic record entered under editor. Then rules changed and it was entered under title. Under rule 21.23C1, it is to be entered under the first of the three performers. There is a collective title and the three performers are named on the chief source of information with equal prominence.

Name-title added entries are used here. One might want to make title added entries as well.

Rules for notes are, in order, 6.7B19, 6.7B6, 6.7B11, 6.7B18.

Front of album

Record label, side one

Example 17: Great American Women's Speeches

Back of album

A 2 RECORD ALBUM TC 2067 CAEDMON

GREAT AMERICAN WOMEN'S SPEECHES

Susan B. Anthony · Carrie Chapman Catt · Florence Kelley · Lucretia Mott · Ernestine Potowski Rose
Anna Howard Shaw · Elizabeth Cady Stanton · Lucy Stone · Sojourner Truth

read by   Eileen Heckart, Claudia McNeil and Mildred Natwick

Edited by Sharon Donovan

Side 1

Declaration of Sentiments and Resolutions: The First Woman's Rights Convention
Seneca Falls, New York, July 19-20, 1848 read by Mildred Natwick   11:15

Lucretia Mott (1793-1880): A Demand for the Political Rights of Women (Philadelphia, 1849) read by Mildred Natwick   7:57

Side 2

Sojourner Truth (c. 1797-1883): Ain't I a Woman? (Convention in Akron, Ohio,
May 28-29, 1851) read by Claudia McNeil   2:40

Ernestine Potowski Rose (1810-1892): Remove the Legal Shackles from Woman
(Second National Woman's Convention, Worcester, Mass., 1851) read by Mildred
Natwick   5:07

Sojourner Truth (c. 1797-1883): The Women Want Their Rights! (Broadway
Tabernacle, September 6, 1853) read by Claudia McNeil   5:00

Lucy Stone (1818-1893): Disappointment is the Lot of Woman (Convention in
Cincinnati, October 18, 1855) read by Eileen Heckart   4:47

Side 3

Elizabeth Cady Stanton (1815-1902): Address to the New York State Legislature
(1860) read by Eileen Heckart   7:54

Susan B. Anthony (1820-1906): Are Women Persons? (New York, New York,
1873) read by Mildred Natwick   4:12

Elizabeth Cady Stanton (1815-1902): Womanliness (National American Woman
Suffrage Convention, 1890) read by Eileen Heckart   3:13

Elizabeth Cady Stanton (1815-1902): Solitude of Self (House Judiciary Committee, 1892) read by Eileen Heckart   6:05

Side 4

Carrie Chapman Catt (1859-1947): Address to the National American Woman
Suffrage Association (Washington, D. C., 1902) read by Mildred Natwick   12:03

Florence Kelley (1859-1932): Working Women Need the Ballot (Massachusetts
Woman Suffrage Association, 1903) read by Mildred Natwick   5:27

Anna Howard Shaw (1847-1919): Emotionalism in Politics (National Woman
Suffrage Association Convention, 1913) read by Eileen Heckart   3:00

Elizabeth Cady Stanton (1815-1902): "We who like the Children of Israel" (International Council of Women, 1888) read by Eileen Heckart   1:13

"The women should keep silence in the churches," declared St. Paul, "for they are not permitted to speak, but should be subordinate, as even the law says. If there is anything they desire to know, let them ask their husbands at home. For it is shameful for a woman to speak in church." Anne Hutchinson, the outspoken Puritan, was the first woman to learn the depth of Paul's misogyny in America. Hutchinson didn't speak in church but about the church, in her own home. For giving her opinions on the established doctrines of the Massachusetts Bay Colony to large groups of men and women, she was arrested, tried and banished from the colony. Anne Hutchinson's punishment was severe not merely for what she said but because she encouraged other women to speak. Her murder by Indians was seen as a sign by the Puritan fathers that they had acted in God's will when they silenced the woman. That female silence lasted for over 150 years in American history.

"Public speech," said Frances Hosford, "was outside a mystic geometrical entity called 'woman's sphere.' The religious called it unscriptural for a woman, the cultured thought it unseemly, the cynical found in it material for their bitterest sneers, the evil-minded felt free to make a woman orator the target of vulgarity." This view, held by women as well as men, was upheld by religion, law and custom.

The Abolition and other reform movements attracted many women in the late 1830's and 1840's. Women often spoke to all-female audiences in "sewing circles." This was acceptable as a "woman's sphere." If a speech was to be given to mixed audiences, which were called "promiscuous," the woman's speech was read by a man. Catherine Beecher and Dorothea Dix used this method. Catherine Beecher worked for equal public education for girls while Dorothea Dix fought for hospital and prison reform.

When women did begin to speak publicly it was not for their rights but against the evils of slavery. Frances Maria W. Stewart, a former slave, was the first American woman to speak for abolition. Her speaking career was short-lived and she was widely ridiculed. In defense of her outspokenness, her farewell address delivered in Boston in 1833 stated:

"Men of eminence have mostly risen from obscurity; nor will I, although a female of a darker hue, and far more obscure than they, bend my head, nor hang my harp upon the willows; for though poor, I will virtuous prove."

Denied the right to speak against the oppression of slaves, women quickly realized their own oppression. Public speaking became a political act. The times were charged with reformist zeal and some women felt it was more immoral to remain silent in their sphere than to shock public sensibilities by having their voices heard.

During the early 1900's the base of support for women's rights grew. Society women marched with factory women, led in their fight for protective labor laws by Florence Kelly.

When Susan B. Anthony retired from the suffrage movement she knew that Carrie Chapman Catt and Florence Kelly would carry on with the organization for the vote, but she also knew that they would need a great orator. Dr. Anna Howard Shaw won the position easily. Shaw, who was both a minister and a physician, was an eloquent speaker. She followed Catt into the presidency of the NWSA.

In 1920 American women finally won the vote. The struggle had been a long one. American society had changed greatly since the 1848 Seneca Falls Declaration of Rights. Women were taking active parts in all levels of life. For women in the flapper and jazz age of the 20's it must have seemed incredible that their mothers had been stoned and ridiculed for speaking their minds in public. It is even more incredible in the space age. Who would have thought that these women orators could have caused such an uproar? When they spoke in public the women did far more than call for their rights. They committed a political act that challenged the very roots of established sex-prejudice. It took nearly one hundred years to win the vote; but this was only one of many demands our grandmothers so bravely spoke for. How much longer will it take to end the other "sex-prejudices"?

—SHARON DONOVAN

copyright © 1973, Caedmon Records, Inc.   Jacket Design: (Designs in toto) New York, N.Y.   Library of Congress Number—72-750988

Example 17: Great American Women's Speeches

```
HQ          Heckart, Eileen.
1423            Great American women's speeches [sound
            recording]. -- New York, N.Y. : Caedmon, p1973.
324.623         2 sound discs (ca. 70 min.) : analog, 33 1/3
            rpm, stereo. ; 12 in.


                Caedmon: TC 2067.
                Read by Eileen Heckart, Claudia McNeil, and
            Mildred Natwick ; edited by Sharon Donovan.
                Notes by Sharon Donovan on container.
                Contents: Declaration of sentiments and
            resolutions : the first Woman's Rights Conven-
            tion, Seneca Falls, New York, July 19-20, 1848
            (11 min., 15 sec.) -- A demand for the political
            rights of women / Lucretia Mott (7 min., 57
            sec.) -- Ain't I a woman? / Sojourner Truth (2
            min., 40 sec.) -- Remove the legal shackles from
            woman / Ernestine Potowski Rose (5 min., 7 sec.)
            -- The women want their rights / Sojourner Truth
            (5 min.) -- Disappointment is the lot of women /
            Lucy Stone (4 min., 47 sec.) -- Address to the
            New York State Legislature (1860) / Elizabeth
            Cady Stanton (7 min., 54 sec.) -- Are women
            persons? / Susan B. Anthony (4 min., 12 sec.) --
            Womanliness (3 min., 13 sec.) ; Solitude of self
            (6 min., 5 sec.) / Elizabeth Cady Stanton --
            Address to the National American Woman Suffrage
            Association, Washington, D. C., 1902 / Carrie
            Chapman Catt (12 min., 3 sec.) -- Working women
            need the ballot / Florence Kelley (5 min., 27
            sec.) -- Emotionalism in politics? / Anna Howard
            Shaw (3 min.) -- "We who like the children of
            Israel" / Elizabeth Cady Stanton (1 min., 13
            sec.).

                1. Feminists.  2. Social reformers--United
            States.  3. Women--Suffrage.  [1. Feminism. 2.
            Women--Civil rights. 3. Women--Suffrage.]  I.
            Donovan, Sharon.  II. McNeil, Claudia.  III.
            Natwick, Mildred.  IV. Mott, Lucretia, 1793-
            1880.  Demand for the political rights of women.
            1973.  V. Truth, Sojourner, 1797-1883.  Ain't I
            a woman?  1973.  VI. Rose, Ernestine Potowski,
            1810-1892.  Remove the legal shackles from
            woman.  1973.  VII. Truth, Sojourner, 1797-1883.
            Women want their rights!  1973.  VIII. Stone,
            Lucy, 1818-1893.  Disappointment is the lot of
            woman.  1973.  IX. Stanton, Elizabeth Cady,
            1815-1902. Address to the New York State Legis-
            lature.  1973.  X. Anthony, Susan B., 1820-1906.
            Are women persons?  1973.  XI.  Stanton, Eliza-
            beth Cady, 1815-1902.  Womanliness.  1973.  XII.
```

Example 17: Great American Women's Speeches

Stanton, Elizabeth Cady, 1815-1902. Solitude of
self. 1973. XIII. Catt, Carrie Chapman, 1859-
1947. Address to the National American Woman
Suffrage Association. 1973. XIV. Kelley,
Florence, 1859-1932. Working women need the
ballot. 1973. XV. Shaw, Anna Howard, 1847-
1919. Emotionalism in politics. 1973. XVI.
Stanton, Elizabeth Cady, 1815-1902. We who like
the children of Israel. 1973. XVII. Declaration of sentiments and resolutions. XVIII.
Title.

Example 18: Coronation Service

The term "mono." is used because it is given on the record label.

Rules for notes are, in order, 6.7B19, 6.7B6, 6.7B6.

The two 6.7B6 notes could be combined into one note.

The introductory portion of the record manufacturer's number note (EMI Records) is supposed to match the name given in the publication, distribution, etc., area.

This example is a liturgical work and has the main entry as shown. Rule 21.39A1 calls for the use of a uniform title. Rule 25.19 tells us how to construct this uniform title.

Information from record label

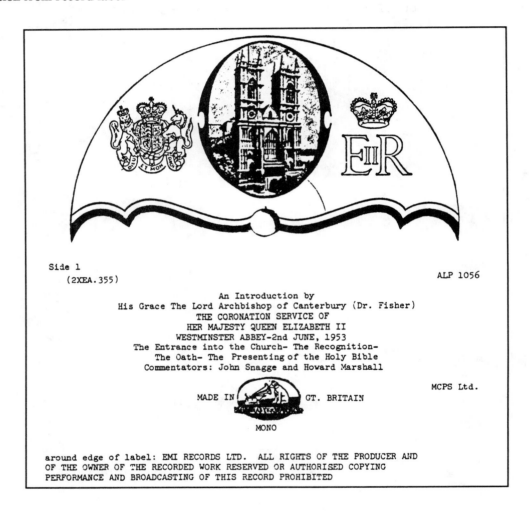

Example 18: Coronation Service

```
DA        Church of England.
112           [Coronation service]
          The coronation service of Her Majesty, Queen
941.085  Elizabeth II [sound recording] : Westminster Abbey,
         2nd June, 1953. -- London : EMI Records, [1953]
              3 sound discs (120 min.) : analog, 33 1/3 rpm,
         mono. ; 12 in. + 1 set of program notes (4 p. ; 26
         cm.)

              EMI Records: ALP 1056--ALP 1058.
              Service conducted by G. Fisher, Archbishop of
         Canterbury.
              Commentators: John Snagge, Howard Marshall.

              1. Elizabeth II, Queen of Great Britain, 1926-
         --Coronation. [1. Elizabeth II, Queen of Great
         Britain, 1926-        --Coronation.]  I. Elizabeth
         II, Queen of Great Britain, 1926-        II. Fisher,
         Geoffrey, 1887-        III. Snagge, John.  IV.
         Marshall, Howard.  V. Title.
```

Example 19: They Chose America

    There are two ways to catalog this, either as a set or each title separately. One would choose to catalog each title separately if one wanted to include separate summaries and distinctive subject headings for each title.

    The chief source of information in either case is the cassette label. The container would be used only if it furnished a collective title not given on the cassette labels.

    The name of the publisher is given in a shortened form as permitted in rule 1.4D2.

    In the physical description area we do not give the playing speed or the number of tracks, because they are standard for the item; for the same reason we do not list the size of the cassette. Nowhere does the cassette say it is monophonic, so we don't include that information.

    A summary was used rather than a contents note, because the separate titles were repetitious and the same information could be presented more concisely in the summary note.

    The producer was not listed in the statement of responsibility, because the information was not given in the chief source, nor was the information given prominently elsewhere.

    Rules for notes are, in order, 6.7B6, 6.7B10, 6.7B11, and 6.7B17.

Two albums of cassettes

Cassette label

Example 19: They Chose America

Volume one open showing notes

```
E          They chose America [sound recording]. -- Princeton,
184            N.J. : Visual Education, p1975.
.A1              12 sound cassettes : analog.

325.73         Producer-director, Scott McDade.
               In two containers.
               Notes on containers.
               Summary: Interviews with Jewish immigrants
           and with immigrants from China, Ireland, Italy,
           Mexico, Poland, Cuba, Germany, Greece, Hungary,
           Japan, Finland, Norway, Denmark, and Sweden, who
           arrived in America between 1902 and 1968.

               1. United States--Emigration and immigration.
           [1. United States--Immigration and emigration.]
           I. McDade, Scott.  II. Visual Education Corpora-
           tion.
```

Example 20: Mothers and Daughters

There is some information on the slip of paper inserted in the cassette container. We don't know who is speaking nor do we know the date.

Rules for notes are 6.7B19, 6.7B17.

Cassette with container, notes

Facsimile of notes from cassette container

Pgm. no. BC 0860   Time   38 min   Reel 1 of 1

MOTHERS AND DAUGHTERS
An examination of the relationship between mothers and
daughters, drawn from the words of poets, writers, and
suffragettes: Sylvia Plath, George Sand, Colette, Harriet
Beecher Stowe, Adrienne Rich and Sappho.

PACIFICA TAPE LIBRARY
5316 Venice Boulevard — Los Angeles, California 90019
No tapes may be reproduced in whole or part without written permission

Example 20: Mothers and Daughters

```
HQ          Mothers and daughters [sound recording]. -- Los
755.85        Angeles, Calif. : Pacifica Tape Library, [197-]
                1 sound cassette (38 min.) : analog.
306.8743
                Pacifica Tape Library: BC 0860.
                Summary: Explores relationships between
            mothers and daughters through words of poets,
            writers, and suffragettes.

                1. Mothers and daughters.  2. Daughters. [1.
            Girls. 2. Mothers. 3. Parent and child.]  I.
            Pacifica Tape Library.
```

Example 21: Cardiology

This is one of a set of 15 tapes. We could choose to catalog the set as a whole with a contents note listing the individual titles.

The statement of responsibility appears on the box, but not on the label. It could be bracketed into the statement of responsibility; I chose to use it as a note.

Notice the punctuation of the bibliographic information in the two notes citing other works. This punctuation is explained in rule 1.7A3. The two notes could be combined into one note if desired. These notes are based on rule 6.7B18.

The series is given with an "&" on the chief source of information, with an "and" on the container.

Tape box and reel showing label placement

Example 21: Cardiology

Facsimile of text on the reel

Gregg Publishing Division, McGraw-Hill Book Co., Inc.
GREGG TEXT TAPES
Medical Dictation & Transcription
CARDIOLOGY
Track 1
WPM 50-60-70-60

Gregg Publishing Division, McGraw-Hill Book Co., Inc.
GREGG TEXT TAPES
Medical Dictation & Transcription
CARDIOLOGY
Track 2
WPM 60

```
R          Root, Kathleen Berger, 1891-
728.8          Cardiology [sound recording] -- New York :
           Gregg, [1967?]
651.3741       1 sound tape reel : analog, 3 3/4 ips, ; 5 in.
           -- (Gregg text tapes, medical dictation &
           transcription)

           By Root and Byers.
           Track 1: 50, 60, 70, 60 wpm from: The medical
       secretary : terminology and transcription. 3rd ed.
       New York : McGraw-Hill, c1967.
           Track 2: 60 wpm from: Medical typing practice.
       2nd ed. New York : McGraw-Hill, c1967.

           1. Dictation (Office practice)  2. Medical
       shorthand--Study and teaching. [1. Shorthand--
       Study and teaching.]  I. Byers, Edward Elmer.  II.
       Title.  III. Series.
```

Example 22: The Mysterious Traveler

Reel-to-reel tapes are almost obsolete, but still in use in some institutions.

The word "Mysterious" is capitalized because this bibliographic record is entered under a title that begins with an article (*AACR 2* Appendix A.4D).

There was little information on the container, none on the reel, and only the quoted phrase was heard before the program began.

The note contains information that might have been split into two or three notes; we are permitted to combine such information. The note is based on rule 6.7B1.

We purchased this material during the 1970s; I used an approximate date as shown.

Radio program on tape, with container

Information on container

Example 22: The Mysterious Traveler

```
PN          The Mysterious traveler [sound recording]. --
3448            Croton-on-Hudson, N.Y. : Radio Yesteryear, [197-]
.S45              1 sound tape reel : analog, 7 1/2 ips ; 7 in.

808             Radio programs from Dec. 29, 1946, and July
.838762         27, 1947, that "journey into the realm of the
                strange and the terrifying."

                   1. Science fiction.  [1. Science fiction--
                Collections.]  I. Radio Yesteryear (Firm).
```

Example 23: Funeral of Sir Winston Churchill

This is included as an example of an "In" analytic (Rule 13.5A). The note is based on rule 6.7B6.

Sound sheet, as received in *National Geographic*

```
DA          The Funeral of Sir Winston Churchill [sound
566.9          recording] : London, January 30, 1965 : with
.C5            excerpts from his speeches.
                  1 sound sheet between p. 198 and 199 :
941.0856       analog, 33 1/3 rpm, mono. ; 7 in.

               Narrator: David Brinkley.
               In National geographic. -- Vol. 128, no. 2
            (Aug. 1965).

               1. Churchill, Winston, Sir, 1874-1965--
            Funeral. [1. Churchill, Winston, Sir, 1874-
            1965--Funeral.]  I. Churchill, Winston, Sir,
            1874-1965.  II. Brinkley, David.
```

If the sound recording were removed from the magazine, a local note would be added to this bibliographic record to explain what was done.

Example 24: Mighty and Majestic Birds

These sound recordings have a small transparent sound disc or sound sheet (it is square with circular grooves cut into it) fastened to the back of a card on which there is a picture of a bird. On the back of the card, beneath the sound recording, is a description of the bird and comments about it. These sound cards are inserted into a special player in which the head revolves while the card remains stationary. The user can examine the picture of the bird while listening to the narration and the bird call. Eighty bird calls and sixty animal sounds are available in sets of ten.

I used the term "sound disc card" rather than "sound picture." Examination of the other terms used as specific material designations in chapter 6 of *AACR 2* seemed to lead to this description.

The place of publication is not given, but is assumed to be in the United States. According to *AACR 2* Appendix B.14A3, "United States" may be abbreviated to "U. S." only when used as an *addition* to the place name.

Rule numbers for notes are 6.7B10, 6.7B17, 6.7B18.

Player, packet, and cards. Transparent disk is on side of card with description of bird.

```
QL          Mighty and majestic birds [sound recording]. --
698.5          [United States] : National Audubon Society,
            c1977.
598.259        10 sound disc cards : analog ; 13 x 7 cm. --
            (Audible Audubon ; set B)

               For use on Microphonograph manufactured by
            Microsonics Corporation.
               Summary: Each card has copy of painting by
            Allan Brooks on one side; notes covered by clear
            plastic sound recording on the other. Sound
            recording includes brief description of the bird
            and its calls, followed by some of the bird
            calls.
               Contents: Red-shouldered hawk -- Red-tailed
            hawk -- American kestrel -- Chuck-will's-widow
            -- Great horned owl -- Barred owl -- Whip-poor-
            will -- Long-eared owl -- Bald eagle -- Screech
            owl.

               1. Bird-song.  [1. Bird song.]  I. Brooks,
            Allan.  I. National Audubon Society.  II. Se-
            ries.
```

Example 25: Wynton Marsalis

This is the only musical example in this manual and is included to show the cataloging of a compact disc.
See example 67 for the cataloging of the interactive compact disk version of Beethoven's Symphony no. 9.
This is a collection of works by different persons. It has a collective title. The principal performer is chosen as main entry, according to rule 21.23.
Rule numbers for notes are, in order, 6.7B19, 6.7B1, 6.7B6, 6.7B10, 6.7B11, 6.7B18.

Plastic container and compact disc

Back of the container

Label information covers one side of disc, other side has recorded sound

Example 25: Wynton Marsalis

```
M        Marsalis, Wynton, 1961-
1366         Wynton Marsalis [sound recording]. -- N[ew]
         Y[ork], N.Y. : CBS, p1982.
781.65       1 sound disc : digital, stereo. ; 4 3/4 in. + 1
         set of program notes.

             CBS: CK 37574.
             Jazz ensembles.
             Wynton Marsalis, trumpet, with Branford
         Marsalis, saxophone ; Herbie Hancock or Kenny
         Kirkland, piano ; Clarence Seay, Charles Fambrough,
         or Ron Carter, double bass ; Jeff Watts or Tony
         Williams, drums.
             Compact disc.
             Program notes by Stanley Crouch inserted in
         container.
             Contents: Father Time / W. Marsalis -- I'll be
         there when the time is right / H. Hancock -- RJ /
         R. Carter -- Hesitation / W. Marsalis -- Sister
         Cheryl / T. Williams -- Who can I turn to (when
         nobody needs me) / L. Bricusse-A. Newley -- Twi-
         light / W. Marsalis.

             1. Jazz ensembles.  [1. Jazz ensembles--Col-
         lected works. 2. Jazz music--Collected works.]  I.
         Marsalis, Branford. II. Hancock, Herbie, 1940-
         III. Kirkland, Kenny.  IV. Seay, Clarence.  V.
         Fambrough, Charles. VI. Carter, Ron, 1937-
         VII. Watts, Jeff.  VIII. Williams, Tony, 1945-
         IX. Marsalis, Wynton, 1961-     Father Time. 1982.
         X. Hancock, Herbie, 1940-      I'll be there when
         the time is right. 1982. XI. Carter, Ron, 1937-
         RJ.  1982.  XII. Marsalis, Wynton, 1961-    Hesi-
         tation. 1982.  XIII. Williams, Tony, 1945-
         Sister Cheryl. 1982.  XIV. Bricusse, Leslie. Who
         can I turn to. 1982.  XV. Marsalis, Wynton, 1961-
         Twilight. 1982.
```

Example 26: Various sources of retirement income

The manufacturer calls this a sound page, so I used that term. We don't know the playing speed so that part of the physical description area is omitted. The measurements of the page are given. A note is made of the equipment needed to play the page, based on rule 6.7B10. This system was developed by 3M, but it doesn't seem to have gone into commercial production.

A sound page and an advertising brochure

A sound page is a flexible sheet of plastic which has a sound recording on one side and pictures and/or printed material on the other side. The pages fit on a special machine, and the page is stationary while the playing mechanism revolves. The whole system is made by 3M (Minnesota Mining and Manufacturing).

```
HQ          Various sources of retirement income [sound
1062           recording] / Career Research Associates. --
               [St. Paul, Minn. : 3M Visual Products Division],
332            c1977.
.02401            1 sound page : analog ; 30 x 22 cm. --
               (Retirement plans ; 8.1)

                  For use on 3M Sound Page Player.

                  1. Retirement.  [1. Retirement.]  I. Career
               Research Associates.  II. Series.
```

Chapter 5

MOTION PICTURES AND VIDEORECORDINGS

AACR 2 Chapter 7

This chapter includes examples of cataloging for all types of motion pictures and videorecordings.

Special Rules for Cataloging Motion Pictures and Videorecordings

In this section the special rules for cataloging motion pictures and videorecordings will be discussed. Parts of some of the rules are given; the user is referred to the rules themselves for complete text and examples. All of the Library of Congress rule interpretations (LCRIs) for this chapter are included.

The Library of Congress has published a manual on cataloging archival film and video (*Archival Moving Image Materials: A Cataloging Manual*, compiled by Wendy White-Hensen. Washington, D.C.: Library of Congress, 1984). Excerpts from the manual are included in this chapter.

For 40 more examples and additional discusion, see *Cataloging Motion Pictures and Videorecordings*, by Nancy B. Olson. (Lake Crystal, Minn.: Soldier Creek Press, 1991).

Chief Source of Information

Title proper

The chief source of information for motion pictures and videorecordings is the material itself, including all title and credits frames.

Title and Statement of Responsibility Area

A problem with film titles is that of "presents" and other information appearing before the title, as discussed in chapter 2 of this manual.

Television series and movie serials might have segment, part, or individual titles and/or numbers in addition to the series title, as discussed in chapter 2 of this manual. *Archival Moving Image Materials* (p. 25-29) suggests the following methods of handling these titles, which you might want to consider. As always, your cataloging should be based on your patron's needs. The practice suggested here is one method that could be used. The same type of access is provided if the name of the series and episode number are used as a series statement.

> Enter the following types of moving image material under their series and episode, part, individual, or segment titles: television series, theatrical serials, newsreels, and educational and technical series that are intended to be viewed consecutively (if this can be determined). The principle that the primary access point includes both the series and episode titles is a cataloging standard in archives for several reasons. In most cases individual titles of parts or episodes are almost meaningless without the title of the series or serial to which they are subordinate. Placing series title and episode title in two different places in a catalog description is confusing and misleading to users.

Examples: Mary Tyler Moore. Chuckles bites the dust.
General Hospital. No. 237.
The March of Time. Vol. 14, no. 18, Watchdogs of the mail.

As noted above, enter television series programs by the series and episode title, separated by a period, space. The name of a news program (or part of the program name) is often the same as the company that produced it and is capitalized because it is a corporate body name.

Example: CBS News special report. The Duke, 1907-1979.

In addition to a series title and a title of an individual segment or episode, a television series title may also include a title for a subseries, i.e., a series within a series. A subseries is a group of programs which appears in conjunction with another, more comprehensive, series of which the subseries forms a part. Though they may not formally be designated a subseries, a group of programs with the same title that is subordinate to or part of a larger series is treated as a subseries.

Example: ABC scope. The Vietnam War. How much dissent?

In television particularly, but not exclusively, there may be a secondary series title that more broadly identifies the context of a particular series title. An example would be public television's programming group, Masterpiece Theater, which includes separate series such as *Upstairs, Downstairs*, and of course individual episodes within the series.

Theatrical serials are always intended to be viewed in a specified order.

Example: Captain Midnight. Chapter 14, Scourge of revenge.

An educational or technical series title and episode title should be considered the title proper when it can be determined that the work is part of a series intended to be viewed consecutively or as a group, or, that the episodes or segments build upon one another in a cumulative manner. The presence of numbers is one of the major, though not the only, indicators of this situation. Segments that are quite short and that are intended to be viewed together, rather than independently, should be described using their series and segment title. Good judgment must be exercised in making the determination to describe a work using both the series and segment or episode titles.

Examples: Biblical masterpieces. Song of Songs.
Music as a language. Music as emotion.
Music as a language. Music as sound.
The Nature of communism. No. 1, Introduction to the course.

Statement of responsibility

A problem in film cataloging is the proliferation of credits given on the title and credits frames. The early films usually listed one producer, one director, and one production company, together with the writers and the cast. Now films give credit to many corporate bodies, and the producer and director functions seem to be done by committees.

ARLO AND JANIS ® by Jimmy Johnson

Reprinted by permission of United Feature Syndicate, Inc.

Several rule interpretations guide us in deciding which names go in the statement of responsibility, which go in the credits note, and which are to be ignored.

7.1F1. Transcribe statements of responsibility relating to those persons or bodies credited in the chief source of information with participation in the production of a film (e.g., as producer, director, animator) that are considered to be of major importance. Give all other statements of responsibility (including those relating to performance) in notes.

LCRI 7.1F1. Primarily this means giving the names of corporate bodies credited with the production of the work. Personal names should also be transcribed when the person's responsibility is important in relation to the content of the work. For example, names of persons who are producers, directors, and writers are given in most instances; the name of an animator is given if animation is a significant feature of the work; the name of a photographer is given if the work is a travelog. (*CSB* 11)

LCRI 7.1F1. When deciding whether to give names in the statement of responsibility or in a note, generally give the names in the statement of responsibility when the person or body has some degree of overall responsibility; use the note area for others who are responsible for only one segment or one aspect of the work. Be liberal about making exceptions to the general policy when the person's or body's responsibility is important in relation to the content of the work, i.e., give such important people and bodies in the statement of responsibility even though they may have only partial responsibility. For example, the name of a rock music performer who is the star of a performance on a videorecording may be given in the statement of responsibility even if his/her responsibility is limited to the performance.

```
Ain't that America / John Cougar Mellencamp
```

Normally the Library of Congress considers producers, directors, and writers as having some degree of overall responsibility and gives them in the statement of responsibility. (*CSB* 36)

Richard Thaxter, Library of Congress, discusses this matter further:

There is a larger issue here; that is, whether an agency which causes a film to be made should be given in the statement of responsibility. In general I think the answer is yes. If one body hires another to produce a film, one can usually assume that the originating agency will have a role in determining the intellectual and artistic content of the finished product. If we decide this is the case then we give both bodies in the statement of responsibility.

At the other end of the spectrum from those works created by one body under the direction of another, are films, etc., for which one agency merely provides funding for another body, or individual, who then produces the work. In this case we do not usually record the name of the sponsor. This would almost always be true in the case of "Made possible by a grant from ..." There are, of course, many situations that fall between the two obvious cases mentioned above, and in the borderline situations catalogers must make a judgment based on interpretation of statements in the work and knowledge of the bodies involved.

Statements found on the actual items are often ambiguous; it often is difficult to determine the relationship of a body to the work in hand (Online Audiovisual Catalogers. *Newsletter*, 3 (Sept. 1983), 11).

Another question in this same article refers to the phrase "produced in cooperation with." Thaxter says this phrase may be included in the statement of responsibility.

7.1F3. If a statement of responsibility names both the agency responsible for the production of a motion picture or videorecording and the agency for which it is produced, give the statement as found.

The following excerpts from *Archival Moving Image Materials* may be helpful.

A statement of responsibility is a statement, transcribed from the material being described, accompanying material, or from secondary sources, which relates all those corporate bodies and persons credited with participation in the original production of a moving image work and who are considered to be of major importance to the work. Credits and their functions are synonymous with the concept of statement of responsibility.

Standard cataloging practice for archival moving image material is to give the production company as the first statement of responsibility. With few exceptions, such as amateur-produced material and the instances in which an individual does in fact perform all production activities, the production company is responsible, in a broad sense, for the overall creation of the work. The production company often serves as the coordinating body responsible for the participation of all persons and other companies in the production of a moving image work (Wendy White-Hensen, *Archival Moving Image Materials*, p.48).

Because responsibility for moving image materials is most often complex and highly diverse, archives—particularly those with special interests—should determine the types of functions they wish to include in this area. These functions may vary from institution to institution according to the types of moving image material. For example, an archive holding television material would probably consider the function of producer more important than that of director. The opposite would be the case for archives whose collections are comprised of motion picture material (Wendy White-Hensen, *Archival Moving Image Materials*, p.49).

With the exception of production company, which is always the first statement of responsibility for moving image material, the order of the statements of responsibility should be determined by the requirements of individual archives (Wendy White-Hensen, *Archival Moving Image Materials*, p.50).

Choose the credit function/type of responsibility terms as found on the item unless [it is misleading] (Wendy White-Hensen, *Archival Moving Image Materials*, p.51).

If a statement of responsibility names both the production company and the sponsor or agency for which it is produced, give the production company first. The word "presents" may imply the function of sponsor. Use the terminology on the item unless it is misleading; use judgment to distinguish corporate bodies that are sponsors from those that are production companies. Likewise, use judgment to distinguish bodies whose contribution is significant, e.g., providing major funding, from those whose participation is minor (Wendy White-Hensen, *Archival Moving Image Materials*, p.52).

In some cases, the same credit term has been used for differing functions during different periods of history, [and] in different parts of the moving image industry. For example, the use of the credit term, "presents," has been and continues to be ambiguous (Wendy White-Hensen, *Archival Moving Image Materials*, p. 53).

Edition Area

We are seeing various versions of feature films being released. Each version is to be considered an edition, and the wording on the item is used as an edition statement.

Restored version
Color version
25th anniversary edition
Letterbox format

Publication, Distribution, Etc., Area

Note: 7.0B2 of AACR2, 2ND ed., 1998 rev. → container now a prescribed source

The prescribed sources of information for area 4 include the chief source of information (the title and credits screens) and any accompanying material. Accompanying material would include a teacher's guide, but not the container of a videocassette. Therefore, any information taken from the container of a videocassette must be bracketed.

This place of publication or distribution for videocassettes is given only on the container in many cases. If so, it must be bracketed.

> **7.4D1.** Give the name of the publisher, etc., and, *optionally* of the distributor, releasing agency, etc., and/or production agency or producer not named in the statements of responsibility (see 7.1F) as instructed in 1.4D.

The intent of this rule, according to Richard Thaxter, is to provide a way to get a name in this area that could not be entered in the statement of responsibility. We can record a producer's name, if that producer is also the distributor, in both places. The name of the publisher or distributor usually appears on the first of the title/credits frames of the motion picture or video.

> Moving image materials are not published or distributed in the traditional manner of books and periodicals. The agency which most nearly matches the function of publisher for books, is, for films, the distributor or releasing company. For television, it is the network or local broadcasting station (Wendy White-Hensen, *Archival Moving Image Materials*, p. 80).

Dates

See the discussion of dates in chapter 2 of this manual, particularly the comments on "made in" dates.

> **7.4F2.** *Optionally*, give a date of original production differing from the date of publication/distribution, etc. ... in the note area (see 7.7B9).

If the date of publication of the item in hand is taken from the container, it must be bracketed. The film might show only the original date of production, and the container might list a copyright date that is more recent. This latter date is used as an assumed date of publication of the item.

The date on the container might be contained in some phrase indicating it is the date of copyright of the container artwork and/or text. It still might be used as the assumed date of publication of the item in hand. It would be bracketed as an assumed date, or bracketed as coming from the container; it would only be given without brackets if it was found on the film itself or on a guide or printed material accompanying the item.

> "*Xiidigitation*. n. The practice of trying to determine the year a movie was made by deciphering the roman numerals at the end of the credits" (A "Sniglet" as reprinted in Op-Ed, *Columbus* (Ohio) *Citizen-Journal*, Apr. 28, 1984).

Physical Description Area

Extent of item

The following terms are to be used for specific material designation. A more specific term may be used if needed.

        film cartridge
        film cassette
        film loop
        film reel
        videocartridge
        videocassette
        videodisc
        videoreel

Playing time

7.5B2. Give the playing time of a motion picture or videorecording as instructed in rule 1.5B4.

```
1 videocassette (57 min.)
2 film reels (ca. 25 min. each)
1 film loop (3 min., 27 sec.)
```

The type of video is no longer named here, but is given in a note.

Playing time for videodiscs

If the videodisc is of moving images, give the playing time as shown above.

```
1 videodisc (42 min.)
1 videodisc (ca. 120 min.)
```

If the videodisc consists of frames of still images, give the playing time if stated. If the number of frames is available, that information may be given.

```
1 videodisc (32,242 fr.)
```

If the videodisc has both still and moving images, the playing time may be given in this area, or the playing time and number of still frames may be given in a note.

Other physical details:

7.5C1. Give the following details, as appropriate, in the order set out here:

        aspect ratio and special projection characteristics (motion pictures) [archival]
        sound characteristics
        colour
        projection speed (motion pictures) [if not standard for the item]

Series Area

Prescribed sources of information for the series area are the chief source of information and accompanying material. This does not include the video package. If the series statement is taken from the package it must be bracketed.

Example: ([The Rodgers & Hammerstein collection])

Notes Area

Notes permitted in this chapter are:

7.7B1. Nature or form
7.7B2. Language
7.7B3. Source of title proper
7.7B4. Variations in title
7.7B5. Parallel titles and other title information
7.7B6. tatements of responsibility
7.7B7. Edition and history
7.7B9. Publication, distribution, etc., and date
7.7B10. Physical description
7.7B11. Accompanying material
7.7B12. Series
7.7B13. Dissertations
7.7B14. Audience
7.7B16. Other formats
7.7B17. Summary
7.7B18. Contents
7.7B19. Numbers
7.7B20. Copy being described, library's holdings, and restrictions on use
7.7B21. "With" notes

1.7A5. ... When appropriate, combine two or more notes to make one note.

Example: Senator Hubert H. Humphrey speaks at a workshop held July 6, 1977, at Mankato State University, on the use of politics and the applications of power in advancing the program, objectives, and goals of handicapped and disabled persons

7.7B1. Nature or form of a motion picture or videorecording

To be used to name or explain the form of the item as necessary.

Examples: An experimental film
Documentary

7.7B2. Language

To be used to name the language(s) of the item cataloged if they are not obvious from other information given. Closed-captioning is indicated by a symbol that looks like a television set with a tail. The words "captioned" or "closed captioned" or the letters "cc" in a box sometimes are used in addition to, or instead of, the symbol.

Figure 2

> *Examples:* `Sound track in German; subtitles in English`
> `Closed-captioned for the hearing impaired`

7.7B3. Source of title proper

To be used if the title proper is taken from other than the chief source of information.

> *Examples:* `Title from container`
> `Title supplied by cataloger`

7.7B4. Variations in title

To be used to note any title appearing on the item that differs significantly from the title proper.

> **LCRI 7.7B4.** When considering 7.7B4 for a variation in title, decide first whether an added title entry is needed under the variant title. Decide this primary issue by consulting 21.2. If the variation in title is as great as the differences in titles described in 21.2, make the added entry and justify the added entry by means of a note formulated under 7.7B4, otherwise, do not apply 7.7B4. (*CSB* 13)

> *Example:* `Title on cartridge and container: Trisecting a straight line`
> `with triangles`
> (*Title proper:* Trisecting a line with triangles)

7.7B5. Parallel titles and other title information

To be used for parallel titles and important other title information not recorded in the title and statement of responsibility area.

> *Example:* `Title on manual: Getting ready to read and add`
> (*Title proper:* Préparation à la lecture et à l'addition)

7.7B6. Statements of responsibility

To be used to record important information not recorded in the statement of responsibility area.

Cast: List featured players, performers, narrators, and/or presenters.

Examples: Narrator: Walter Cronkite.
        Cast: Gene Kelly, Donald O'Connor, Debbie Reynolds, Jean Hagen, Millard Mitchell, Cyd Charisse

Credits: List persons other than the cast who have contributed to the artistic and technical production of a motion picture or videorecording and who are not named in the statement of responsibility. Do not include assistants, associates, etc., or any other persons making only a minor contribution. Preface each name or group of names with a statement of function.

Example: Credits: Screenplay, Harold Pinter ; music, John Dankworth ; camera, Gerry Fisher ; editor, Reginald Beck

Notice the punctuation within the note. This type of spacing and punctuation is used because this formal note contains statement of responsibility information.

Notice also this note does not have the function and name information in the same order as that used in the 6.7B6 note. The film note has function followed by name. The music note has name followed by function. The difference is confusing to those of us who must catalog both types of media.

The difference has been in place for several decades. I see some sense in both cases: screen credits usually give function first; music credits tend to put the name in primary position, probably because normally the names are rather well known. The notes we make are more or less copied from what appears, as far as order is concerned, and there are different conventions for order from one kind of material to another. (Ben R. Tucker, letter to the author, 17 Dec. 1984).

    LCRI 7.7B6. For audiovisual items, generally list persons (other than producers, directors, and writers) or corporate bodies who have contributed to the artistic and technical production of a work in a credits note (see RI 7.1F1).

    Give the following persons or bodies in the order in which they are listed below. Preface each name or group of names with the appropriate term(s) of function:

        photographer(s), camera, cameraman/men, cinematographer,
        animator(s),
        artist(s), illustrator(s), graphics,
        film editor(s), photo editor(s), editor(s),
        narrator(s), voice(s),
        music,
        consultant(s), adviser(s).

Do not include the following persons or bodies performing these functions:

        assistants or associates,
        production supervisors or coordinators,
        project or executive editors,
        technical advisers or consultants,
        audio or sound engineers,
        writers of discussion, program, or teacher's guides,
        other persons making only a minor or purely technical contribution.

    (CSB 22)

Richard Thaxter commented on this LCRI: "The list of persons to include and the order in which they should go is neither prescriptive nor exhaustive. The list in rule interpretation 7.7B6 was designed to solve data sheet cataloging problems at LC" (Online Audiovisual Catalogers. *Newsletter,* 3 (Sept. 1983), 10).

7.7B7. Edition and history

To be used for information about earlier editions, or the history of the item being cataloged.

LCRI 7.7B7. When an item is known to have an original master in a different medium and the production or release date of the master is more than two years earlier than that of the item being cataloged, give an edition/history note.

```
Originally produced as motion picture in [year]
Originally issued as filmstrip in [year]
```

Make a similar note when an item is known to have been previously produced or issued (more than two years earlier) if in a different medium, but the original medium is unknown.

```
Previously produced as motion picture in [year]
Previously issued as slide set in [year]
```

If the date of production or release of an original master or an earlier medium is unknown or if the difference between its production or release date and the production or release date of the item being cataloged is two years or less, indicate the availability of the other medium or media in a note according to 7.7B16.
Note: The use of production versus release dates is left to the cataloger's judgment. Make the note that seems best to give information about either production or release of other formats on a case-by-case basis. (*CSB* 15)

See also the discussion on the above topic in chapter 2 of this manual.

Examples:
```
Issued in 1945 as motion picture
    Revised version of the filmstrip issued in 1967 under the same
title
```

7.7B9. Publication, distribution, etc., and date

To be used for important information not recorded in the publication, distribution, etc. area.

LCRI 7.7B9. When a foreign firm, etc., is given in the source as emanator or originator, do not assume that the item was either made or released in that country if not so stated. Instead use the note

```
A foreign film (Yugoslavia)
```

For a U.S. emanator and a foreign producer or a foreign emanator and a U.S. producer, do not make the note. (*CSB* 13)

7.7B10. Physical description

Ten different physical description characteristics may be given in the notes. The most common notes are explained here.
Stereo sound is indicated in a note rather than in area five.
Dolby sound is indicated on the container by the Dolby symbol of back-to-back upper-case Ds in an oblong, or by the word "stereo" enclosed in a pair of Ds. The container may say Dolby stereo, Dolby system, Dolby surround, or other wording.

Figure 4

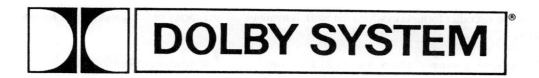

The videorecording system (VHS, Beta, LaserVision) is given in a note rather than in area five. If desired, this information may be given as the first note in the bibliographic record.
Give the information as found on the item.

```
VHS hi-fi stereo, Dolby system, on linear tracks
VHS hi-fi, Dolby stereo
VHS hi-fi, stereo, Dolby surround, videophonic sound digitally dupli-
cated
LaserVision CAV
U-matic
Beta
```

Other notes, for archival cataloging, deal with length of film or tape in feet, type of color, form of print, film base, generation of copy, special projection requirements, and any other physical details important for use or preservation.

7.7B11. *Accompanying material*

To be used for any important information not given in the accompanying material part of area 5.

Example: Guide includes bibliography

7.7B12. *Series*

To be used for any important information not recorded in the series area.

Example: Formerly issued as part of series: The Atlantic community

7.7B13. *Dissertations*

To be used for the standard dissertation note when applicable.

Example: Thesis (Ed. Sp.)--Mankato State University, 1982

7.7B14. Audience

To be used to record the intended audience of a work; use this note only if the information is stated on the item. Do not attempt to judge the audience for an item.

> *Examples:*   Intended audience: Grade 3-4
>   Rated R

7.7B16. Other formats

To be used to list other formats in which the work is available. The Library of Congress lists all formats available commercially.

> *Example:*   Issued also as 1/2 in. Beta I videocassette

7.7B17. Summary

To be used for a brief objective summary of the content of the item. Do not use a summary if the rest of the bibliographic record provides enough information.

> *Example:*   Summary: A documentary of the history of the brewing industry
>   in Mankato, Minnesota

7.7B18. Contents

To be used for a formal or informal listing of the contents of the item.

> *Example:*   Contents: 1. Who killed Jesus Christ? -- 2. Let His blood fall
>   on our heads -- 3. And on the heads of our children -- 4. Calvary.
>   The verdict

7.7B19. Numbers

To be used to list any important number appearing on the item other than those to be recorded in area 8. This may include the barcode number if desired.

> *Example:*   RGA 42-95

7.7B20. Copy being described, library's holdings, and restrictions on use

To be used for any notes applicable only to the particular copy of the item being described. Also used for local library restrictions on the material being described or for information of use only to patrons of the local library.

> *Example:*   To be used by nursing students only

7.7B21. "With" notes

To be used for "with" notes.

> *Example:*   In cassette with: Saga of the whale

Example 27: A Star is Born

This video presents a number of cataloging problems. The container and the videocassette label say "restored version" and the container explains the story of the film. The original 181-minute film was cut to 153 minutes before release. Most of the missing footage was recovered in the 1987 restoration, and still photographs with narration were used for the scenes not found. The restored version is considered to be an edition of the original 1954 film.

This same story has been made into film three different times, each with the same title. The first was made in 1937, with Janet Gaynor, Frederick March, and Adolphe Menjou. The second is the one cataloged here, made in 1954 with Judy Garland, James Mason, and Jack Carson. The third was made in 1976 with Barbra Streisand, Kris Kristofferson, and Gary Busey.

A uniform title main entry is needed for each, with the date added to distinguish among them. This restored version needs both the original date (1954) and the version information to distinguish it from the original 1954 version, also available on videocassette.

Uniform titles for the three versions, and for the restored version, would be as follows:

```
Star is born (1937)
Star is born (1954)
Star is born (1954 : Restored version)
Star is born (1976)
```

If your library only owned one of these, and there were no conflict in your catalog, you might choose not to use the uniform title main entry.

Rules for notes area, in order, are 7.7B6 (cast), 7.7B6 (credits), 7.7B7, 7.7B7, 7.7B10f and a, 7.7B17.

Cassette label   **Side of box**

   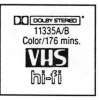

From front of box

From back of box

Example 27: A Star is Born

Transcription of major title and credits screens

Warner Home Video

Warner Bros Pictures

Judy Garland

James Mason

in

A Star is Born

[other cast]

Screen Play by Moss Hart

Based on
the Dorothy Parker, Alan Campbell
Robert Carson Screen Play
From a Story by
William A. Wellman and Robert Carson

New Songs
Music by Harold Arlen
Lyrics by Ira Gershwin

Musical Direction by Ray Heindorf

Produced by Sidney Luft

Directed by George Cukor

Example 27: A Star is Born

PN
1995.9
.M86

791
.43653

Star is born (1954 : Restored version)
    A star is born [videorecording] / Warner Bros
Pictures ; screen play by Moss Hart ; produced by
Sidney Luft ; directed by George Cukor. --
Restored version. -- [Burbank, CA]: Warner Home
Video, [1987]
    2 videocassettes (176 min.) : sd., col. ; 1/2
in.

    Cast: Judy Garland, James Mason, Jack Carson,
Charles Bickford.
    Credits: Music, Harold Arlen ; lyrics, Ira
Gershwin.
    "Based on the Dorothy Parker, Alan Campbell,
Robert Carson screen play from a story by William
A. Wellman and Robert Carson."
    Originally released as motion picture in 1954.
    VHS hi-fi; Dolby stereo.
    Rated PG.
    Summary: A classic story of fame, innocence,
and destruction, as a matinee idol (Mason) falls
in love with a young girl (Garland) and propels
her to stardom.

    1. Musical films. 2. Feature films. 3. Mo-
tion picture actors and actresses. I. Hart,
Moss, 1904-1961. II. Luft, Sid. III. Cukor,
George Dewey, 1899- IV. Garland, Judy. V. Ma-
son, James, 1909- VI. Carson, Jack, 1910-1963.
VII. Bickford, Charles, 1899-1967. VIII. Arlen,
Harold, 1905-1986. IX. Gershwin, Ira, 1896- X.
Warner Bros. Pictures. XI. Warner Home Video.

Example 28: Sound of Music 25th Anniversary Edition

This example shows the use of an edition statement. The edition information may be taken from the chief source or from accompanying material. This does not include the container, so the edition statement is bracketed.

The series statement must be in brackets because it is taken from the package.

This video included an interview and a commercial in addition to the main feature. Some videos also include cartoons or "special added attractions." These added features should always be described in the notes, and may need their own added entries, or they may need a separate bibliographic record (see example 36, *Honey, I Shrunk the Kids* and *Tummy Trouble*).

Rules for notes are, in order, 7.7B10 (moved to first position because of importance to the patrons), 7.7B2, 7.7B6 (cast), 7.7B6 (credits), 7.7B7, 7.7B7, 7.7B10a, 7.7B14, 7.7B17, 7.7B18, 7.7B19.

On the overwrap

Silver Anniversary Edition

On the front of the box

Silver Anniversary

Also on the box

THE RODGERS & HAMMERSTEIN COLLECTION

Example 28: Sound of Music 25th Anniversary Edition

Transcription of significant title and credits screens

CBS Fox Video
c1990

[sales pitch for Rodgers & Hammerstein Collection of videos]

Stereo Surround

[Interview with Robert Wise]

20th Century Fox

A Robert Wise Production
of
Rodgers and Hammerstein's

The
Sound of Music

starring
Julie Andrews
Christopher Plummer
...
Music by Richard Rodgers
Lyrics by Oscar Hammerstein II
Additional Words and Music by
Richard Rodgers

Music supervised, arranged, and conducted by Irwin Kostal

From the stage musical with music and lyrics
by
Richard Rodgers and Oscar Hammerstein II

Book by Howard Lindsay and Russel Crouse

originally produced on the stage by
Leland Hayward,
Richard Halliday,
Richard Rodgers, and
Oscar Hammerstein II

Screenplay by Ernest Lehman

Directed by Robert Wise

Example 28: Sound of Music 25th Anniversary Edition

```
PN          Rodgers and Hammerstein's The Sound of music
1995.9          [videorecording] / 20th Century Fox ; directed
.M86            by Robert Wise ; screenplay by Ernest Lehman. --
                [Silver anniversary ed.] -- [New York, N.Y.] :
782.141         CBS Fox, c1990.
                    2 videocassettes (175 min.) : sd., col. ; 1/2
                in. -- ([The Rodgers & Hammerstein collection])

                VHS.
                Closed-captioned for the hearing impaired.
                Cast: Julie Andrews, Christopher Plummer,
                Richard Haydn, Peggy Wood, Eleanor Parker,
                Charmian Carr, the Bil Baird Marionettes.
                Music by Richard Rodgers, lyrics by Oscar
                Hammerstein II, with additional words and music
                by Richard Rodgers; music supervised, arranged,
                and conducted by Irwin Kostal.
                Originally released as motion picture in
                1965.
                Based on the stage musical with music and
                lyrics by Richard Rodgers and Oscar Hammerstein
                II, book by Howard Lindsay and Russel Crouse
                which was based on the lives of the Trapp Family
                Singers.
                Stereo sound.
                Rated G.
                Summary: A young girl named Maria is uncer-
                tain about her decision to enter a religious
                order. While deciding what to do, she becomes
                the governess of the seven Von Trapp children
                who live with their widowed father, a former
                captain in the Austrian navy. Set in Austria
                just before its takeover by the Nazis.
                Feature preceded by 1990 interview with
                director Robert Wise and by advertisement for
                titles in the CBS/Fox Rodgers & Hammerstein
                collection.
                1829.

                1. Musical films.  2. Trapp Family Singers.
                3. Video recordings for the hearing impaired.
                I. Wise, Robert.  II. Lehman, Ernest.  III.
                Andrews, Julie.  IV. Plummer, Christopher.  V.
                Haydn, Richard.  VI. Wood, Peggy.  VII. Parker,
                Eleanor.  VIII. Carr, Charmian.  IX. Rodgers,
                Richard, 1902-  X. Hammerstein, Oscar, 1895-
                1960.  XI. Lindsay, Howard.  XII. Crouse,
                Russel.  XIII. Twentieth Century-Fox Film Corpo-
                ration.  XIV. CBS Fox Video.  XV. Bill Baird
                Marionettes.  XVI. Title: The sound of music.
```

Example 29: Cathedral

This video has both animated and live action portions, resulting in twice the normal number of credits for producer, director, etc. The video was originally produced for television, then sold in the 60-minute version, and in a 30-minute edited version. It is based on a book of the same title.

Nowhere on the item or its packaging does it indicate any location for Dorset Video, which is named only on the container. We assume it was produced in England and place both "England" and "Dorset Video" in brackets.

Rules for notes are, in order, 7.7B6, 7.7B7, 7.7B7, 7.7B10f, 7.7B17.

Illustration on the front of the box

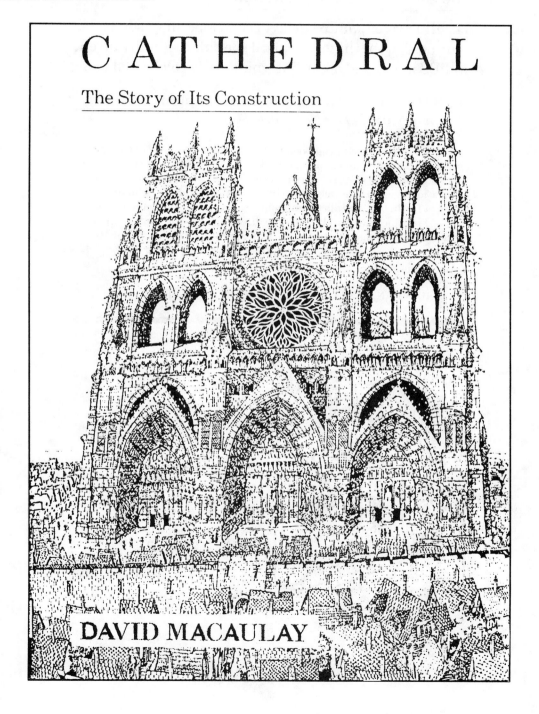

Example 29: Cathedral

Illustration on the back of the box

CATHEDRAL
The Story of Its Construction

The illustrator *par excellence*, David Macaulay, serves as your host in this highly-praised special, originally aired on PBS and based on his internationally celebrated book.

"CATHEDRAL is a delight...a great plum pudding of a program." – *The New York Times*

Based on the award-winning book by David Macaulay, CATHEDRAL uses live-action film and cinema-quality animation to illustrate the planning, building and cultural importance of the Gothic cathedral. Filmed on location at eight awe-inspiring churches, this wonderful film provides a look at Gothic cathedrals throughout France, while animated portions inspired by Macaulay's acclaimed line drawings trace the design and construction of an imaginary but historically accurate cathedral near Paris.

The locations include: Amiens, Chartres, Bourges, Reims, Beauvais, Notre-Dame de Paris and the Royal Abbey Church of St. Denis.

© 1985, UNICORN PROJECTS INC. DISTRIBUTED BY DORSET VIDEO.

Host
David Macaulay, with French actress Caroline Berg

Narrator
Derek Jacobi (animated sequences)

Animation
Animation Partnership Ltd., London

Producer
Unicorn Projects, Inc., Washington, DC
Presented on PBS by WGBH Boston

Underwriters
National Endowment for the Humanities and the Arthur Vining Davis Foundations

Project Advisors
John Baldwin, Johns Hopkins University
William Clark, Queens College
David Herlihy, Harvard University
Robert Mark, Princeton University
Gabrielle M. Spiegel, University of Maryland

Illustration from CATHEDRAL by David Macaulay
© 1973. Published by Houghton Mifflin Company

Example 29: Cathedral

Transcription of significant title and credits screens

The National Endowment for the Humanities
The Arthur Vining Davis Foundations
Unicorn Projects
A Unicorn Project

Cathedral

Based on the book by David Macaulay
with David Macaulay and Caroline Beny

Executive Producer Ray Hubbard

Written and Produced by Mark Olshaker and Larry Klein

Animation Created and Directed by Tony White

Original Music Score by Ian Llande and Steve Parr

Live Action Sequences by Carl Gover Associates
Directed by Tim King
Producer Colin Leighton
c1985

```
NA         Cathedral [videorecording] / Unicorn Projects ;
5543            written and produced by Mark Olshaker and Larry
                Klein ; animation created and directed by Tony
726.64          White ; live action sequences by Carl Gover
                Associates ; directed by Tim King ; producer, Colin
                Leighton. -- [England? : Dorset Video], c1985.
                   1 videocassette (60 min) : sd., col. ; 1/2 in.

                Credits: Music, Ian Llande, Steve Parr.
                Based on the book by David Macaulay.
                Originally produced for television in 1985.
                VHS.
                Summary: Follows, through animation, the plan-
                ning and construction of a Gothic cathedral in the
                imaginary French town of Beaulieu during the thir-
                teenth century. In live-action sequences David
                Macaulay and Caroline Beny explain why and how the
                great cathedrals of Europe were built.

                   1. Cathedrals--France.  2. Architecture,
                Gothic--France.  I. Olshaker, Mark, 1951-  II.
                Klein, Larry.  III. White, Tony.  IV. King, Tim.
                V. Leighton, Colin.  VI. Llande, Ian.  VII. Parr,
                Steve.  VIII. Beny, Caroline.  IX. Macaulay, David.
                Cathedral.  X. Unicorn Projects, Inc.  XI. Carl
                Gover Associates.  XII. Dorset Video.
```

Example 30: Frosty the Snowman

This animated film was produced for television and later distributed in videocassette.
Rules for notes: 7.7B6, 7.7B7, 7.7B7, 7.7B10f, 7.7B14, 7.7B17
The date is given on the container, and so must be bracketed, because the container is not one of the prescribed sources for this information. The place of publication and distributor information also come from the container, so they must be bracketed.

Notice the use of the ISBN found on the package.

Distribution information on the container with ISBN.

Christmas Classics
S·E·R·I·E·S

ISBN 1-55658-336-2
Exclusively Distributed By
MCA DISTRIBUTING CORP.

0 1223-27311-3 3

Transcription of most title and credits screens

Family Home Entertainment

Rankin/Bass Present

Frosty the Snowman

Told & Sung by Jimmy Durante

Starring Billy DeWolfe as The Magician

and

Jackie Vernon as "Frosty"

Produced & Directed by Arthur Rankin, Jr. & Jules Bass

Written by Romeo Mueller

Example 30: Frosty the Snowman

```
PN          Frosty the Snowman [videorecording] / produced &
1995.9          directed by Arthur Rankin, Jr. & Jules Bass ;
.C5             writen by Romeo Muller. -- [Van Nuys, Calif.] :
                Family Home Entertainment ; [exclusively
791.433         distributed by MCA Distributing Corp., 1989]
                    1 videocassette (30 min.) : sd., col. ; 1/2
                in. -- (Christmas classics series)

                    Cast: Told and sung by Jimmy Durante ; Billy
                DeWolfe (Magician), Jackie Vernon (Frosty).
                    Based on the song by Steve Nelson and Jack
                Rollins.
                    Produced for television in 1969.
                    VHS.
                    "Suitable for all ages."
                    Summary: When Frosty the Snowman is acci-
                dently brought to life, he must outwit the plans
                of the evil magician before finding safety at
                the North Pole.
                    ISBN 1-55658-336-2.


                    1. Christmas stories.  2. Children's films.
                3. Animated films.  I. Rankin, Arthur.  II.
                Bass, Jules.  III. Muller, Romeo.  IV. Durante,
                Jimmy.  V. DeWolfe, Billy.  VI. Vernon, Jackie.
                VII. Family Home Entertainment.  VIII. Series.
```

Example 31: New York, New York

If you were adding this to a collection that included an earlier version of this title not in letterbox format, you would need to use a uniform title main entry for this version:

```
New York, New York (Motion picture : Letterbox format)
```

Rules for notes, in order, 7.7B2, 7.7B6, 7.7B6, 7.7B7, 7.7B7, 7.7B10a, 7.7B10f, 7.7B14, 7.7B17.

Transcription of significant title and credits screens

MGM/UA Home Video

A Robert Chartoff—Irwin Winkler Production

A Martin Scorsese Film

Liza Minnelli   Robert DeNiro

New York New York

Lionel Stander   Barry Primus

Original Songs by John Kander and Fred Ebb

Screenplay by Earl Mac Rauch and Mardik Martin

Story by Earl Mac Rauch

Produced by Irwin Winkler and Robert Chartoff

Directed by Martin Scorsese

Example 31: New York, New York

PN
1995.9
.M86

791
.436353

New York, New York [videorecording] / United
Artists ; directed by Martin Scorsese ; produced
by Irwin Winkler and Robert Chartoff ;
screenplay by Earl Mac Rauch and Mardik Martin ;
story by Earl Mac Rauch. -- Letterbox format. --
[Universal City, Calif.] : MGM/UA Home Video,
[1989]
2 videocassettes (164 min.) : sd., col. ; 1/2
in.

Closed-captioned for the hearing impaired.
Cast: Liza Minnelli, Robert DeNiro, Lionel
Stander, Barry Primus.
Original songs by John Kander and Fred Ebb.
"Original uncut version"--Package.
Originally produced as motion picture in
1977.
"Hi-fi, enhanced for stereo, digital video
transfer"--Package.
VHS.
Rated PG.
Summary: Musical celebrating the big band
era, set in post-war Manhattan. A jazz saxophone
player (DeNiro) and an ex-WAC (Minnelli) who
dreams of singing, meet, marry, and work to-
gether, but their ambitions and the pressures of
show business do not permit a happy ending.

1. Musicals. 2. Feature films. 3. Video
recordings for the hearing impaired. 4. Enter-
tainers. I. Scorsese, Martin. II. Winkler,
Irwin. III. Chartoff, Robert. IV. Rauch, Earl
Mac, 1949- V. Martin, Mardik. VI. Minnelli,
Liza, 1946- VII. DeNiro, Robert. VIII.
Stander, Lionel. IX. Primus, Barry. X. Kander,
John. XI. Ebb, Fred. XII. United Artists.
XIII. MGM/UA Home Video.

Example 32: Sorrowful Jones

   This example has a personal possessive included as part of the title proper. It could have a uniform title main entry for the title *Sorrowful Jones*, but I have used a title added entry for this. The uniform title main entry could be used because the "real" title is obscured.
   Rules for notes are, in order, 7.7B6 (cast), 7.7B6 (narrator), 7.7B6 (credits), 7.7B7, 7.7B7, 7.7B10f, 7.7B17.

Transcription from the back of box

PARAMOUNT presents
BOB HOPE • LUCILLE BALL
in DAMON RUNYON'S **"SORROWFUL JONES"**
with WILLIAM DEMAREST • BRUCE CABOT
THOMAS GOMEZ and introducing MARY ANNE SAUNDERS
Forward narrated by WALTER WINCHELL • Produced by ROBERT L. WELCH
Directed by SIDNEY LANDFIELD • Screenplay by MELVILLE SHAVELSON, EDWARD HARTMANN
and JACK ROSE • Adapted from a story by DAMON RUNYON and a screenplay by
WILLIAM R. LIPMAN, SAM HELLMAN and GLADYS LEHMAN
© 1949 Paramount Pictures Inc. Renewed 1976 by EMKA. All Rights Reserved.

70 UNIVERSAL PLAZA, UNIVERSAL CITY, CA 91608
©1988 MCA Home Video, Inc. All Rights Reserved. Printed in U.S.A.

Transcription of most title and credits screens

MCA Home Video

A Paramount Picture

Bob Hope and Lucille Ball
in
Damon Runyon's

Sorrowful Jones

with
William Demarest
Bruce Cabot
Thomas Gomez
Tom Pedi
Paul Lees
Houseley Stevenson
and introducing
Mary Jane Saunders

Screenplay by Melville Shavelson, Edward Hartmann and Jack Rose

Adapted from a story by Damon Runyon
and a screenplay by William R. Lipman, Sam Hellman, and Gladys Lehman

Produced by Robert L. Welch
Directed by Sidney Lanfield

Example 32: Sorrowful Jones

```
PN          Damon Runyon's Sorrowful Jones [videorecording] /
1995.9         a Paramount Picture ; produced by Robert L.
.C55           Welch ; directed by Sidney Lanfield ; screenplay
               by Melville Shavelson, Edward Hartmann, and Jack
791.43617      Rose. -- [Universal City, Calif.] : MCA Home
               Video, [1988]
                   1 videocassette (88 min) : sd., b&w ; 1/2 in.

               Cast: Bob Hope, Lucille Ball, William
           Demarest, Bruce Cabot, Mary Jane Saunders.
               Narrator: Walter Winchell.
               Music score, Robert Emmett Dolan.
               Adapted from a story by Damon Runyon and a
           screenplay by William R. Lipman, Sam Hellman,
           and Gladys Lehman.
               Originally produced as motion picture in
           1949.
               VHS.
               Summary: A penny-pinching Broadway bookie,
           Sorrowful Jones (Hope), inherits a five-year-old
           girl on a bet. Big Steve (Cabot) is a bad guy
           with a horse in the big race. Gladys O'Neill
           (Ball) is a night club singer friendly with both
           Hope and Cabot.

               1. Feature films.  2. Comedy films.  I.
           Welch, Robert L.  II. Lanfield, Sidney, 1898-
           1972.  III. Shavelson, Melville.  IV. Hartmann,
           Edward.  V. Rose, Jack.  VI. Hope, Bob, 1903-
           VII. Ball, Lucille, 1911-1989.  VIII. Demarest,
           William.  IX. Saunders, Mary Jane.  X. Winchell,
           Walter.  XI. Dolan, Robert Emmett.  XII. Runyon,
           Damon, 1880-1946.  XIII. Paramount Pictures.
           XIV. MCA Home Video.  XV. Title: Sorrowful
           Jones.
```

Example 33: From Page to Screen

This film is about the activities of Weston Woods Studios, and it is produced and distributed by Weston Woods, but it does not fit the narrow definition of rule 21.1B2 for entry under corporate body.

Information on the title screens is a bit confusing. Morton Schindel is not the title proper, though the positioning might indicate this. He is the narrator of the film, and Weston Woods is his company.

Label on cassette

Transcription of all title and credits screens

Weston Woods
Presents

Morton Schindel

From Page to Screen

```
LB        From page to screen [videorecording] / Weston Woods
1044          ; Morton Schindel. -- [Weston, Ct.] : Weston
          Woods, [1981]
791.4         1 videocassette (26 min.) : sd., col. ; 1/2
          in.

              VHS.
              Summary: Morton Schindel recounts the history
          of Weston Woods Studios, and shows how they
          adapt children's books to filmstrips and movies,
          including writing music, recording narration,
          and adapting and/or animating artwork.

              1. Weston Woods Studios.  2. Motion pictures
          -- Production and direction.  3. Animated films.
          I. Schindel, Morton.  II. Weston Woods Studios.
```

Figure 4 — Videocassette boxes

Example 34: Ciao, Italia

This music video has personal main entry, permitted under the LC rule interpretation for 21.23.

21.23C1, 21.31D1 [in part]. Apply rules 21.23C1 and 21.23D1 to the following:

1) Videorecordings that contain collections of music performed by a principal performer. (*CSB* 45)

This rule interpretation permits us to enter music videos under the principal performer.
One must be sure to use the birth date for the singer Madonna. OCLC users can tell a funny story about what happens to that main entry when the date is omitted, and the authority file is used in a machine-conversion.
The word "stereo" is not permitted in area 5 of chapter 7, but must be used in a note.
Rules for notes are, in order, 7.7B1, 7.7B6, 7.7B6, 7.7B10a, 7.7B10f, 7.7B18.

Transcription of some title and credits screens

Madonna

Ciao, Italia
Live from Italy

Produced by Riccardo Mario Corato Network
for RAI Radiotelevisione Italiana

Director Egbert Van Hees
ID TV Amsterdam

Live Recording Produced by ID TV Amsterdam
in cooperation with Cinevideogroep

Executive Producer Harry De Winter

Producer Marijke Klasema

Editor Michael Snoway

Example 34: Ciao, Italia

```
M          Madonna, 1957-
1630.18        Ciao, Italia [videorecording] : live from Italy
           / Madonna ; produced by Ricardo Mario Corato
781.63     Network for RAI Radiotelevisione Italiana ;
           director Egbert Van Hees. -- [Burbank, Calif. :
           Warner Reprise Video, 1988]
               1 videocassette (100 min.) : sd., col. ; 1/2 in.

               Concert performance.
               Songs written and performed by Madonna, with
           vocal and instrumental accompaniment.
               Credits: Musical director, Pat Leonard ; concert
           directed and staged by Jeffrey Hornaday.
               Dolby stereo.
               VHS format.
               Contents: Open your heart -- Lucky star -- True
           blue -- Papa don't preach -- White heat -- Causing
           a commotion -- The look of love -- Medley: Dress
           you up, Material girl, Like a virgin -- Where's the
           party -- Live to tell -- Into the groove -- La isla
           bonita -- Who's that girl -- Holiday.

               1. Music videos. 2. Popular music--1981-  3.
           Rock music--1981-  I. Van Hees, Egbert.  II.
           Leonard, Pat.  III. Hornaday, Jeffrey.  IV. Ricardo
           Mario Corato Network.  V. RAI--Radiotelevisione
           italiana.  VI. Warner Reprise Video.  VII. Title.
           VIII. Madonna, 1957-    Open your heart
           (Videorecording).  1988.  IX. Madonna, 1957-
           Lucky star (Videorecording).  1988.  X. Madonna,
           1957-    True blue (Videorecording).  1988.  XI.
           Madonna, 1957-    Papa, don't preach
           (Videorecording).  1988.  XII. Madonna, 1957-
           White heat (Videorecording).  1988.  XIII. Madonna,
           1957-    Causing a commotion (Videorecording).
           1988.  XIV. Madonna, 1957-    Look of love
           (Videorecording).  1988.  XV. Madonna, 1957-
           Dress you up (Videorecording).  1988.  XVI. Ma-
           donna, 1957-    Material girl.  XVII. Madonna,
           1957-    Like a virgin (Videorecording).  1988.
           XVIII. Madonna, 1957-    Where's the party
           (Videorecording).  1988.  XIX. Madonna, 1957-
           Live to tell (Videorecording).  1988.  XX. Madonna,
           1957-    Into the groove (Videorecording).  1988.
           XXI. Madonna, 1957-    Isla bonita
           (Videorecording).  1988.  XXII. Madonna, 1957-
           Who's that girl (Videorecording).  1988.  XXIII.
           Madonna, 1957-    Holiday (Videorecording).  1988.
```

Example 35A: Singin' in the Rain VHS

The place of publication is given on the container as "NY, NY." Because it is on the container, it must be bracketed. One does not use brackets within brackets. Because it's going to be bracketed anyway, one would simply supply the full form of the place.

A cross reference is needed from Singing in the rain to Singin' in the rain.

Rules for notes are, in order, 7.7B6, 7.7B6, 7.7B7, 7.7B10f, 7.7B17.

The VHS, CAV, and CLV versions of Singin' in the Rain

Transcription of title and credits screens

MGM/UA Home Video

Metro Goldwyn Mayer

| Gene | Debbie | Donald |
| Kelly | Reynolds | O'Connor |

in

Singin' In The Rain

with

| Jean | Millard |
| Hagen | Mitchell |

Cyd
Charisse

Story and Screen Play by
Adolph Green and Betty Comden

Suggested by the Song "Singin' in the Rain"

Example 35A: Singin' in the Rain VHS

Songs:
Lyrics by Arthur Freed
Music by Nacio Herb Brown

Produced by Arthur Freed

Directed by Gene Kelly and Stanley Donen

```
PN        Singin' in the rain [videorecording] / Metro
1995      Goldwyn Mayer ; produced by Arthur Freed ;
.M86      directed by Gene Kelly and Stanley Donen ; story
          and screen play by Adolph Green and Betty
791       Comden. -- [New York, NY] : MGM/UA Home Video,
.43653    [1983]
               1 videocassette (103 min.) : sd., col., 1/2
          in.

               Cast: Gene Kelly, Debbie Reynolds, Donald
          O'Connor, Jean Hagen, Millard Mitchell, Cyd
          Charisse.
               Lyrics by Arthur Freed ; music by Nacio Herb
          Brown.
               Originally released as a motion picture in
          1952.
               VHS.
               Summary: Musical comedy parody of Hollywood's
          transition to "talking pictures" in the 1920s.

               1. Musical films.  2. Feature films.  I.
          Freed, Arthur, 1894-1973.  II. Kelly, Gene,
          1912-     III. Donen, Stanley.  IV. Green,
          Adolph.  V. Comden, Betty.  VI. Reynolds,
          Debbie.  VII. O'Connor, Donald, 1925-
          VIII. Hagen, Jean, 1924-1977.  IX. Mitchell,
          Millard.  X. Charisse, Cyd.  XI. Brown, Nacio
          Herb, 1896-     XII. Metro-Goldwyn-Mayer.
          XIII. MGM/UA Home Video.
```

Example 35B: Singin' in the Rain CLV

This two-sided videodisc is in the CLV format that permits search by "chapters" of the film. Rules for notes are 7.7B6, 7.7B6, 7.7B7, 7.7B10f, 7.7B14, 7.7B17, 7.7B19. The CLV note is given as found on the item.

Transcription of title and credits screens

Criterion

MGM/UA Home Video

Turner

Metro Goldwyn Mayer

Gene	Debbie	Donald
Kelly	Reynolds	O'Connor

in

Singin' In The Rain

with

Jean	Millard
Hagen	Mitchell

Cyd
Charisse

Story and Screen Play by Adolph Green and Betty Comden

Suggested by the Song
"Singin' in the Rain"

Songs:
Lyrics by Arthur Freed
Music by Nacio Herb Brown

Produced by
Arthur Freed

Directed by
Gene Kelly and Stanley Donen

Example 35B: Singin' in the Rain CLV

```
PN          Singin' in the rain [videorecording] / Metro
1995        Goldwyn Mayer ; produced by Arthur Freed ;
.M86        directed by Gene Kelly and Stanley Donen ; story
            and screen play by Adolph Green and Betty
791         Comden. -- [Santa Monica, CA : Distributed by
.43653      the Voyager Co., 1990]
                 1 videodisc (103 min.) : sd., col.; 12
            in. -- (The Criterion Collection ; 52A)

                 Cast: Gene Kelly, Debbie Reynolds, Donald
            O'Connor, Jean Hagen, Millard Mitchell, Cyd
            Charisse.
                 Lyrics by Arthur Freed ; music by Nacio Herb
            Brown.
                 Originally released as a motion picture in
            1952.
                 Extended play (CLV).
                 Rated G.
                 Summary: Musical comedy parody of Hollywood's
            transition to "talking pictures" in the 1920s.
                 "CC1210L."
                 ISBN 0-55940-072-2.

                 1. Musical films.  2. Feature films.  I.
            Freed, Arthur, 1894-1973.  II. Kelly, Gene,
            1912-        III. Donen, Stanley.  IV. Green,
            Adolph.  V. Comden, Betty.  VI. Reynolds,
            Debbie.  VII. O'Connor, Donald, 1925-
            VIII. Hagen, Jean, 1924-1977.  IX. Mitchell,
            Millard.  X. Charisse, Cyd.  XI. Metro-Goldwyn-
            Mayer.  XII. Voyager Company.  XIII. Series.
```

Example 35C: Singin' in the Rain CAV

This CAV disc allows random access, slow and fast motion, and freeze frame functions. The supplementary material is on side 4. I gave the length of the film in the note rather than in area 5. The total length of the package is not given on the item, and it is that length that would go in area 5.

Rules for notes are, in order, 7.7B6, 7.7B6, 7.7B7, 7.7B10f, 7.7B17, 7.7B18, 7.7B18, 7.7B19.

The CAV note is given as found on the item.

Transcription of title and credits screens

Criterion

MGM/UA Home Video

Turner

Metro Goldwyn Mayer

Gene	Debbie	Donald
Kelly	Reynolds	O'Connor

in
Singin' In The Rain

with

Jean	Millard
Hagen	Mitchell

Cyd
Charisse

Story and Screen Play by Adolph Green and Betty Comden

Suggested by the Song
"Singin' in the Rain"

Songs:
Lyrics by Arthur Freed
Music by Nacio Herb Brown

Produced by Arthur Freed

Directed by
Gene Kelly and Stanley Donen

Example 35C: Singin' in the Rain CAV

```
PN         Singin' in the rain [videorecording] / Metro
1995         Goldwyn Mayer ; produced by Arthur Freed ;
.M86         directed by Gene Kelly and Stanley Donen ; story
             and screen play by Adolph Green and Betty
791          Comden. -- [Santa Monica, CA : Distributed by
.43653       the Voyager Co., 1988]
                  2 videodiscs : sd., col.; 12 in. -- (The
             Criterion Collection ; 52)

                  Cast: Gene Kelly, Debbie Reynolds, Donald
             O'Connor, Jean Hagen, Millard Mitchell, Cyd
             Charisse.
                  Lyrics by Arthur Freed ; music by Nacio Herb
             Brown.
                  Originally released as a motion picture in
             1952.
                  Full feature format (CAV).
                  Summary: Musical comedy parody of Hollywood's
             transition to "talking pictures" in the 1920s.
                  Audio essay by Ronald Haver is on the second
             audio track.
                  Following the film (103 min.) are original
             film versions of the songs Singin' in the rain
             (Cliff Edwards), Beautiful girl (Bing Crosby),
             and You were meant for me (Charles King and
             Anita Page). Also included are an early demon-
             stration of talking movies, and an outtake from
             the film.
                  "CC1152L."
                  ISBN 0-931393-98-1.

                  1. Musical films.  2. Feature films.  I.
             Freed, Arthur, 1894-1973.  II. Kelly, Gene,
             1912-      III. Donen, Stanley.  IV. Green,
             Adolph.  V. Comden, Betty.  VI. Reynolds,
             Debbie.  VII. O'Connor, Donald, 1925-
             VIII. Hagen, Jean, 1924-1977.  IX. Mitchell,
             Millard.  X. Charisse, Cyd.  XI. Metro-Goldwyn-
             Mayer.  XII. Voyager Company.  XIII. Series.
```

Example 36: Honey, I Shrunk the Kids *and* Tummy Trouble

Here are two titles on one cassette with no collective title, and each with its own title and credits frames. They could be cataloged on one bibliographic record with all the information about the cartoon combined in one note, or both titles could be given in the title area with credits for each done in separate notes. I chose to catalog each separately and link them using "with" notes.

Back and side of cassette box

Example 36A: Tummy Trouble

Rules for notes are 7.7B1, 7.7B2, 7.7B10f, 7.7B17, 7.7B21.

General credits at beginning of videocassette

Walt Disney Home Video

Walt Disney Pictures

(preview of Dick Tracy)

Transcription of title screens and credits

Walt Disney Pictures
R. K. Maroon presents A Maroon Cartoon in color
© 1990
Walt Disney Pictures and Steven Spielberg present

Tummy Trouble

Animation directed by Rob Minkhoff
Live action directed by Frank Marshall
Produced by Don Hahn
AMBLIN Entertainment
Distributed by
Buena Vista Pictures Distribution, Inc.

```
PN        Tummy trouble [videorecording] / Walt Disney
1995.9        Pictures ; [presented by] Steven Spielberg ;
.C55       Amblin Entertainment ; produced by Don Hahn ;
          animation directed by Rob Minkhoff ; live action
791        directed by Frank Marshall. -- [Burbank, Calif.]
.43617     : Walt Disney Home Video ; distributed by Buena
          Vista Pictures, c1990.
              on 1 videocassette (8 min.) : sd., col. ; 1/2
          in.

              "A Maroon cartoon"
              Closed-captioned for the hearing impaired.
              VHS, stereo.
              Summary: "When Baby Herman swallows a rattle,
          it's Roger Rabbit who's all shook up as these
          two toons take over a hospital and stir up a
          little medical mayhem"--Container.
              With: Honey, I shrunk the kids.

              1. Animated films.  2. Rabbit, Roger.  3.
          Baby Herman.  I. Spielberg, Steven, 1947-
          II. Hahn, Don.  III. Minkhoff, Rob.  IV.
          Marshall, Frank.  V. Walt Disney Pictures.  VI.
          Amblin Entertainment (Firm).  VII. Walt Disney
          Home Video.  VIII. Buena Vista Pictures.
```

Example 36B: Honey, I Shrunk the Kids

Rules for notes are, in order, 7.7B2, 7.7B6, 7.7B7, 7.7B10a and f, 7.7B14, 7.7B17 and 7.7B6 combined, 7.7B18, 7.7B21.

Transcription of title screens and credits

Walt Disney Pictures
presents

in association with
Silver Screen Partners III

Rick Moranis
in

Honey, I Shrunk the Kids

Story by Stuart Gordon, Brian Yuzna, Ed Naha

Screenplay by Ed Naha, Tom Schulman

Produced by Penney Finkelman Cox

Directed by Joe Johnston

Example 36B: Honey, I Shrunk the Kids

PN
1995.9
.C55

791
.43617

Honey, I shrunk the kids [videorecording] / Walt
Disney Pictures ; Silver Screen Partners III ;
produced by Penney Finkelman Cox ; directed by
Joe Johnston. -- [Burbank, Calif.] : Walt Disney
Home Video ; [distributed by Buena Vista Home
Video], c1990.
   1 videocassette (101 min.) : sd., col. ; 1/2
in.

   Closed-captioned for the hearing impaired.
   Credits: Story, Stuart Gordon, Brian Yuzna,
Ed Naha ; screenplay, Ed Naha, Tom Schulman.
   Originally produced as motion picture in
1989.
   VHS, stereo.
   Rated PG.
   Summary: An absent-minded inventor (Rick
Moranis) working on a shrinking machine acciden-
tally shrinks his kids down to 1/4 inch in
height! When they are tossed out with the trash
they have to make their way home through a
backyard that has become a jungle.
   Preceded by a preview of the movie Dick
Tracy.
   With: Tummy trouble.
   ISBN 1-55890-909-5.

   1. Comedy films. 2. Video recordings for the
hearing impaired. I. Cox, Penney Finkelman.
II. Johnston, Joe. III. Gordon, Stuart. IV.
Yuzna, Brian. V. Naha, Ed. VI. Schulman, Tom.
VII. Moranis, Rick. VIII. Walt Disney Pictures.
IX. Silver Screen Partners III. X. Walt Disney
Home Video. XI. Buena Vista Home Video.

Example 37: Mitosis

This is the standard type of film loop, a very popular type of media in the early 1970's. The next example, *Trisecting a line with triangles* is a non-standard type.

Box, guide, and cartridge

Title page of the guide

A
SELF-INSTRUCTION
INQUIRY GUIDE

For the film

Mitosis

Created and developed by
Biological Sciences Curriculum Study (BSCS)
Boulder, Colorado.

Published and distributed by
Hubbard Scientific Company,
Northbrook, Illinois

Example 37: Mitosis

Transcription of title and credits frames:

Mitosis
c1967
Produced by the
Biological Sciences
Curriculum Study

```
QH          Mitosis [motion picture] / produced by the
605.2       Biological Sciences Curriculum Study. --
            Northbrook, Ill. : Hubbard, c1967.
574
.87623         1 film loop (4 min.) : si., col. ; super 8
            mm. + 1 self-instruction inquiry guide. -- (A
            BSCS single topic inquiry film)

               Summary: Uses time-lapse photography to show
            the process of mitosis.

               1. Mitosis.  2. Cell division.  [1. Cells. 2.
            Reproduction.]  I. Biological Sciences Curricu-
            lum Study.  II. Hubbard Scientific Company.
            III. Series.
```

Example 38: Trisecting a Line

Variant titles should be noted and added entries made when the title variation is significant for filing or retrieval purposes, as this variation is. The difference is in the third word of the title.

This type of motion picture cartridge can only be used on one type of projector, so the type of projector must be named in a note.

The statement of responsibility is given on the container, not on the film itself (the chief source of information), so the statement of responsibility information is given as a note rather than in area 1.

The Walden Film Corporation is named only in the copyright statement; this statement is included as a note to justify the added entry.

No subject heading in *LCSH* is as specific as the topic of this film, so a general subject heading is used.

Rules for notes are, in order, 7.7B5, 7.7B6, 7.7B10, 7.7B17.

Film cartridge and container (cartridge propped up)
This is a super 8 film in a cartridge. The cartridge contains a reel of film rather than the more familiar film loop.

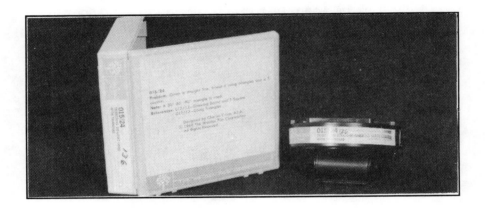

Title frame for series

BASIC
DRAFTING
TECHNIQUES

015/24

Title frame

TRISECTING A LINE
WITH TRIANGLES

© 1969 The Walden Film Corporation

Example 38: Trisecting a Line

```
QA          Trisecting a line with triangles [motion picture].
459             -- [United States] : Heath, c1969.
                1 film cartridge (ca. 4 min.) : sd., col. ;
516.2076    super 8 mm. -- (Basic drafting techniques ;
            015/24)

                Title on cartridge and container: Trisecting
            a straight line with triangles.
                Credits: Designed by Charles Coiro ; copy-
            right by the Walden Film Corporation.
                For use on Kodak Supermatic Projector.
                Summary: Shows how to trisect a straight line
            using a 30/60/90 triangle and a T-square.

                1. Geometry--Problems, exercises, etc.  [1.
            Geometry--Problems, exercises, etc.]  I. Coiro,
            Charles.  II. Walden Film Corporation.  III.
            Title: Trisecting a straight line with tri-
            angles.  IV. Series.
```

Example 39: News Images

There are many choices to be made concerning title proper for this example. I made added entries for all possibilities in addition to my title proper choice.

The name of the distributor appears in the statement of responsibility so may be given in area 4 in shortened form.

Rules for notes are, in order, 7.7B6, 7.7B6, 7.7B10f, 7.7B17.

Title screen information

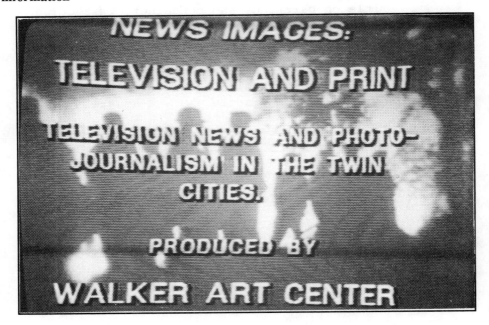

```
PN        News images, television and print [videorecording]
4888          : television news and photojournalism in the
.T4        Twin Cities / produced by Walker Art Center ;
           director, Charles Helm ; producer and script
070.4      writer, Maud Lavin. -- Minneapolis : The Center,
           c1978.
               1 videocassette (15 min.) : sd., col. ; 1/2
           in.

               Narrator, Dave Moore.
               Produced with the assistance of WCCO-TV.
               VHS.
               Summary: Describes and compares television
           journalism and press photography using examples
           of Minneapolis and St. Paul news items.

               1. Broadcast journalism.  2. Photography,
           Journalistic.  3. Television broadcasting of
           news.  [1. Television broadcasting. 2. Photogra-
           phy, Journalistic.]  I. Moore, Dave.  II. Helm,
           Charles.  III. Lavin, Maud.  IV. Walker Art
           Center.  V. WCCO-TV (Television station : Minne-
           apolis, Minn.)  VI. Title: Television and print.
           VII. Title: Television news and photojournalism
           in the Twin Cities.  VIII. Title: News images.
```

Example 40: 100 Years of Brewing

This bibliographic record makes note of, and added entries for, people that might not ordinarily be mentioned (project advisor, music). These people are faculty members at Mankato State University, and, following our local policy, I make added entries for them for our catalog. The credits note is constructed according to rule 7.7B6 and its LCRI.

This is a locally produced videorecording that was distributed to all of the Regional Production Centers in Minnesota, so it is considered to be published.

Transcription of title and credits frames:

100 Years of Brewing
Written and Produced by Joyce Peterson and Rod Terbeest
Directed by Rod Terbeest
Narrated by Curt Crandall
Music Lowell Schreyer, Michael Scullin
Project Advisor William McGinley
Special thank you to:
Dorothy Steil,
Bill Thilgen,
August Schell Brewing Company,
New Ulm, Minnesota,
Carl Busch,
Frank Hecht,
Frank Roetzler,
St. Paul Pioneer Press
Produced in association with
The Regional Production Center
Mankato State College
Mankato, Minnesota.

```
HD          100 years of brewing [videorecording] / written
9397           and produced by Joyce Peterson and Rod Terbeest
.U53           ; directed by Rod Terbeest ; produced in
               association with the Regional Television
663            Production Center, Mankato State College. --
.309776        Mankato, Minn. : The Center, [1971]
                    1 videocassette (30 min.) : sd., b&w ; 3/4
               in.

                    Credits: Narrator, Curt Crandall ; music,
               Lowell Schreyer, Michael Scullin ; project
               adviser, William McGinley.
                    U-matic.
                    Summary: A documentary of the history of the
               brewing industry in Mankato, Minnesota.

                    1. Brewing industry--Minnesota.  [1. Bever-
               ages.]  I. Peterson, Joyce.  II. Terbeest, Rod.
               III. Crandall, Curt.  IV. McGinley, William A,
               1943-      V. Schreyer, Lowell.  VI. Scullin,
               Michael.  VII. Mankato State College. Regional
               Television Production Center.  VIII. Title: One
               hundred years of brewing.
```

Example 41: Out of the Closet

This off-air videorecording was taped with permission of WCCO. The title was announced by Dave Moore, but it did not appear in print on a title or credit frame.

Rules for notes are, in order, 7.7B3, 7.7B6, 7.7B9, 7.7B10f, 7.7B17.

The qualifier "(Television program)" is always added to an added entry for the name of a program (rule 25.5B LCRI, *CSB* 25).

Transcription of title and credits frames:

Moore on Sunday
Produced and Written by Jim Hayden
A Presentation of the Public Affairs Unit
WCCO Television News

```
HQ          Out of the closet [videorecording] / produced and
76.25          written by Jim Hayden. -- [1977]
                  1 videocassette (30 min.) : sd., col. ; 1/2
306.7       in. -- (Moore on Sunday)


            Title from narration.
            A presentation of the Public Affairs Unit,
            WCCO Television News.
            Broadcast on WCCO-TV Oct. 23, 1977; taped
            with permission.
            VHS-SP.
            Summary: Commentary on the oppression of
            gays, role of Anita Bryant, and Minneapolis
            reaction.

                1. Homosexuality.  [1. Gay men. 2. Gay women.
            3. Homosexuality.]  I. Moore, Dave.  II. Bryant,
            Anita.  III. WCCO-TV (Television station :
            Minneapolis, Minn.)  III. Series: Moore on
            Sunday (Television program)
```

Example 42: Power, Politics, & Current Issues in Rehabilitation

This is an example of an unpublished videorecording. It records a workshop on rehabilitation issues. Only the date appears in area 4. The word "Department" may be abbreviated to "Dept." in added entries according to the LCRI to *AACR 2* Appendix B.9. A note is made for local Mankato State faculty so that added entries may be made for them.

Transcription of title and credits frames:

Power, Politics & Current Issues in Rehabilitation
Workshop
Presented by Rehabilitation Counseling Department
Mankato State University
Staff: Dr. Robert Hopper, Department Chairman
Dr. Richard Ugland, Project Director
Dr. Ward Thayer, Workshop Director

```
HD        Power, politics & current issues in rehabilitation
7255           [videorecording] : workshop / presented by
               Rehabilitation Counseling Department, Mankato
362.4          State University. -- [1977]
                  1 videoreel (60 min.) : sd., b&w ; 1/2 in.

               Workshop director, Ward Thayer ; project
           director, Richard Ugland ; department chairman,
           Robert Hopper.
               Summary: Senator Hubert H. Humphrey speaks at
           a workshop held July 6, 1977, at Mankato State
           University, on the use of politics and the
           applications of power in advancing the program,
           objectives, and goals of handicapped and dis-
           abled persons.

               1. Rehabilitation  [1. Physically handi-
           capped--Rehabilitation.]  I. Humphrey, Hubert H.
           (Hubert Horatio), 1911-1978.  II. Thayer, Ward.
           II. Ugland, Richard.  II. Hopper, Richard.  II.
           Mankato State University.  Rehabilitation Coun-
           seling Dept.  III. Title: Power, politics, and
           current issues in rehabilitation.
```

Example 43: The Age of Steam

This videorecording is a master's thesis. Rules for notes are, in order, 7.7B6, 7.7B10f, 7.7B13, 7.7B17.

Transcription of title and credits frames:

The Age of Steam
Written, Produced and Directed by
William A. McGinley
Special Assistance by
Thomas E. Harmening
and
George H. Collins
Produced In Association With
Indiana University
Department
of
Radio and Television
1968

```
TJ         McGinley, William A., 1943-
615           The age of steam [videorecording] / written,
           produced, and directed by William A. McGinley ;
385.09     special assistance by Thomas E. Harmening and
           George H. Collins. -- 1968.
              1 videocassette (30 min.) : sd., b&w ; 3/4 in.

              Produced in association with Indiana University
           Department of Radio and Television.
              U-matic.
              Thesis (M.A.)--Indiana University, 1968.
              Summary: Brief historical study of the steam
           locomotive from its inception to its replacement by
           the diesel.

              1. Locomotives.  2. Steam engineering.  [1.
           Locomotives. 2. Steam engineering.]  I. Harmening,
           Thomas E.  III. Collins, George H.  III. Indiana
           University.  Dept. of Radio and Television.  IV.
           Title.
```

Chapter 6

GRAPHIC MATERIALS

AACR 2 Chapter 8

Graphic materials of all kinds, whether opaque or intended to be projected or viewed, are cataloged using rules of *AACR 2* chapter 8. Examples for many types of graphic materials are included here. Those materials intended to be projected so as to create the illusion of movement are cataloged by the rules of *AACR 2* chapter 7.

Special Rules for Cataloging Graphic Materials

In this section the special rules for cataloging graphic materials will be discussed. Parts of some of the rules are given; the user is referred to the rules themselves for complete text and examples. All of the Library of Congress rule interpretations are included.

For cataloging original art works and historical collections, refer also to: *Graphic Materials: Rules for Describing Original Items and Historical Collections*, compiled by Elisabeth W. Betz (Washington, D.C.: Library of Congress, 1982).

Chief Source of Information

8.0B1. The chief source of information for graphic materials is the item itself including any labels that are permanently affixed to the item or a container that is an integral part of the item. If the item being described consists of two or more separate physical parts, treat a container that is the unifying element as the chief source of information if it furnishes a collective title and the items themselves and their labels do not....

The chief source of information for a filmstrip is the title and credits frames of the filmstrip. For a set of filmstrips, one would look at all the title and credits frames, and compare that information to the information on the container for the set. If the box/container for the set carries a collective title that does *not* appear on the title and credits frames of the filmstrips, the container is chosen as the chief source of information.

The chief source of information for a set of slides is the title and credits slides and the information on the slide mounts. If a container furnishes a collective title not found on the individual slides or their mounts, the container is used as the chief source of information.

The chief source of information for a set of transparencies is any title/credit transparency and the transparency mounts. Transparencies are less likely to have title/credit information on the film itself. This information is more likely to be on the transparency mounts or on the container.

Title and Statement of Responsibility Area

There are no problems of title that are unique to these materials.

LCRI 8.1F1. This rule is merely a reference to chapter 1. If there is a corporate body responsible overall for the work, usually record in the note area the names of persons responsible for only a segment of the work. Contributors who are considered to be of major importance to the item always may be recorded in the statement of responsibility. (*CSB* 11)

LCRI 8.1F1. When deciding whether to give names in the statement of responsibility or in a note, generally give the names in the statement of responsibility when the person or body has some degree of overall responsibility; use the note area for others who are responsible for only one segment or one aspect of the work. Be liberal about making exceptions to the general policy when the person's or body's responsibility is important in relation to the content of the work, i.e., give such important people and bodies in the statement of responsibility even though they may have only partial responsibility. Normally the Library of Congress considers producers, directors, and writers (or, in the case of slides and transparencies, authors, editors, and compilers) as having some degree of overall responsibility and gives them in the statement of responsibility. (*CSB* 13)

Publication, Distribution, Etc., Area

LCRI 8.4F2. Give a date of original production differing from the dates of publication/ distribution or copyright, etc., in the note area (see 8.7B9). Apply the provision if the difference is greater than two years. When dealing with different media, see 8.7B7. (*CSB* 33)

Physical Description Area

Extent of item

A long list of terms is given for use as specific material designations. At the end of the rule is the option to substitute or add a term more specific than those listed.

The various specific material designations would be apportioned among the GMD's as follows:

Art original	Flash card	Technical drawing
Art original	Flash card	Technical drawing
Art reproduction	Picture	Transparency
Art print	Photograph	Transparency
Art reproduction	Picture	
Chart	Postcard	
Chart	Radiograph	
Flip chart	Study print	
Wall chart	Slide	
Filmstrip	Slide	
Filmslip	Stereograph	
Filmstrip		

The term "activity card" has been approved by the JSC as a GMD and an SMD. We can use these terms after the JSC decision is officially published sometime in 1992.

Counting frames of a filmstrip

LCRI 8.5B2. When counting unnumbered frames, generally do not consider any number too numerous to count. Begin counting with the first content frame and end with the last content frame, thereby counting any noncontent frame interspersed, but excluding noncontent frames that precede the first content frame or follow the last content frame. Give the number resulting from this count as the total, within brackets. (Small groups of unnumbered optional content frames may be ignored.)

As with separately numbered title frames, give separate totals of test frames.

```
60 fr., 4 test fr.
```

(*CSB* 33)

This rule interpretation led to several letters that appeared in successive issues of the Online Audiovisual Catalogers *Newsletter*. The last of these includes the following information from Richard Thaxter, Library of Congress:

I must confess that the major part of RI 8.5B2 was lifted directly from the appropriate rule (228D1) in *AACR 1* chapter 12, revised. We offered this rule interpretation because *AACR 2* did not give any guidance on counting filmstrip frames, and we decided that we could just count them as we did previously. The definition of content frame, I'm afraid, excludes title frames. The definition we would follow would again be that included in *AACR 1* chapter 12, revised: "A filmstrip frame which presents subject matter, rather than title, credits, etc. (If titles, credits, etc., are superimposed on a frame which presents subject matter, the frame is considered as a content frame)."

Since we catalog very few filmstrips "from scratch" at LC, the issue of frame counting does not loom so large on our list of cataloging problems. I will say that the old *AACR 1* rule never presented any controversy in the past so we simply extended it in the absence of any guidance in *AACR 2*. I do like Margaret Maxwell's simple solution, i.e., count from the first frame to the last, regardless of whether they are title, credits, or "content" frames. But the definition as worded leaves a problem which I believe Nancy Olson has pointed out, namely, that the first title frame may appear many frames after the beginning of the filmstrip (similar to many modern motion pictures where the credits are almost at the end of the first reel) ... I have never thought that the number of frames on a filmstrip is as crucial in identification as, for example, the pagination of a book (Verna Urbanski. "The Last Word on Counting Frames in Filmstrips." Online Audiovisual Catalogers. *Newsletter*, 3 (June 1983), 7).

Measuring filmstrips

A useful aid for counting filmstrips is a piece of white tape fastened to the edge of the work table, marked off in frame lengths. Stretch the filmstrip out against the scale (like measuring yard goods) and read the frame count directly from the scale.

Other physical details

Directions are given in *AACR2* for describing all types of graphic material. Rule 8.5C1e refers to filmstrips where the sound is integral; this means the sound is on the film or is packaged with the filmstrip in a permanent container. Rule 8.5C1h refers to slides with integral sound; these slides are individually packaged in cassettes with sound, or have sound on the film in some way, such as the Dia-cassettes for the Pixtron IIs that have 90 seconds of sound for each slide.

There is no provision in area 5 for including the information that captions are on the frames of a filmstrip. This information is given in a note.

Dimensions

Directions are given for measuring all types of graphic materials. Note that in rule 8.5D4 we are directed to *exclude* the mount in measuring for transparencies and for art works and their reproductions.

Accompanying material

We are directed to record the number and name of accompanying material; physical description of that material is optional, but when done is in parentheses following the name of the material.

If the sound is on the item, it is mentioned under other physical details; if it is on a separate physical item, it is mentioned as accompanying material.

Notes Area

Notes permitted in this chapter are:

8.7B1.   Nature or artistic form
8.7B2.   Language
8.7B3.   Source of title proper
8.7B4.   Variations in title
8.7B5.   Parallel titles and other title information
8.7B6a. Statements of responsibility
8.7B6b. Donor, source, etc., and previous owners
8.7B7.   Edition and history
8.7B9.   Publication, distribution, etc.
8.7B10. Physical description
8.7B11. Accompanying material
8.7B12. Series
8.7B13. Dissertations
8.7B14. Audience
8.7B16. Other formats
8.7B17. Summary
8.7B18. Contents
8.7B19. Numbers
8.7B20. Copy being described, library's holdings, and restrictions on use
8.7B21. "With" notes
8.7B22. Notes relating to the original

Explanation of notes

Each of the notes will be explained in the following section and examples of their use given.

1.7A5. ... When appropriate, combine two or more notes to make one note.

Example: `Designed and copyright by Richard Miller; to be assembled into`
`model of human skull`

8.7B1. Nature or artistic form

To be used to name or explain the form of the item as necessary.

Example: `Original watercolor`

8.7B2. Language

To be used to name the language or languages of the item cataloged if not obvious from other information given.

Examples: `Captions in French`
`Description in German`

8.7B3. Source of title proper

To be used if the title proper is taken from other than the chief source of information.

Examples: `Title from publisher's catalog`
`Title supplied by cataloger`

8.7B4. Variations in title

To be used to note any title appearing on the item that differs significantly from the title proper.

> *Example:* `Title on first slide: Make the case with surveillance`
> (*Title proper:* Surveillance)

8.7B5. Parallel titles and other title information

To be used for parallel titles and important other title information not recorded in the title and statement of responsibility area.

> *Example:* `English title: Maintaining workers' interest`
> (*Title proper:* Conserve el interes de sus empleades)

8.7B6. Statements of responsibility

To be used to record important information not recorded in the statement of responsibility area.

> **LCRI 8.7B6.** For audiovisual items, generally list persons (other than producers, directors, and writers) who have contributed to the artistic and technical production of a work in a credits note (see 8.1F1). Give the following persons in the order in which they are listed below. Preface each name or group of names with the appropriate term(s) of function:
>
> > photographer(s); camera; cameraman/men; cinematographer
> > animator(s)
> > artist(s); illustrator(s); graphics
> > film editor(s); photo editor(s); editor(s)
> > narrator(s); voice(s)
> > music
> > consultant(s); adviser(s)
>
> Do not include the following persons:
>
> > assistants or associates
> > production supervisors or coordinators
> > project or executive editors
> > technical advisers or consultants
> > audio or sound engineers
> > writers of discussion, program, or teacher's guides
> > other persons making only a minor or purely technical contribution
>
> (*CSB* 22)

In response to a question referring to the fact that a "Credits:" note is not authorized in chapter 8, Richard Thaxter stated:

> LC's rule interpretation 8.7B6 was intended to show that we will continue to use formally captioned "Credits:" notes for filmstrips, slide sets, etc. Chapter 8 encompasses a wide range of materials, most of which would never have a "Credits:" note.
>
> One of the advantages of the integrated structure of *AACR 2* is that one can usually borrow from one chapter when a provision is lacking in another ... The list of persons to include and the order in which they should go (RI 8.7B6) is neither prescriptive nor exhaustive ... If more than three persons perform the same function only the first will be listed, marks of omission and the phrase "et al." will be used (Verna Urbanski. "LC Answers Questions on 508 "Credits" RI." Online Audiovisual Catalogers. *Newsletter*, 3 (Sept. 1983), 9).

This LCRI is intended as guidelines for general cases. When cataloging photographs by a famous photographer, or reproductions of those photos, the photographer's name should go in the statement of responsibility rather than in a note if that name appears in a prominent position in the chief source of information.

8.7B6. Donor, source, etc., and previous owners

To be used for information about the donor, source, and previous owners of an original graphic item.

> *Example:*   `Donated in 1989 by Aileen Marcy`

8.7B7. Edition and history

To be used for information about earlier editions, or the history of the item being cataloged.

> **LCRI 8.7B7.** When an item is known to have an original master in a different medium and the production or release date of the master is more than two years earlier than that of the item being cataloged, give an edition/history note:
>
> `Originally issued as filmstrip in [year]`
>
> Make a similar note when an item is known to have been previously produced or issued (more than two years earlier) in a different medium, but the original medium is unknown.
>
> `Previously issued as slide set in [year]`
>
> If the date of production or release of an original master or an earlier medium is unknown or if the difference between its production or release date and the production or release date of the item being cataloged is two years or less, indicate the availability of the other medium or media in a note according to 8.7B16.
>
> `Issued also as slide set and videorecording`
> `Produced also as slide set`
>
> Note: The use of production versus release dates is left to the cataloger's judgment. Make the note that seems best to give information about either production or release of other formats on a case-by-case basis. (*CSB* 15)

8.7B9. Publication, distribution, etc.

To be used for important information not recorded in the publication, distribution, etc., area.

> **LCRI 8.7B9.** When a foreign firm, etc., is given in the source as emanator or originator, do not assume that the item was either made or released in that country if not so stated. Instead use the note:
>
> `A foreign filmstrip (Yugoslavia)`
> `A foreign slide set (Yugoslavia)`
>
> For a U.S. emanator and a foreign producer, or a foreign emanator and a U.S. producer, do not make the note. (*CSB* 13)

8.7B10. Physical description

To be used for any important information not given in area 5, the physical description area.

Examples: `Transparencies and duplicating masters perforated for removal`

8.7B11. Accompanying material

To be used for any important information not given in the accompanying material part of area 5.

Example: `Guide includes bibliography`

8.7B12. Series

To be used for any important information not recorded in the series area.

Example: `Series on container: America and world power`

8.7B13. Dissertations

To be used for the standard dissertation note when applicable.

Example: `Thesis (M.S.)--Iowa State University, 1979`

8.7B14. Audience

To be used to record the intended audience of a work; use this note only if the information is stated on the item. Do not attempt to judge the audience for an item.

Example: `Intended audience: Construction management personnel`

8.7B16. Other formats

To be used to list other formats in which the work is available. The Library of Congress lists all formats commercially available in this note.

Example: `Issued also as slide set`

8.7B17. Summary

To be used for a brief objective summary of the content of the item.

Example: `Summary: Illustrates simple random sampling and some of its`
`          applications`

8.7B18. Contents

To be used for a formal or informal listing of the contents of the item. Number of frames may be added. Playing time may also be added after each title.

Examples: `Careers (80 fr.) -- …`
`           What's your point? (55 fr., 13 min., 2 sec.) -- …`
`           Residential architecture, tools (15 min., 10 sec.) -- …`

The following examples show both formal and informal contents notes.

Examples: `Contents: Pottery painters at work -- Silversmith at work`
`-- Building with adobe bricks -- Drying sisal -- Printing`
`textiles -- Fishermen at work -- Refining petroleum -- Port`
`of Veracruz`
`Bibliography in guide, p. 70-77`

8.7B19. Numbers

To be used to list any important number appearing on the item other than those to be recorded in area 8.

Example: `"S 1967"`

8.7B20. Copy being described, library's holdings, and restrictions on use

To be used for any notes applicable only to the particular copy of the item being described. Also used for local library restrictions on the material being described, or for information of use only to patrons of the local library.

Example: `Use restricted to Film 404 class`

8.7B21. "With" notes

To be used for "with" notes.

Example: `With: Sneetches`

8.7B22. Notes relating to original

To be used for information about the original of a reproduced art work.

Example: `Original in National Gallery of Art`

Helpful Hints

A 20X magnifying lens is useful for reading dates and other information directly from films and filmstrips. This size hand lens can be purchased from a scientific supply house or a "rockhounds" shop. Bausch & Lomb carries three different 20X magnifiers; a Hastings triplet magnifier (least distortion), a Coddington, and a folding pocket magnifier (5X to 20X).

Figure 5

For slides in carousel trays, a spiral line drawn on the top edge of the slides makes it easy for the circulation staff to see if a slide is missing, or if any slides are out of order or inserted incorrectly. This line is easily produced. Load the slides into the tray and check to make sure they are positioned correctly. Remove the slides, keeping them in the same order and orientation as they were in the tray. Hold the group of slides in the corner of a box (to keep them squared properly), with the side up that shows on the top of the carousel, and draw a diagonal line from one corner of the stack to the other with a felt tip pen. When the slides are replaced in the tray, the diagonal line becomes an even spiral.

Figure 6

Filmstrips for Controlled Reading Machines

If one is cataloging filmstrips for one of the controlled reading machines for which filmstrip frames are only 4 mm in height instead of the usual 18.5 mm, do not attempt to count frames, but explain in a note that each frame is one line of text.

Filmstrip Cartridges

The filmstrip cartridges for use in the Duo 16 projectors contain a continuous loop of 16 mm film in a cartridge with up to 250 vertical, single-frame visuals. The cartridge also contains a continuous loop of 1/4 in. two-track sound tape that plays 18 min. at 3 3/4 ips or 36 min. at 1 7/8 ips. The tape has automatic advance signals for the film. This is not designed to give the illusion of motion; the frames are advanced one-by-one and the narration accompanies the individual frames. The physical description and explanatory note for this material would be (for a set called *Fundamentals of N/C*):

```
10 filmstrip cartridges : sd., col. ; 16 mm. + 1 student guide

Each cartridge contains continuous 16 mm film loop of single
frame visuals and continuous sound tape loop (analog, 1 7/8 ips ;
1/4 in.) with automatic advance signals; for use on LaBelle Duo 16
projector
```

Activity Cards

While *AACR 2* does not specifically mention activity cards, we can catalog them by the rules of chapter 8 if they are pictures or chapter 10 if they are games. Physical description and notes are prepared as appropriate. "Activity card" has been approved as a GMD and as an SMD for use beginning sometime in 1992.

Example 44: Selecting Leisure Activities

This is an example of one of the most common types of audiovisual material: a filmstrip and a sound cassette and teaching material all packaged together in a container. The filmstrip is the dominant medium, therefore the set is cataloged as a filmstrip with accompanying material.

The title and credits frames of the filmstrip all are part of the chief source of information. The statement of responsibility is transcribed from these frames. The note is based on rule 8.7B17.

One filmstrip with cassette in container

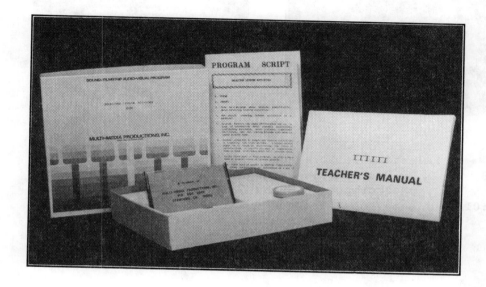

Example 44: Selecting Leisure Activities

Title frame of filmstrip

Credits frame of filmstrip

```
BJ          Selecting leisure activities [filmstrip] / produced
1498            by Multi-Media Productions, Inc. ; written and
                photographed by John Loughary, Theresa Ripley,
790.013         and Vanesa Tsang. -- Stanford, CA : Multi-Media
                Productions, c1979.
                   1 filmstrip (61 fr.) : col. ; 35 mm. + 1
                sound cassette + 1 program script + 1 teacher's
                manual.

                   Summary: Discusses 15 satisfactions of lei-
                sure activities as well as conditions to be
                considered such as time, costs, physical needs,
                skills, and aptitude.

                   1. Leisure.  2. Recreation.  3. Time alloca-
                tion.  [1. Leisure. 2. Recreation. 3. Hobbies.]
                I. Multi-Media Productions, Inc.  II. Loughary,
                John.  III. Ripley, Theresa.  IV. Tsang, Vanesa.
```

Example 45A: Word Processing

Here are bibliographic records for a set as a whole and for one of its parts cataloged independently. The chief source of information for the set is the container, because it furnishes the collective title and the individual parts do not. The chief source of information for separate cataloging of the individual parts is the title and credits frames of the individual filmstrips. The collective title is used as a series title when individual parts of the set are cataloged. The set title used as a series title with series numbering serves to tie the bibliographic records together when the set is repackaged.

The notes are based on rules 8.7B17, 8.7B18 for 45A, 8.7B11, 8.7B17 for 45B.

Set of filmstrips with cassettes

This set of filmstrips is cataloged as received, and one title is also cataloged separately as it would be if the set were split up and repackaged.

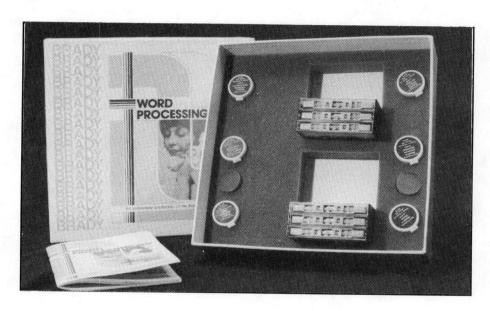

Example 45A: Word Processing

```
HF          Word processing [filmstrip] / an audiovisual
5548.115    production of the Robert J. Brady Co. --
            Bowie, MD : Brady, c1978.
652.5           6 filmstrips : col. ; 35 mm. + 6 sound
            cassettes + 1 instructional guide in container
            33 x 33 x 8 cm.

                Summary: Designed to introduce word process-
            ing systems to students in business programs or
            to office workers in traditional settings.
                Contents: module 1. Introducing word process-
            ing (95 fr.) -- module 2. Word processing orga-
            nizations (80 fr.) -- module 3. Work flow (106
            fr.) -- module 4. Careers (80 fr.) -- module 5.
            Equipment orientation (101 fr.) -- module 6.
            Office of the future (79 fr.).

                1. Word processing.  [1. Word processing.]
            I. Robert J. Brady Company.
```

Example 45B: Careers

```
HF          Careers [filmstrip] / produced by Robert J. Brady
5548            Co. -- Bowie, Md. : Brady, c1978.
                   1 filmstrip (80 fr.) : col. ; 35 mm. + 1
652             sound cassette + 1 manual. -- (Word processing
.54023          ; module 4)

                Title on manual: Career paths.
                Summary: Discusses career possibilities using
            word processing systems and explains tasks and
            levels of responsibility in a word processing
            center and in an administrative office.

                1. Career education.  2. Word processing--
            Vocational guidance.  [1. Occupations.]  [2.
            Word processing--Study and teaching.]  I. Robert
            J. Brady Company.  II. Title: Career paths.
            III. Series.
```

Example 46: Surveillance

The container, guide, and cassette used the title *Surveillance*. No title appeared on the notes or question sheets. The container was chosen as chief source of information because it provided the title used by most of the parts.

The plus sign is repeated for each item of accompanying material in the physical description area.

Contents of container

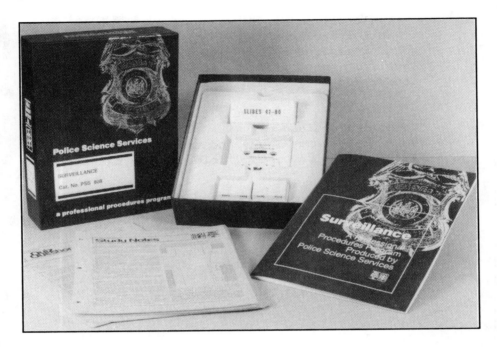

Title slide   **Last slide**

Example 46: Surveillance

HV 8080 .P2 363.232	Surveillance [slide] / produced for United Learning by Police Science Services. -- Niles, Ill. : United Learning, c1976. 80 slides : col. + 1 sound cassette + 1 manual + 1 set study notes + 1 set quiz questions.

   Title from container. Title on title frame of
filmstrip: Make the case with surveillance.
   Summary: Includes instruction on foot, ve-
hicular, and fixed surveillance, as well as
information on avoiding detection, working with
non-surveillance officers, equipment, and re-
porting. Safety precautions are emphasized.

   1. Police patrol--Surveillance operations.
2. Criminal investigation. [1. Criminal investigation. 2. Law enforcement--Techniques.] I.
United Learning (Firm) II. Police Science
Services, Inc. III. Title: Make the case with
surveillance.

Example 47: Mount Rainier

This illustrates the cataloging of a single slide. The only note is for the number found on the slide. It is quoted to indicate it is exactly as found on the item.

A single slide

```
GB          Mount Rainier, Wash. [slide] : aerial of glaciers.
2425           -- [United States] : Pana-Vue, [197-?]
.W3            1 slide : col.

917            "S 1967."
.97782
               1. Rainier, Mount (Wash.)  2. Glaciers.  [1.
           Rainier, Mount (Wash.)]  I. Pana-Vue (Firm)  II.
           Title: Aerial of glaciers.
```

Example 48: MV 20 Film Card Sample

    This sample was called by the manufacturer "film card"; it could be made up from any slides (color or black and white or combination) and was available in two formats, 20 slides per card and 40 slides per card.

    No GMD is used in this cataloging as neither "slide" nor "microfiche" seems appropriate.

    The note is based on rule 8.7B1.

A film card sample

```
LB          MV 20 film card sample. -- Tempe, Ariz. : Multi
1043.7      Vue, [1982]
                 1 film card (20 fr.) : col. ; 7 x 10 cm.
371.335
                 Sample of "film card" made from color slides.

                 1. Audio-visual materials.  [1. Audio-visual
            materials.]  I. Multi Vue (Firm).
```

Example 49: Random Sampling

This example shows the cataloging of a set of transparencies. Ordinarily I would not use the lengthy contents note as the title and brief summary are sufficient to inform the patron about the purpose of this set.

The label on the container is the chief source.

Rule numbers for notes are, in order, 8.7B11, 8.7B17, 8.7B18.

Set of transparencies with container

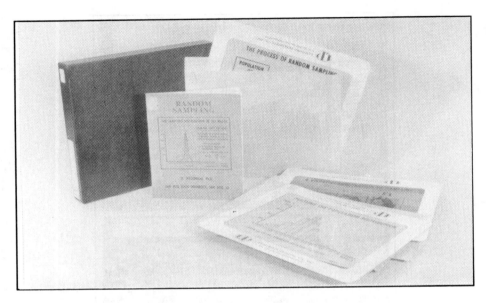

Label on container

Example 49: Random Sampling

QA
276.6

519.52

Random sampling [transparency]. -- San Jose, Calif.
: Lansford Pub. Co., c1973.
15 transparencies : col. ; 19 x 26 cm. + 1
teacher's guide.

Guide by D. Wassenaar.
Summary: Illustrates simple random sampling
and some of its applications.
Contents: The process of random sampling -- A
visual demonstration of sampling -- Plotting the
population distribution -- Calculating population mean and standard deviation -- How to draw
a random sample -- Practical methods for drawing
random samples -- Calculating a sample mean and
standard deviation -- The sampling distribution
of the means -- The normal distribution --
Confidence level estimates -- Determining required sample size -- Balancing cost versus
accuracy -- The binomial distribution -- Relationship between population size and required
sample size -- Political polls.
"W340T"

1. Sampling (Statistics) [1. Sampling (Statistics)] I. Wassenaar, D. (Dirk Jan) II.
Lansford Publishing Company.

Example 50: Composition of the Earth

This is included as an example of media purchased in book form. The book must be taken apart for use, although the teacher's guide will remain in the binding. The transparencies included are on heavy plastic, in full color, and are perforated for easy removal from the book.

The notes are based on rule numbers 8.7B1, 8.7B10.

Teachers guide

Example 50: Composition of the Earth

Title and contents page

Earth Science Series

COMPOSITION OF THE EARTH

written by Virginia Powers Leftwich
illustrated by Larry Weaver

CONTENTS

Page
*   1. Atomic Theory
 1A. Atomic Theory
*   2. Subatomic Particles
 2A. Atomic Structure
*   3. Atomic Models
*   4. Periodic Table of the Elements
 4A. Periodic Table of the Elements
 4B. Atomic Models
*   5. Distribution of the Elements
 5A. Distribution of the Elements
*   6. Chemical Bonding
 6A. Atomic Bonding
 6B. Atomic Bonding
*   7. The Six Crystal Systems
*   8. The Inner Structure of Crystals
 8A. Six Crystal Systems
*   9. Berzelian System of Major Mineral Classes
 9A. Minerals
* 10. Genetic Classification of Rocks
10A. Genetic Classification of Rocks
* 11. Rock Cycle
11A. The Rock Cycle
* 12. Model of the Earth
12A. The Earth's Structure
13—16. Unit Test
Composition of the Earth

* Indicates full color transparency.

```
QE        Leftwich, Virginia Powers.
509           Composition of the earth [transparency] /
          written by Virginia Powers Leftwich ; illustrated
551.1     by Larry Weaver. -- St. Louis, Mo. : Milliken
          Pub. Co., c1971.
              12 transparencies : col. ; 21 x 28 cm. + 16
          duplicating pages + 1 teacher's guide (12 p. ; 28
          cm.). -- (Earth science series)

              "A Milliken full color transparency-duplicating
          book"--Cover.
              Transparencies and duplicating masters are
          perforated for removal.

              1. Earth--Internal structure.  [1. Earth--
          Internal structure.]  I. Weaver, Larry.  II.
          Milliken Publishing Co.  III. Title.  IV. Series.
```

Example 51: Dependent Clauses

   This is an example of print material that is really a form of media; these originals are to be used to make transparencies and to make duplicated pages for class use. The originals are in black and white, but transparencies could be made on colored sheets.

   No GMD was used here since none really fit; "transparency" would be the closest. There is no GMD in rule 8.5B1 that matches this item. The rule permits us to use the specific name of the item in area 5, so I have used the term "printed originals" as specific material designation.

   The note is based on rule 8.7B1.

Title page of packet

Example 51: Dependent Clauses

Cover of packet

```
PE        Searles, John R.
1385         Dependent clauses / by John R. Searles. -- St.
          Paul, Minn. : 3M, [196-?]
425          31 printed originals : b&w ; 28 x 22 cm. --
          (English packet ; number 5)

             "Printed originals for preparing overhead pro-
          jection transparencies"--Cover.

             1. English language--Clauses. [1. English
          language--Grammar.]  I. Title.  II. Series.
```

Example 52: 50 Puzzles

Here is another GMD problem. These spirit masters are to be used to make classroom sets of the puzzles and games and to make transparencies for use by the teacher. The set is an item of media and one that is fairly common. Some of these sets contain all games, and such a set could be cataloged as a game.

Box, title page, one spirit master

50 Puzzles for Distributive Education Classes is designed to supplement the instructional program and create learning experiences for students enrolled in distributive education courses at the middle school, junior high, senior high, or vocational school level.

The teacher can use the puzzles to introduce, reinforce, or evaluate the academic area in an informative and enjoyable way. The puzzles can be used to promote competition: between individual class members, groups within a class, or entire classes. Teaching strategies such as placing a time limit for completing a puzzle and awarding grade points based on the fastest completion time or priority of finish, or using them for extra-credit purposes will further motivate and excite students.

The puzzles vary in degree of difficulty. Some puzzles will be completed by students with minimum effort, while others will take considerable time and may require the use of reference materials. For some of the puzzles, the teacher may wish to furnish clues by making flash cards, writing words and information on the chalkboard or transparencies, or supplying information on handouts. These techniques will provide an incentive for the student to participate in a learning experience and to complete an assignment.

My distributive education colleagues will find the enclosed educational material a useful supplement to their instructional programs. Suggestions and recommendations concerning any aspect of the puzzles are welcomed.

WILLIAM R. MUSCATELLO

Example 52: 50 Puzzles

```
HF          Muscatello, William R.
5415.4          50 puzzles for distributive education classes /
            William R. Muscatello. -- Portland, Me. : J. Weston
650.07      Walch, c1979.
                50 spirit masters : b&w ; 28 x 22 cm. + 1 answer
            key in box.

                Summary: Educational puzzles for use in junior
            high through vocational school.

                1. Distributive education.  2. Business educa-
            tion.  [1. Business education.]  I. J. Weston Walch
            (Firm).  II. Title.  III. Title: Fifty puzzles for
            distributive education classes.
```

Example 53: Environmental Values Action Cards

These are activity cards. Each picture has suggested activities on the back. The GMD "picture" is used for this particular set. We can use the GMD "activity card" when the 1991 JSC decision is published.

Rule numbers for notes are 8.7B6, 8.7B10, 8.7B17.

Activity cards

The EVA cards are intended to be used as idea banks for teachers, and it is suggested that teachers explore many ways of introducing them to students. The cards may be used with individual children or with groups. It is important to note that each card contains a metaphor plus activities that extend it. In this way the cards should encourage children to explore their own values and become more aware of themselves. The cards also encourage means of expression that are significantly different from those normally used in the classroom.

Extra special thanks to Marc Wanveg, Minneapolis Schools, who did the photography and supervised the art work for this project.

Richard C. Clark

Project Director

Example 53: Environmental Values Action Cards

```
BF          Environmental values action cards [picture]. --
408             [Saint Paul, Minn.] : Minnesota Dept. of
                Education, 1976.
153.42          50 activity cards : b&w ; 21 x 21 cm.

                Project director: Richard C. Clark.
                On the back of each photograph or illustra-
            tion are suggested activities.
                Summary: Intended to help children explore
            their values, become aware of themselves, and
            express their ideas creatively.

                1. Creative thinking (Education)  2. Social
            values.  3. Self-perception.  [1. Creative
            thinking. 2. Self perception. 3. Social values.]
            I. Clark, Richard C.  II. Minnesota. Dept. of
            Education.
```

Example 54: Mexico, Crafts and Industries

These are typical study prints with big pictures reproduced on heavy paper and questions, maps, and activities printed on the back of each.

Rules for notes are, in order, 8.7B6, 8.7B10, 8.7B18.

From the SVE *Picture-Story Study Print* Set
MEXICO, CRAFTS AND INDUSTRIES—SP 145
(Series: Mexico, Central America, and the West Indies Today)

Consultant: Carroll J. Schwartz, Ph.D.
  Assistant Professor of Geography
  Northeastern Illinois State College
  Chicago, Illinois

SINGER
EDUCATION & TRAINING PRODUCTS

Produced and
Distributed by
SVE SOCIETY FOR VISUAL EDUCATION INC.
1345 DIVERSEY PARKWAY   CHICAGO, ILL. 60614

Example 54: Mexico, Crafts and Industries

```
F            Mexico, crafts and industries [picture] / produced
1210              by Society for Visual Education. -- Chicago,
                  Ill. : Distributed by SVE, c1968.
338.0972          8 study prints : col. ; 23 x 46 cm. in
                  portfolio. -- (Mexico, Central America, and the
                  West Indies today)

                  Consultant: Carroll J. Schwartz.
                  Notes, research questions, enrichment activi-
              ties, key words, maps, picture, and list of
              related filmstrips on back of study prints.
                  Contents: Pottery painters at work -- Silver-
              smith at work -- Building with adobe bricks --
              Drying sisal -- Printing textiles -- Fishermen
              at work -- Refining petroleum -- Port of
              Veracruz.

                  1. Mexico--Industries.  [1. Mexico--Indus-
              tries.]  I. Schwartz, Carroll J.  II. Society
              for Visual Education.  IV. Series.
```

Example 55: Transportation

  These items are reproductions of photographs. A "guidesheet" gives background information. There is a line of information at the bottom of each picture; no information is on the back of the pictures.
  Rules for notes are 8.7B11, 8.7B17.

```
HE        Transportation [picture] / the State Historical
151          Society of Wisconsin. -- [Madison, Wis.] : The
             Society, [197-?]
380          23 reproductions of photographs : b&w ; 22 x
.50973       28 cm. + 1 guidesheet.

             Title on guide: Transportation in the 1890's.
             Summary: Photographs from 1870 to 1930 of
          streetcars, excursion boats and schooners,
          bicycles, stagecoaches, trolleys, early automo-
          biles and buses, railroad parlor cars, horse-
          drawn buggies, wagons, sleds and sleighs, carts,
          fire and hose wagons, milk wagons, school buses,
          and streetcars.

             1. Transportation--United States--History.
          [1. Transportation--History.]  I. State Histori-
          cal Society of Wisconsin.  II. Title: Transpor-
          tation in the 1890's.
```

Example 56: Portrait of Mister Rogers

This is cataloging for a photograph that was not published or distributed commercially.
Rules for notes are 8.7B1, 8.7B3, 8.7B10.

```
PN          [Portrait of Mister Rogers][picture]. -- [1984?]
1992.4         1 photograph : col. ; 13 x 18 cm.
.R6
               Photograph of Fred Rogers of the television
921         program Mister Rogers' neighborhood.
               Title supplied by cataloger.
               Inscription: For Nancy with kindest regards and
            gratitude for your help with our "history." Fred
            Rogers, 1984, "Mister Rogers".

               1. Rogers, Fred.  [1. Rogers, Fred.]  I. Rogers,
            Fred.
```

Example 57: Motivational Curriculum Chart

Note the physical description for this chart can include the size of the chart itself as well as its folded size.

Title area of chart

Information on publisher, date

Example 57: Motivational Curriculum Chart

```
LB          Cherry, Clare.
1570            Motivational curriculum chart. No. 1,
            For early childhood [chart] / by Clare Cherry. --
375.001     Belmont, CA : Fearon, c1969.
                1 chart : b&w ; 48 x 61 cm. folded to 18 x 31
            cm.

                Summary: Chart has 54 horizontal rows divided
            into 7 general areas of learning. The 17 columns
            contain specific activity suggestions. Designed to
            be used as a motivational reminder for curriculum
            planning.

                1. Curriculum planning.  [1. Education--Cur-
            ricula.]  I. Fearon Publishers.  II. Title.
```

Example 58: Public access to government documents

This is a bibliographic record for a poster. The author of this poster is only named in the copyright statement. This statement may be transcribed in a note.

Rules for notes are 8.7B1, 8.7B6, 8.7B10.

Full view of poster, reproduced by permission of USHDI

Printed along left margin of poster

United States Historical Documents Institute, Inc. • Carrollton Press, Inc. • Washington, D.C. • © 1975 •
William W. Buchanan

Example 58: Public access to government documents

```
KF          Buchanan, William W.
4774            "Public access to government documents is
            essential to the successful operation of a
323.445     democracy". -- Washington, D.C. : United States
            Historical Documents Institute, c1975.
                1 poster : col. ; 76 x 56 cm.

                Poster designed as sales promotion for sets of
            indexes to government documents; used during the
            U.S. Bicentennial year.
                Quotation by William S. Moorhead, Congressman
            from Pennsylvania. Poster copyright by William W.
            Buchanan.
                Red, white, and blue books arranged like stripes
            and star field of American flag, on dark blue
            background.

                1. Freedom of information.  2. Government publi-
            cations.  [1. Freedom of information. 2. Government
            publications.]  I. Moorhead, William S.  II. United
            States Historical Documents Institute.  III. Title.
```

Example 59: The Black Cat

   This is the bibliographic description for a reproduction of a movie poster. The GMD "picture" is used, although it might be better to omit the GMD in this case, as "picture" is not really accurate.
   The note combines information from rule 8.7B1 and 8.7B7.

Full view of poster

Copyright information from lower left edge of poster

© 1976 PORTAL PUBLICATIONS LTD. • CORTE MADERA, CALIFORNIA 94925

```
PN          Carl Laemmle presents Karloff and Bela Lugosi in
1995.9      Edgar Allan Poe's The black cat [picture]. --
.H6         Corte Madera, Calif. : Portal Publications,
            c1976.
813.3          1 poster : col. ; 74 x 48 cm.

               Reproduction of poster for 1934 movie by
            Universal Pictures.

               1. Horror films.  2. Film posters.  3. Poe,
            Edgar Allan, 1809-1849. Black cat.  [1. Horror--
            Motion pictures.]  I. Laemmle, Carl, 1867-1939.
            II. Karloff, Boris, 1887-1969.  III. Lugosi,
            Bela, 1882-1956.  IV. Universal Pictures Com-
            pany.  V. Portal Publications.  VI. Black cat
            (Motion picture).
```

Example 60: Division

These are flash cards. Each has the answer on the back. The container is the chief source of information for these, because the individual items do not contain title information. Because this container is the substitute for the chief source, a note is needed giving the source of the title.

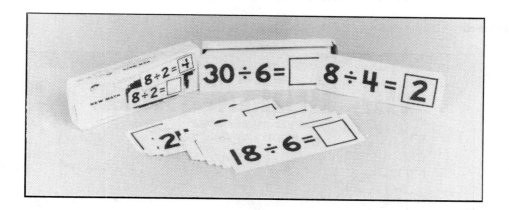

NEW MATH

Flash Cards ideal

IDEAL SCHOOL SUPPLY CO.

CHICAGO, ILLINOIS • 60620

DIVISION

No. 789

```
QA          Division [flash card]. -- Chicago, Ill. : Ideal
115             School Supply Co., 1963.
.D4                90 flash cards : b&w ; 8 x 23 cm. -- (New
                math flash cards)
513.214
                Title from container.
                "No. 789."

                1. Division.  2. Arithmetic.  [1. Division.]
            I. Ideal School Supply Company.  II. Series.
```

Example 61: The Human Skull

This bibliographic record describes a drawing. It is perforated, to be punched out and assembled into a model. At this stage, however, it is not a model. I did not use any GMD as none really fits.

See chapter 8 in this manual for the cataloging of the assembled model.

The note combines information from rules 8.7B1, 8.7B6, 8.7B10.

Item as purchased

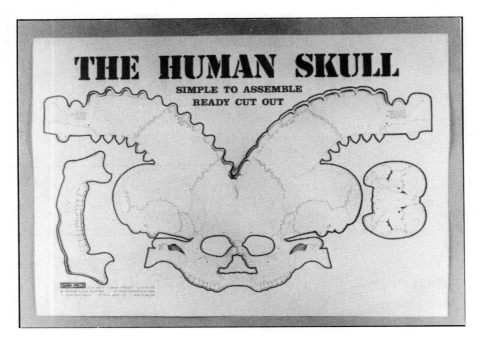

Information from lower left corner of sheet

```
QM        Miller, Richard.
105           The human skull. -- London : Fisher-Miller,
          c1980.
611.91        1 drawing : brown & tan ; 46 x 64 cm. + 1 sheet
          of assembly instructions.

              Design and copyright by Richard Miller; to be
          assembled into model of human skull.

              1. Skull.  2. Head.  [1. Anatomy, Human. 2.
          Head.]  I. Fisher-Miller (Firm)
```

Example 62: Common Loon

This bibliographic record describes a reproduction of a work of art.
The notes are based on rule numbers 8.7B1, 8.7B18.

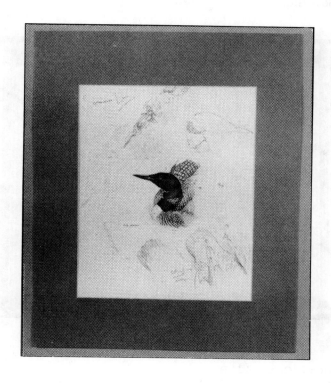

```
QL        Loates, Martin Glen, 1945-
696           Common loon [art reproduction] / M.G. Loates. --
.G33       Kenyon, Minn. : Nature Incentives, U.S.A., [198-?]
              1 art reproduction : col. ; 36 x 31 cm. in mat
598.442   51 x 41 cm.

           Watercolor of loon head with sketches of loon.
           Sketch in lower right labeled: Tail and wing
        movement diving.

           1. Loons.  [1. Loons.]  I. Nature Incentives,
        U.S.A.  II. Title.
```

Example 63: Common Loons

This bibliographic record describes an original work of art. *Graphic Materials* was helpful in preparing the physical description.

The note is based on rule 8.7B6.

```
QL        Danbom, Carroll D.
696            Common loons [art original] / C. Danbom. --
.G33       1982.
               1 art original : pastel on paper ; visible image
598.442    32 x 43 cm. in frame 50 x 60 cm.

               Signed on back: Common loons, a pastel by
           Carroll D. Danbom.

               1. Loons.  [1. Loons.]  I. Title.
```

Chapter 7

COMPUTER FILES

AACR 2 Chapter 9

Computer files are cataloged using rules found in *AACR 2* chapter 9.

Special Rules for Cataloging Microcomputer Software

A publication that might be helpful, with 100 exmples, is:

> *Cataloging Microcomputer Software: a Manual to Accompany AACR 2 Chapter 9, Computer Files,* by Nancy B. Olson. (Littleton, Colo.: Libraries Unlimited, 1988).

Chief Source of Information

The chief source of information for computer files is the title screen(s). If there is no title screen, or if the cataloger does not have access to the equipment needed to use the computer file, information is to be taken from the physical carrier and its labels, the documentation, or the container. Prefer the source with the most complete information.

A note is always made stating the source of the title proper.

Title and Statement of Responsibility Area

There are no title proper problems unique to computer software.

The GMD for this chapter is "computer file".

Edition Area

Where a statement of change in the content of a computer file is indicated, generally accept the statement as an edition statement. It might be called an *edition, issue, version, release, level,* or *update.*

One must be careful when cataloging computer files to differentiate between a new version of the file and the version of the operating system needed to run that file. Both might be expressed as "version 3.3" or some other decimal number. The term that refers to the operating system generally will be prefaced by the letters "DOS" or "CP/M" or some combination of numbers and letters, frequently including the letters "os" for operating system. A statement referring to the version of the software is recorded as an edition statement; a statement referring to the version of the operating system needed to run that software is included in the System requirements note.

Publication, Distribution, Etc., Area

There are no unique problems with computer software in this area of bibliographic description.

File Characteristics Area

This area must be used when a file is available only by remote access.

Designation

One of the following terms is used when the information is readily available:

> Computer data
> Computer program(s)
> Computer data and program(s)

Number of records, statements, etc.

For computer data, the number of files and the number of records and/or bytes may be added.

Examples: `Computer data (1 file : 90 records)`
`Computer data (300 records, 3000 bytes)`

For computer programs, the number of files and the number of program statements and/or bytes may be given.

Example: `Computer program (1 file : 94 statements)`

Physical Description Area

If a computer file is available only by remote access, there is no area 5 in the bibliographic record.

Extent of item

Terms used as specific material designations include:

> computer cartridge
> computer cassette
> computer disk
> computer reel

Note that computer disk is spelled with a "k" rather than the "c" used in chapters 6 and 7.

More specific terms may be used:

> computer chip cartridge
> computer tape cartridge
> computer tape reel
> computer laser optical disk
> computer laser optical card

If none of these terms is appropriate, use the exact term needed.

All disks are counted. If one or more are backup disks, they are included in the extent, and described in a note.

Other physical details

The presence of sound is indicated by "sd."
A display in two or more colors is indicated by "col."

Examples: 1 computer disk : sd.
          3 computer disks : col.
          2 computer disks : sd., col.

Dimensions

The diameter of a computer disk is given to the next higher ¼ inch.

Examples: 1 computer disk : sd., col. ; 5 1/4 in.
          2 computer disks ; 3 1/2 in.

The length of the side of a cartridge that is inserted into the machine is measured to the next highter ¼ inch.
The length and height of the face of a cassette are measured to the next higher ⅛ inch.
No dimension is given for reels.
For other carriers, measurements are given, rounded, in centimeters.

Notes Area

Types of notes:

9.7B1.   Nature and scope and systems requirements
9.7B2.   Language and script
9.7B3.   Source of title proper
9.7B4.   Variations in title
9.7B5.   Parallel titles and other title information
9.7B6.   Statements of responsibility
9.7B7.   Edition and history
9.7B8.   File characteristics
9.7B9.   Publication, distribution, etc.
9.7B10. Physical description
9.7B11. Accompanying material
9.7B12. Series
9.7B13. Dissertations
9.7B14. Audience
9.7B16. Other formats
9.7B17. Summary
9.7B18. Contents
9.7B19. Numbers
9.7B20. Copy being described, library's holdings, and restrictions on use
9.7B21. "With" notes

1.7A5. ... When appropriate, combine two or more notes to make one note.

9.7B1. Nature and scope and system requirements

This note is divided into three parts.

9.7B1a. Nature and scope

To be used to name or explain the nature of the item as necessary.

Examples: An educational game for two or more players
Role-playing game

9.7B1b. System requirements

The systems requirement note gives information concerning the computer system on which the computer file will run. The characteristics are given in the following order:

> make and model of the computer(s) on which the file is designed to run
> the amount of memory required
> the name of the operating system
> the software requirements, including the programming language
> the kind and characteristics of any required or recommended peripherals

The type of computer needed to use the item must be named. Any special equipment needed to use the item also must be described in this note.

Examples: System requirements: Apple II or higher; printer
System requirements: IBM PC or compatible

9.7B1c. Mode of access

If the file is available only by remote access, the mode of access must be specified here.

Example: Available through Corvus system

9.7B2. Language and script

To be used if the information is given and not recorded elsewhere.

Example: Language of text: German

9.7B3. Source of title proper

Must be used to give the source from which the title proper was taken.

Examples: Title from title screens
Title from container
Title supplied by cataloger
Title from disk label

9.7B4. Variations in title

To be used to note any title appearing on other than the chief source of information that differs significantly from the title proper.

Examples: Title on user's guide: Cartels and cutthroats
(*Title proper:* Cartels & cutthroats)
Title on disk label: Genetics
(*Title proper:* Elementary genetics)

9.7B5. Parallel titles and other title information

To be used for parallel titles and other title information that were not recorded in the title and statement of responsibility area; give only if considered important.

Example: Title on guide: Getting ready to read and add
(*Title proper:* Préparation à la lecture et à l'addition)

9.7B6. Statements of responsibility

To be used to record the information not given in the chief source of information, or not given prominently there, concerning programmers, system designers, etc.

Example: James Bach, Scott Bailey, programmers

9.7B7. Edition and history

To be used for information about earlier editions.

Example: First ed. called: Step by step
(*Title proper:* New step by step)

9.7B8. File characteristics

To be used for important file characteristics not included in area 3.

Example: File size unknown

9.7B9. Publication, distribution, etc.

Any detail not given in the publication, distribution, etc., area, but considered important, would be given in this note.

Example: "Published in the U.K. for the Schools Council by Longman"--T. p.
of guide

9.7B10. Physical description

To be used for any important information not given in area 5.

Example: One disk is back-up

9.7B11. Accompanying material

To be used for any important details not given in area 5 concerning accompanying material.

Example: User's manual includes 5-lesson tutorial

9.7B12. Series

To be used for any important information not given in area 6.

Example: Issued also as part of Tax management series

9.7B13. Dissertations

To be used for the standard dissertation note when applicable.

Example: Thesis (M.S.)--Mankato State College, 1972

9.7B14. Audience

To be used to note the intended audience or intellectual level if the information is given on the item or in its documentation.

Example: For children 3 to 8 years old

9.7B16. Other formats

To be used to list other formats in which the work is available.

Example: Issued also on disk for IBM-PC

9.7B17. Summary

To be used for a brief objective summary of the content of the software unless the information is obvious from the rest of the bibliographic description.

Example: Summary: Simulation for one to three players of presidential campaigning from Labor Day to election night; players decide how to allocate campaign funds. Includes six historical scenarios, hypothetical scenarios, and minute-by-minute election returns

9.7B18. Contents

To be used to list the contents of the item, either formally or informally.

Examples: Includes nine versions of the game
Contents: ABC time -- Letter game -- Spelling zoo

9.7B19. Numbers

Give any numbers on the item in this note if they seem important. The numbers should be quoted.

Example: "No. 1881"

9.7B20. Copy to being described, library's holdings, and restrictions on use

To be used for notes that apply only to the copy being cataloged. To provide information of importance to patrons of the library cataloging the item.

Examples: On Reserve in the ERC
Use restricted to Sociology 454 class

9.7B21. "With" notes

To be used for "with" notes.

Example: `With: Hypercard`

Access Points

It may be important to provide access to the computer make and model.

For those of us using a MARC-based online system, this access to computer make and model is available through field 753 in the MARC format, which provides an added entry for machine and model number, programming language, and operating system.

Examples: `IBM PC`
`Apple IIe`
`Macintosh Plus`

Processing Material for Circulation

Paper clips on date due cards or on package inserts can become entangled with disk covers and scratch disk surfaces. Labels put on the front or back of the disk can peel back slightly, as can the write-protect tabs, catching in disk drives. These are some things to watch for when preparing materials for circulation.

Automated check-out devices can be harmful to magnetic computer materials, as can theft-protection systems. A new 3M system is supposed to be safe for these materials.

Example 64: MacInTax 1989

The first example shows capital letters embedded in the title proper and in the name of the publisher. This is typical of computer software.

Rules for notes are 9.7B1b, 9.7B3, 9.7B17.

This could be cataloged as a serial.

Title screen

```
MacInTax® 1989
version V1.1.1

Copyright © 1985-89 by Softview®.

All Rights Reserved.
```

```
HJ          MacInTax 1989 [computer file]. -- Version v1.1.1.
4652             -- Oxnard, Calif. : SoftView, c1989.
                 4 computer disks ; 3 1/2 in. + 1 user's
336.24      guide.

                 System requirements: Macintosh 512KE;
            printer.
                 Title from title screen.
                 Summary: Designed to aid user in preparing
            federal income tax return. Performs calcula-
            tions, moves results to appropriate forms, and
            prints completed forms.

                 1. Income tax--United States.  I. SoftView,
            Inc.  II. Macintosh 512KE.
```

Example 65A: Aldus PageMaker

With this example we show the title screens for versions 1.1, 2.0a, 3.0, and 4.0. Note how inconsistent the information given as title is in these title screens.

PageMaker
PageMaker
Aldus PageMaker
Aldus PageMaker 4.0

We transcribe the title proper as found. In each case we must determine what, if any, title added entries are needed. Rules for notes are, in order, 9.7B1b, 9.7B3, 9.7B11, 9.7B11, 9.7B17.

Version 1.1 title screen

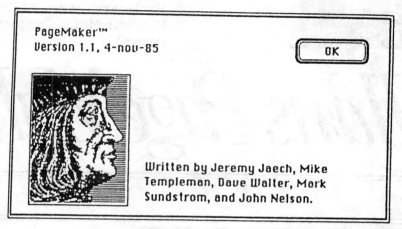

Version 2.0a title screen

Example 65A: Aldus PageMaker

Version 3.0 title screen

199926 bytes free
System version 4.20

OK

Version 3.0

© 1985-1988 Aldus Corporation.
All rights reserved. Portions Ranked
Hyphenator System © 1986-1987
Houghton Mifflin Company. All rights
reserved.

Aldus PageMaker®

Version 4.0 title screen

OK

Help...

Sharon Olson
Apple Blossom Books

861784 bytes free
System version 6.05

Aldus PageMaker 4.0

Example 65A: Aldus PageMaker

```
Z          Aldus PageMaker 4.0 [computer file]. -- Version
286            4.0. -- Seattle, WA : Aldus, c1990.
.D47           4 computer disks : col. ; 3 1/2 in. + 5
           manuals + 1 training package.
005.3
               Systems requirements: Macintosh Plus, SE
           family, or Mac II family; 1-2MB RAM; hard disk
           with minimum of 5MB; laser printer.
               Title from title screen; title on box: Aldus
           PageMaker.
               Includes reference manual, "getting started"
           manual, including quick reference guide, intro-
           duction to PageMaker, table editor guide, and
           templates guide.
               Training package includes 1 computer disk, 1
           sound cassette, 1 command summary card.
               Summary: A desktop publishing package allow-
           ing the user to integrate text and graphics and
           to control the appearance of documents.

               1. Desktop publishing.  2. Printing, Practi-
           cal.  I. Aldus Corporation.  II. Title: Aldus
           PageMaker.  III. Title: PageMaker.  IV. Title:
           Page maker.  V. Macintosh Plus.  VI. Macintosh
           SE.  VII. Macintosh II.
```

Example 65B: PageMaker 4 by Example

This shows the cataloging of a book related to a computer program. In this case the computer disk is accompanying the book, rather than the book acompanying the disk.

Title page

PageMaker 4
by Example

Macintosh Version

David Webster
Tony Webster

Adapted to PageMaker 4 by
Paul Webster
Caroline Webster

Example 65B: PageMaker 4 by Example

```
Z          Webster, Tony, 1940-
286            PageMaker 4 by example : Macintosh version /
.D47       Tony Webster, David Webster ; adapted to
           PageMaker 4 by Paul Webster and Carolyn Webster.
005.3      -- 1st ed. -- Redwood City, Calif. : M&T Books,
           1990.
               593 p. : ill. ; 24 cm. + 1 computer disk (3
           1/2 in.)

               System requirements: Macintosh Plus, SE, or
           II; hard disk; PageMaker computer program ver-
           sion 4.0.
               Cover title: PageMaker 4 by example for the
           Macintosh.
               Includes index.
               Computer disk contains self-paced exercises.

               1. PageMaker (Computer program).  2. Desktop
           publishing.  I. Webster, David, 1967-      II.
           Webster, Carolyn.  III. Title: PageMaker 4 by
           example for the Macintosh.  IV. Title: PageMaker
           four by example.
```

Example 66: Image Gallery

This package contains artwork on a compact disk for use in desktop publishing programs. It would take a stack of 5¼ or 3½ inch computer disks to hold all the images included here.

The place of publication did not appear anywhere on the disk, container, manual, advertising, or license agreement. The version information and copyright date were on the disk label.

Disk and user's manual

```
Z        Image gallery [computer file] / NEC. -- Version
286          1.1. -- [United States] : NEC, c1989.
.D47           1 computer disk ; 4 3/4 in. + 1 user's
             manual.
005.3
               System requirements: Macintosh 512E, Plus, SE
             or II; desktop publishing software; CD-ROM
             reader.
               Images by Metro ImageBase, Inc.
               User's manual shows each image.
               Summary: Includes "2,800 professionally hand-
             drawn images" divided among 20 categories; in
             TIFF or EPS file format, for use in desktop
             publishing.

               1. Desktop publishing.  2. Copy art.  I. NEC
             Home Electronics (U.S.A.) Inc.  II. Metro
             ImageBase, Inc.  III. Macintosh 512E.  Title:
             NEC Image gallery.
```

Example 67: Ludwig van Beethoven Symphony no. 9

The earlier version of this title had the computer files on 2 computer disks accompanying the sound recording compact disc. In that case I would have cataloged the package as a sound recording accompanied by 2 computer disks.

Both music and computer files are on this disk (disc?). The user can play the music as any music compact disc (skipping the first track that contains the computer programs) or can use any of the interactive features at any time.

Rules for notes are 9.7B1a, 9.7B1b, 9.7B3, 9.7B6, 9.7B6, 9.7B17.

Disk and user's guide

Example 67: Ludwig van Beethoven Symphony no. 9

From disk container

Example 67: Ludwig van Beethoven Symphony no. 9

```
M          Ludwig van Beethoven Symphony no. 9 [computer
1001       file]. -- Upgraded version. -- Santa Monica,
.B4        Calif. : Voyager, c1991.
op. 125        1 computer disk : sd. ; 4 3/4 in. + 1 user's
           guide. -- (CD companion series)
```

Interactive media.

System requirements: Macintosh Plus, SE, or II; HyperCard 2.0; hard disk drive; CD-ROM drive, earphones or speakers.

Title from container.

Program by Robert Winter ; program design by Robert Winter, Robert Stein.

Music recorded: Symphony no. 9 / Ludwig van Beethoven. London: Decca, c1988. Joan Sutherland, soprano ; Marilyn Horne, contralto ; James King, tenor ; Martti Talvela, bass ; Vienna State Opera Chorus, Wilhelm Pitz, chorus master ; Vienna Philharmonic, Hans Schmidt-Issersdtedt, conductor. Originally released by Decca, 1966.

Summary: Allows user to examine the music itself along with the historical and personal setting in which it was created. Features include detailed real-time commentary on the entire work and explanation of music showing excerpts from the score.

1. Beethoven, Ludwig van, 1770-1827. Symphonies, no. 9, op. 125, D minor--Analysis, appreciation. 2. Music appreciation. 3. Musical analysis. 4. Music--19th century--History and criticism. I. Winter, Robert, 1945-   II. Stein, Robert. III. Beethoven, Ludwig van, 1770-1827. Symphonies, no. 9, op. 125, D minor. 1988.

Example 68: Quarterstaff

This is a role-playing fantasy game with lots of accompanying materials. The title screen gives the information we need for cataloging. The summary is quoted from the container. I did not use personal author main entry because the title screen shows many names, all in the same size type. I considered responsibility to be diffuse and used title main entry.

Rules for notes are 9.7B1a, 9.7B1b, 9.7B3, 9.7B17.

Title screen

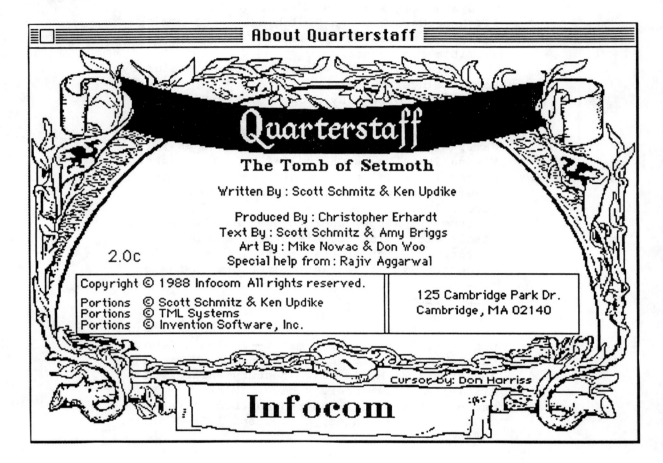

Example 68: Quarterstaff

```
GV          Quarterstaff [computer file] : the tomb of Setmoth
1469.25     / written by Scott Schmitz & Ken Updike ;
.Q3         produced by Christopher Erhardt. -- Cambridge,
            MA : Infocom, c1988.
793.932        3 computer disks ; sd., col. ; 3 1/2 in. + 1
            user's manual + 1 reference guide + 1 chart + 1
            wooden token + 1 poster.

               Role-playing game.
               System requirements: Mac Plus, SE or II; 2MB
            memory; color video card.
               Title from title screen.
               Summary: "Three months ago, the Tree Druid
            colony vanished without a trace. It is your
            mission--and that of your companions--to dis-
            cover what fate has befallen these gentle souls,
            and to save any that may survive"--Container.

               1. Fantasy games.  2. Computer adventure
            games.  I. Schmitz, Scott.  II. Updike, Ken.
            III. Erhardt, Christopher.  IV. Infocom.
```

Example 69: The Manhole

When this runs, it shows a file labeled "credits." Those credits are transcribed here.

The "developed by" phrase was on the package. I chose to bracket it into the statement of responsibility with similar information rather than separate it as a note.

I chose to use "computer disk" in area 5 rather than the more specific "computer laser optical disk." This same technology is recorded as "sound disc" in AACR 2 chapter 6 and "videodisc" in AACR 2 chapter 7. The size of 4¾ in. as well as the system requirements note make it clear what this is.

I quoted the description from the container rather than attempting to construct a summary.

Rules for notes are 9.7B1a, 9.7B1b, 9.7B3.

Disk and container

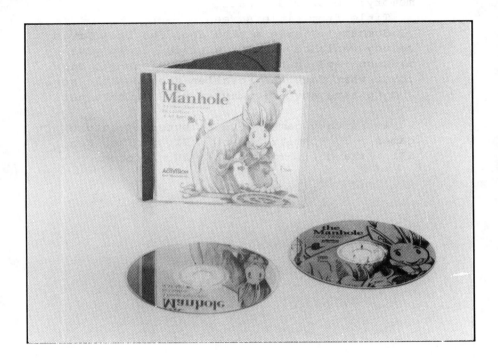

Title and credit screens

Cyan presents

World Design
Robyn Miller

Illustrations
Robyn Miller

Scripting and Editing
Rand Miller

Theme music composed and conducted by
Russell Lieblich

Example 69: The Manhole

Sound effects ...

Voice characterizations ...

Technical production ...

CD-ROM scripting ...

**Produced by
Sherry Whiteley**

**Distributed by
MEDIAGENIC**

© 1988 Activision

The Manhole

```
GV          The Manhole [computer file] / Cyan ; [developed by
1469.2         Robyn Miller and Rand Miller] ; produced by
               Sherry Whiteley. -- Menlo Park, CA : Activision
793          ; distributed by Mediagenic, 1989, c1988.
.932           1 computer disk : sd., col. ; 4 3/4 in.

               "A fantasy exploration for children of all
            ages."
               System requirements: Macintosh Plus, SE, or
            II; 1 megabyte of memory; HyperCard 1.2.1 or
            higher; SCSI hard drive; Apple CD-SC CD-ROM
            drive or equivalent
               Title from title screens.

               1. Computer games.  2. Fantasy games.  I.
            Miller, Robyn.  II. Miller, Rand.  III.
            Whiteley, Sherry.  IV. Cyan Software.  V.
            Activision, Inc.  VI. Mediagenic (Firm).  VII.
            Macintosh Plus.
```

Example 70: Stoneware's DB Master

    The physical description and note reflect the two identical disks included in the package.

    The manual refers to this as "D B master," so a title added entry for that form also must be made; a note must be made to justify the added entry.

    This package is labeled "Version three. Apple II edition." The title screen has the rest of the edition information.

Manual and two identical disks

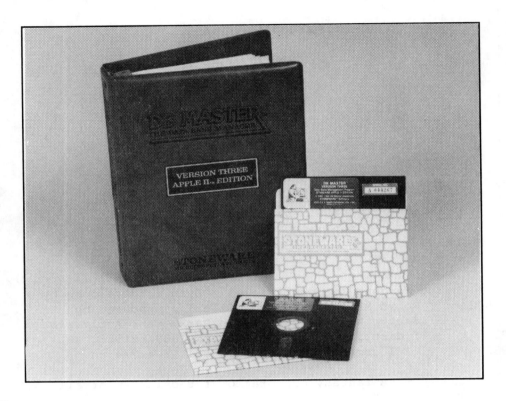

Title screen

```
            STONEWARE'S

      => DB MASTER <=

          (REV. 3.02!)

        SERIAL # 44267A

  (C) 1980,1982 DB MASTER ASSOCIATES
        ALL RIGHTS RESERVED  2222

PRESS 'RETURN' TO CONTINUE ...
```

Example 70: Stoneware's DB Master

```
QA          Stoneware's DB master [computer file]. -- Version
76.9            three, Apple II ed., rev. 3.02. -- San Rafael,
.D3             CA : Stoneware, 1982.
                   2 computer disks ; 5 1/4 in. + 1 manual.
005.74
                   Data base management program.
                   System requirements: Apple II or higher; two
                disk drives, printer.
                   Title from title screen; title on manual: D B
                master.
                   Second disk is back-up.

                   1. Data base management.  [1. Information
                systems--Computer programs.  I. Stoneware, Inc.
                II. Title: DB master.  III. Title: D B master.
                IV. Apple II.
```

Example 71A: Alphabet Zoo

This package includes three different educational games. The author and illustrator are named in the chief source of information. The programmers are not named in the chief source of information, but in the manual, so they are named in a note rather than in the statement of responsibility.

This example is shown cataloged as a unit with a contents note and title added entries. It is then shown with one title cataloged as an "in" analytic.

Disk, user's guide, and container

Note from user's guide

A NOTE TO PARENTS

Any child 3 to 8 years old will enjoy this game.

ALPHABET ZOO contains an alphabet display and two exciting maze games that are fun and educational. Colorful pictures and delightful music accompany all parts of the program.

ABC TIME is a computer alphabet book that helps kids become familiar with the alphabet. The program moves through the alphabet displaying the letters in order from A to Z. Large colorful capital and lower case letters appear on the screen while a full size picture is drawn in slow motion. Every time kids view the program, it will show a different assortment of pictures.

In THE LETTER GAME, kids race through the maze to capture the first letter of the picture shown in the middle of the screen.

THE SPELLING ZOO challenges young players to pick up the letters in the correct order to spell the word pictured on the screen.

ALPHABET ZOO helps children strengthen their letter recognition skills as they associate letters of the alphabet with the sounds that they represent. The games also help sharpen a child's spelling skills. Kids will have fun at every turn of the maze.

Example 71A: Alphabet Zoo

Title screen display

```
A L P H A B E T     Z O O


COPYRIGHT (C) 1983
SPINNAKER SOFTWARE CORP.
ALL RIGHTS RESERVED
```

Displays after title screen

Example 71A: Alphabet Zoo

Menu, which displays after the above

```
┌──────────────────────────────────────────────────┐
│                  ALPHABET ZOO                      │
│  ════════════════════════════════════════════════ │
│  ABC TIME                                          │
│  LETTER GAME                                       │
│  SPELLING ZOO                                      │
│                                                    │
└──────────────────────────────────────────────────┘
```

Example 71A: Alphabet zoo

```
PE        Disharoon, Dale.
1143          Alphabet zoo [computer file] / by Dale Disharoon
          ; artwork by Bill Groetzinger. -- Cambridge, Mass.
421.52    : Spinnaker Software, c1983.
              1 computer disk : sd., col. ; 5 1/4 in. + 1
          user's guide. -- (Early learning series)

              System requirements: Apple II.
              Title from title screens.
              James Bach, Scott Bailey, programmers.
              For children 3 to 8 years old.
              Contents: ABC time -- Letter game -- Spelling
          zoo.

              1. English language--Orthography and spelling.
          [1. English language--Spelling.]  I. Groetzinger,
          Bill.  II. Spinnaker Software Corp.  III. Title.
          IV. ABC time. 1983.  V. Letter game. 1983.  VI.
          Spelling zoo. 1983.  VII. Series.  VIII. Apple II.
```

Example 71B: ABC time

```
PE        Disharoon, Dale.
1143          ABC time [computer file]. -- on 1 computer disk
          : sd., col. ; 5 1/4 in. + 1 user's guide.
421.52
              System requirements: Apple II.
              Title from title screen.
              For children 3 to 8 years old.
              Summary: Shows each letter of the alphabet and
          draws a picture to go with it. Player presses
          letter on keyboard to match letter on the screen.
              In Disharoon, Dale. Alphabet zoo. Cambridge,
          Mass. : Spinnaker Software, c1983.

              1. English language--Orthography and spelling.
          [1. English language--Spelling.]  I. Groetzinger,
          Bill.  II. Spinnaker Software Corp.  III. Title.
          IV. Apple II.
```

Example 72: President Elect

This game has a personal main entry.

On title screen:

**President Elect
by Nelson G. Hernandez, Sr.
Copyright 1981**

Disk and directions

```
JK        Hernandez, Nelson G.
524           President elect [computer file] / by Nelson G.
          Hernandez. -- Mountain View, CA : Strategic
324.973   Simulations, c1981.
              1 computer disk : sd., col. ; 5 1/4 in. + 1 rule
          book + 1 short rule card + 1 pad of campaign
          strategy sheets.

              System requirements: Apple II or higher.
              Title from title screen.
              Summary: Simulation for one to three players of
          presidential campaigning from Labor Day to election
          night; players decide how to allocate campaign
          funds. Includes six historical scenarios, hypo-
          thetical scenarios, and minute-by-minute election
          returns.

              1. Presidents--United States--Election.  [1.
          Elections--United States.]  I. Strategic Simula-
          tions, Inc.  II. Title.  III. Apple II.
```

Example 73: Lode Runner

A uniform title is used for this example because the title proper has words preceding the actual title.

Package, directions, and disk

Title screen display

Example 73: Lode Runner

Game in progress

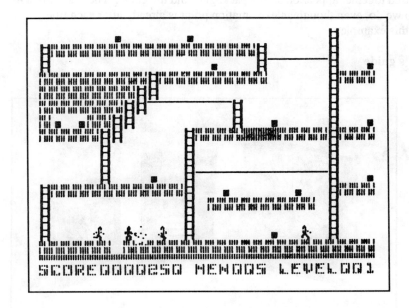

```
GV          Smith, Doug.
1469.35       [Lode runner]
.L6           Broderbund Software presents Lode runner
            [computer file] / by Doug Smith. -- San Rafael,
749.8       Calif. : Broderbund Software, c1983.
              1 computer disk : sd., col. ; 5 1/4 in. + 1 set
            of directions.

              System requirements: Apple II or higher.
              Title from title screen; title in directions:
            Loderunner.
              Summary: Action game and game generator for one
            player. Game has 150 different puzzles or mazes.
            Game generator permits player to design puzzles and
            scenes.

              1. Video games.  [1. Video games.]  I.
            Broderbund Software.  II. Title: Lode runner.  III.
            Title: Loderunner.  IV. Apple II.
```

Example 74: Speedway

There is no title screen for this cartridge, so we use the label as the chief source of information. There is no collective title; the three titles used together appear on all the packaging and the guide. The rules direct us to separate those titles by a period-space, so we do, even though an exclamation point is already after each title.

I used area 3 in this example.

Cartridge and user's guide

```
GV          Speedway!. Spin-out!. Crypto-logic! [computer
1469.35        file]. -- Programs. -- [Los Angeles] : North
.S6            American Philips Consumer Electronics, c1978.
                   1 computer chip cartridge : sd., col. ; 3 1/4
794.8          in. + 1 set of official rules.

                   System requirements: Odyssey2 game system.
                   Title from cartridge label.
                   Summary: Three games for one or more players.
               The first two are car racing games, the third
               (for two players) involves solving secret mes-
               sages.

                   1. Racing.  2. Video games.  3. Cryptography.
               [1. Video games.]  I. North American Philips
               Consumer Electronics Corp.  II. Speedway!. 1978.
               III. Spin-out!. 1978.  IV. Crypto-logic!. 1978.
               V. Odyssey2 game system
```

Chapter 8

THREE-DIMENSIONAL ARTEFACTS AND REALIA

AACR 2 Chapter 10

This chapter covers the cataloging of all types of three-dimensional materials including models, dioramas, games, sculptures, machines, clothing, toys, puppets, and exhibits. It also covers naturally occurring objects ("realia") such as rocks, minerals, shells, and mounted microscopic specimens.

These materials are covered by the rules found in *AACR 2* chapter 10.

Special Rules for Cataloging Three-Dimensional Artefacts and Realia

In this section the special rules for cataloging three-dimensional artefacts and realia will be discussed. Parts of some of the rules are given; the user is referred to the rules themselves for complete text and examples.

Chief Source of Information

The chief source of information for any material covered in this chapter is the item itself, together with any accompanying material.

Title and Statement of Responsibility Area

Frequently the cataloger will have to supply a title for materials cataloged by this chapter. In such a case, the title is to be bracketed and a note citing the source of the title is to be supplied.

The general material designations used for materials in this chapter are:

> diorama
> game
> microscope slide
> model
> realia
> toy
> art original

The GMD "toy" was added in the 1988 revision of *AACR 2*.

Publication, Distribution, Etc., Area

Naturally occurring objects

A naturally occurring object, such as a rock, will not have any information in this area because it is not published or distributed and there is no date of publication. "S.l." and "s.n." are not used because we do not want to imply an unknown publisher for natural objects. If, however, a naturally occurring object is commercially packaged and distributed, the package will have a publisher and/or distributor.

No date is given or implied in area 4. For example, if one were cataloging ash from Mount Saint Helens, one would give the date of the volcanic eruption in a note rather than in area 4.

Manufactured objects

Material cataloged according to *AACR 2* chapter 10 might have been manufactured rather than published. If so, the material will have place of manufacture, name of manufacturer, and date of manufacture.

```
(Place of manufacture : Name of manufacturer, Date)
```

Example: ([United States : s.n., 186-])

Material may be manufactured by one company and distributed by a different company. If the distributor and the manufacturer are both known, include the distributor in the usual way in area 4, bracketing in the words "distributed by" or "distributor" if that function is not clear, and use the information about the manufacture of the item as shown above.

An item may have a date of manufacturing and a date of distribution. If both are known or given on the item, both may be used. If only one date is known, decide whether it is the date of manufacture or the date of distribution and place it accordingly.

```
Place of distribution : Name of distributor, Date of distribu-
tion (Place of manufacture : Name of manufacturer, Date of manu-
facture)
```

Hand-made items

Hand-made three-dimensional items may be cataloged by the rules in *AACR 2* chapter 10. The name of the person who made the item would go in the statement of responsibility if given on the item.

If the person or body who made the item is named in the statement of responsibility, that name is not repeated in the name of manufacturer area. If the place where the item was made is given in the title proper or other title information, that place is not to be repeated as place of manufacture.

"Artefacts not intended primarily for communication"

This phrase is used in 10.4C2 through 10.4F2. I have wondered what was intended when the phrase was written. My cannon ball is an artifact, and definitely communicates something about the horrors of the Civil War.

Ben Tucker explains: "I remember rather clearly the discussion that went into the formulation of the rule. The words 'not intended for communication' mean nothing more than 'not published,' or 'not issued in an edition.' Another term that might have served is 'not commercially available in multiple copies.' 'Artefacts' means man-made or man-manipulated." (Ben R. Tucker, letter to the author, 17 Dec. 1984).

Physical Description Area

Extent of item

The number of physical units is given followed by the specific name of the item or the names of the parts.

Added to this, when appropriate, are the number and name of pieces. The phrase "various pieces" may be used. A note may be used to give further details.

Other physical details

The material or materials of which the item is made is given next, if appropriate. This is followed by "col." or "b&w" or the name(s) of the color(s) if in one or two colors.

Dimensions

The dimensions are given in centimeters, rounded up to the next whole centimeter. Dimensions of a three-dimensional object are given in height times width times depth. Only one dimension is given if appropriate; to this should be added a word to indicate which dimension is given.

If the object is in a container, the container is named and its dimensions given, either as the only dimensions, or after the dimensions of the object.

Accompanying material

The name of any accompanying material is recorded. Physical description of the accompanying material is optional.

Notes Area

Notes permitted in this chapter are:

10.7B1. Nature of the item
10.7B3. Source of title proper
10.7B4. Variations in title
10.7B5. Parallel titles and other title information
10.7B6. Statements of responsibility
10.7B7. Edition and history
10.7B9. Publication, distribution, etc.
10.7B10. Physical description
10.7B11. Accompanying material
10.7B12. Series
10.7B14. Audience
10.7B17. Summary
10.7B18. Contents
10.7B19. Numbers
10.7B20. Copy being described, library's holdings, and restrictions on use
10.7B21. "With" notes

1.7A5. ... When appropriate, combine two or more notes to make one note.

10.7B1. Nature of the item

To be used to name or explain the form of the item as necessary.

   Example: `Electronic game`

10.7B3. Source of title proper

To be used if the title proper is taken from other than the chief source of information.

   Example: `Title supplied by cataloger`

10.7B4. Variations in title

To be used to record any title appearing on the item that differs significantly from the title proper.

   Example: `Title in guide: Pac Man`
              (*Title proper:* Tomytronic Pac Man)

10.7B5. Parallel titles and other title information

To be used for parallel titles and important other title information not recorded in the title and statement of responsibility area.

> *Example:* Subtitle on manual: Implementing institutional self-
> evaluation

10.7B6. Statements of responsibility

To be used to record important information not recorded in the statement of responsibility area.

> *Example:* Crocheted by Betty Robbin

10.7B7. Edition and history

To be used for information about earlier editions or the history of the item being cataloged.

> *Example:* Assembled from: The human skull. London : Fisher-Miller,
> 1980

10.7B9. Publication, distribution, etc.

To be used for important information not recorded in the publication, distribution, etc., area.

> *Example:* Distributed by R. Dakin, San Francisco

10.7B10. Physical description

To be used for any important information not given in area 5, the physical description area.
If the phrase "various pieces" was used in the physical description area, a more complete description may be given here.

> *Examples:* Signed in pencil on base
> Includes 1,000 red wooden beads, 1,000 black plastic
> beads, 20 red shoestrings, 20 black shoestrings, 20 pattern
> boards

10.7B11. Accompanying material

To be used for any important information not given in the accompanying material element of area 5.

> *Example:* Teacher's guide has directions for making artifacts and
> for the educational simulation; includes pages for reproduc-
> tion

Libraries in the United States use American spellings such as "artifact" in the description.

10.7B12. Series

To be used for any important information not recorded in the series area.

> *Example:* Previously issued as part of series: Introduction to the
> crime laboratory

1.7B14. Audience

To be used to record the intended audience of a work. Use this note only if the information is stated on the item. Do not attempt to judge the audience for an item.

Example: Intended audience: Grade 2

10.7B17. Summary

To be used for a brief objective summary of the content of the item.

Example: Summary: Game for two to four players in which players try to accumulate wealth through buying and developing property, gaining power, and acquiring connections

10.7B18. Contents

To be used for a formal or informal listing of the contents of the item.

Example: Contents: A. Checked (grade 2) -- B. Striped (grade 3) -- C. Polka-dot (grade 4) -- D. Plaid (grade 5)

10.7B19. Numbers

To be used to list any important number appearing on the item other than those to be recorded in area 8.

Example: "24/125"

10.7B20. Copy being described, library's holdings, and restrictions on use

To be used for any notes applicable only to the particular copy of the item being described. Also used for local library restrictions on the material being described, or for information of use only to patrons of the local library.

Examples: Library's copy signed by artist
For library use only

10.7B21. "With" notes

To be used for "with" notes.

Example: With: Geodes from Keokuk, Iowa

Example 75: Minnesota Trivia

This is a game patterned after Trivial Pursuit, except the questions are all about Minnesota. In area 5 one could choose to list all the pieces, use "various pieces", or give "1 game."

Notes are based on rules 10.7B10, 10.7B17.

This could be classified with Minnesota history or with "trivia" games.

Game board and pieces

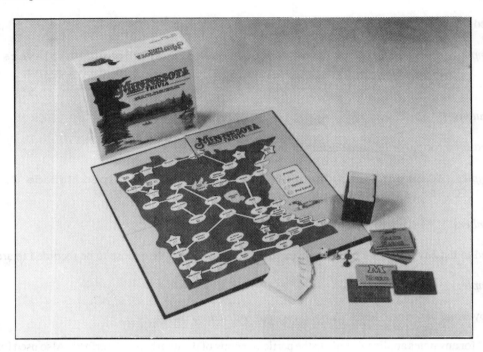

```
F          Minnesota trivia [game]. -- Minnetonka, MN :
606.5          Minnesota Trivia, c1984.
                  1 game ; in box 27 x 27 x 9 cm.
917
                  Includes 1 game board, 4 markers, 1 die, 500
               question/answer cards, 2 card boxes, 28 scoring
               cards, 1 rule sheet.
                  Summary: Game for two or more players or
               teams in which players must answer Minnesota-
               related questions on people, places, sports, or
               "pot-luck" to move from city to city on the
               board.

                  1. Board games.  2. Minnesota--History.  3.
               Educational games.  I. Minnesota Trivia, Inc.
```

Example 76: Cathedral

This game attracted me because it is made of beautifully finished pieces of wood in the shapes of buildings. One player or team uses the buildings made of dark wood, the other uses the buildings of light wood. The cathedral is blue.

There is absolutely no information given about the publisher. It has a New Zealand copyright. The name of the game is the only thing printed on the box.

Rules for notes are 10.7B1, 10.7B6, 10.7B17.

Game board and pieces

```
GV       Cathedral [game] : the game of the mediaeval city.
1469         -- 3rd ed. -- [New Zealand? : s.n.], 1985.
.C3          1 game (playing board, 30 pieces, rules book)
         : wood ; in box 26 x 26 x 7 cm.
793.9
             Game for two players or teams.
             Copyright by Robert P. Moore.
             Summary: Based upon the concept of a mediae-
         val city surrounded by a wall with a cathedral
         as focal point, place of sanctuary, and mediator
         in keeping any one faction from becoming too
         powerful. Playing pieces are buildings; oppo-
         nents attempt to gain control of property within
         the city.

             1. Games.  2. Board games.  I. Moore, Robert
         P.
```

Example 77: Monopoly

This version of Monopoly was issued to celebrate the 50th anniversary of the game. The pieces are gold colored, and the special booklet includes an illustrated history of the game.

We would need to use a uniform title main entry for this if we had more than one version in our catalog. It would be

Monopoly (Game : Deluxe anniversary ed.)

Rules for notes are 10.7B1, 10.7B10, 10.7B11, 10.7B17.

Game board and pieces

```
GV        Monopoly [game]. -- Deluxe anniversary ed. --
1469          Beverly, MA : Parker Brothers, c1985.
.M65          1 game (various pieces) ; in container 26 x
              51 x 7 cm.
793.7
              "Parker Brothers real estate trading game"
          for 2 to 8 players.
              Includes game board, play money, 2 dice, 11
          gold-colored playing pieces, red wooden hotels,
          green wooden houses, title deed cards, chance
          and community chest cards, rules.
              Rule book includes illustrated 50-year his-
          tory of the game.
              Summary: "The object of the game is to become
          the wealthiest player through buying, renting,
          and selling property."

              1. Monopoly (Game).  2. Board games.  I.
          Parker Brothers, inc.
```

Example 78: Human Skull

    This model is assembled from a flat sheet of heavy paper, which is marked and perforated to be punched out. See the example in chapter 6 of this manual for the cataloging of the original marked sheet.

    Notes are based on rules 10.7B3, 10.7B7.

Assembled paper skull

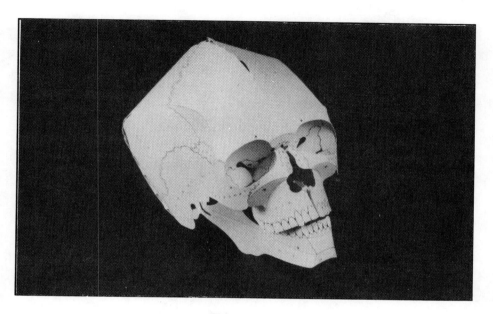

Flat sheet, unassembled

```
QM         [Human skull][model]. -- [1983]
105            1 model : paper, tan ; 22 cm. long.

611.91         Title supplied by cataloger.
               Assembled from: The human skull. London :
           Fisher-Miller, 1980.

               1. Skull.  2. Head.  [1. Anatomy, Human.]  [2.
           Head.]
```

Example 79: Replicas of a Cylinder Seal Impression

These items are mounted replicas of cylinder seals. On the back of each mount is the descriptive information. These beautiful items are models, as they are full-sized reproductions of actual objects.

Rules for notes are 10.7B10, 10.7B18.

Replicas of cylinder seals

Descriptive information

THE BRITISH MUSEUM
REPLICA OF A CYLINDER SEAL IMPRESSION
1   AN AKKADIAN 'CONTEST SCENE'
A seal with a finely-modelled group showing a bull-man and nude hero each holding a rampant bull by the horn and tail. The forelegs of the bulls are engraved to make it appear as if they touched the top of a stylized mountain, on which stands a 'sacred tree'. It has been thought, without much justification, that scenes of this type may represent Gilgamesh, hero of a series of Sumerian epic tales and of the famous Assyro-Babylonian *Epic of Gilgamesh*, and the bull-man his friend and fellow-adventurer, Enkidu.
Akkadian, about 2200 B.C. Greenstone. 3·8 cm high × 2·3 cm diameter.

THE BRITISH MUSEUM
REPLICA OF A CYLINDER SEAL IMPRESSION
2   THE SEAL OF A SCRIBE
A military figure, possibly the prince mentioned in the inscription, wearing a flat cap and bearing an axe on his left shoulder, is attended by three men led by a bowman who wears shoes with turned-up toes. Behind the group are two other attendants, bearing furniture and provisions, depicted on a smaller scale beneath the inscription. This may be read either in Sumerian or in Akkadian:
    '(O) Ubil-Eshtar, brother of the king; KAL-KI, the scribe (is) thy servant' (Sumerian, or 'his servant', Akkadian).
The reading of the name of the scribe is uncertain.
Akkadian, about 2200 B.C. Aragonite. 3·4 cm high × 2·1 cm diameter.

THE BRITISH MUSEUM
REPLICA OF A CYLINDER SEAL IMPRESSION
3   AN EARLY 'CONTEST SCENE'
In this seal a nude hero, in the centre, holds a bull in each hand while a bull-man, shown in profile, fights a rampant lion. Between them is a bird with spread wings. To the right, the bull-man, here full-faced, struggles with two lions to rescue an ibex shown between the contestants. An ibex's head (above, right) is used as a space filler.
Sumerian (Early-Dynastic II); about 2650 B.C. Aragonite. 4·2 cm high × 3·6 cm diameter.

THE BRITISH MUSEUM
REPLICA OF A CYLINDER SEAL IMPRESSION
4   THE SEAL OF A GOVERNOR
A typical 'introduction scene'. A goddess introduces Hashhamer, governor of the city Ishkun-Sin, to the seated King Ur-Nammu, founder of the IIIrd Dynasty of Ur (c. 2050 B.C.). Another goddess is in attendance. The inscription, in Sumerian, reads:
    '(O) Ur-Nammu, mighty male, King of Ur—Hashhamer, governor of Ishkun-Sin, (is) thy servant.
Ur III period, 2050 B.C. Green schist. 5·4 cm high × 3·2 cm diameter.   (Ref. No. 89126)

THE BRITISH MUSEUM
CYLINDER SEAL IMPRESSION
5   SEAL OF THE SCRIBE ADDA
The sun-god, whose rays spring from his shoulder, holds aloft his emblem, the saw, as he rises between two mountains. Ea, god of the Sweet Underground Waters (indicated by the flowing waters), steps over a rising bull and holds a bird in his hand. His Janus-headed attendant, Usmu, stands behind. On the mountain, to the left, stands a winged-goddess of war, perhaps Ishtar, shown full-faced, carrying quivers on her back and an object (a date-cluster?) in her hand. The tree growing from the mountain is a symbol of fertility. Another god, perhaps Ninurta, advances with a bow in hand, followed by a roaring lion.
Akkadian, about 2200 B.C. Green schist. 3·8 cm high × 2·5 cm diameter.

Example 79: Replicas of a Cylinder Seal Impression

```
CD          Replica[s] of a cylinder seal impression [model] /
5344            the British Museum. -- London : The Museum,
                [197-?]
737.6           5 replicas : plastic, tan on black ; 4 x 7-
            6 x 10 cm. on mounts 8 x 10-8 x 14 cm.

                Description on back of each replica.
                Contents: 1. An Akkadian "contest scene"
            (2200 B.C.) -- 2. The seal of a scribe
            (Akkadian, 2200 B.C.) -- 3. An early "contest
            scene" (Sumerian, 2650 B.C.) -- 4. The seal of a
            governor (Ur III period, 2050 B.C.) -- 5. Seal
            of the scribe Adda (Akkadian, 2200 B.C.).

                1. Cylinder seals.  2. Sumerians.  3. Civili-
            zation, Assyro-Babylonian.  [1. Seals (Numismat-
            ics)]  I. British Museum.
```

Example 80: Speedy Andrew's Repair Shop

This completed model is cataloged, rather than the kit from which it was assembled. The date of assembly of the model is given followed by the place and name of the "manufacturer."
See chapter 11 of this manual for the cataloging of the purchased kit from which this model was constructed.
Rules for notes are 10.7B6 and 10.7B7 combined, 10.7B10, 10.7B17.

The finished model

Cover illustration of model

```
TL          Olson, Andrew A., 1960-
153             Speedy Andrew's repair shop [model]. --
            ([Lake Crystal, Minn. : A.A. Olson, 1979])
629.286         1 model : plastic, col. ; 10 x 16 x 14 cm.

                Assembled by Andrew A. Olson from 76-piece
            Tyco-kit manufactured in West Germany by Pola.
                HO scale.
                Summary: Model of automobile repair shop of
            the 1920-1930 period.

                1. Automobiles--Service stations.  [1. Auto-
            mobiles--Service stations.]  I. Title.
```

Example 81: Geode

This is an example of realia that has not been distributed commercially; no place or date is given in area 4, because one would not want to imply any publisher, etc. If "S.l. : s.n." were used, it would indicate there was a publisher with unknown place and name. We want to avoid theological discussions about "makers" of realia.

Notes are based on rules 10.7B3, 10.7B10.

Two halves of a geode

```
QE          [Geode][realia].
471.15          1 geode (2 halves) ; 4 x 5 x 4 cm.
.G4
                Title supplied by cataloger.
549             Geode contains calcite crystals; from the
            Keokuk, Iowa, area.

                1. Geodes.  [1. Mineralogy. 2. Rocks.]
```

Example 82: Golden Adventure Kit of Rocks and Minerals

In processing for circulation, these rocks and minerals would not have to be labeled as they are glued into the box. These naturally-occurring objects are commercially packaged, so place and name of publisher are used (10.4C2, etc.) No notes are needed as the rest of the bibliographic record provides sufficient information for the user.

Box of rocks

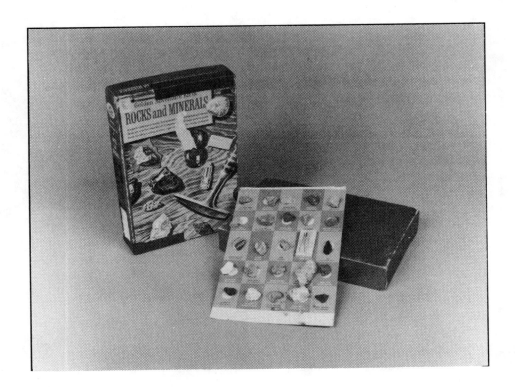

Example 82: Golden Adventure Kit of Rocks and Minerals

```
QE          Golden adventure kit of rocks and minerals
432.2           [realia]. -- [United States] : Golden Press,
                c1957.
549             24 specimens ; mounted in box, 30 x 21 x 5
                cm. + 1 streak plate.

                 1. Rocks.  2. Mineralogy.  [1. Rocks. 2.
            Mineralogy.]  I. Golden Press.
```

Example 83: Cat Skeleton

These are real bones packaged for use by elementary school students. Other titles in the series are: *Rabbit Skeleton*, *Mink Skeleton*, and *Mystery Bones*.

Because these are real bones the GMD "realia" is used in this example. There are too many bones to count and "various pieces" in the physical description area sounds strange, so I used "1 skeleton" for that information.

The entire series could be cataloged in one bibliographic record with a contents note listing the individual titles.

Cat bones and accompanying material

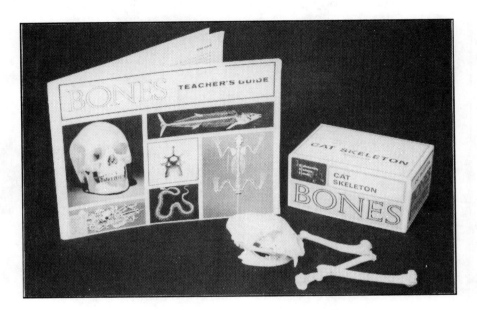

End of container

Top of container

Example 83: Cat Skeleton

```
QL          Cat skeleton [realia] : disarticulated. -- St.
737            Louis : Webster Division, McGraw-Hill, 1968.
.C23           1 skeleton ; in box 17 x 11 x 8 cm. + 1
               teacher's guide (72 p. ; 28 cm.). -- (Bones)
599          (Elementary science study)
.74428
                   Summary: Bones of a cat; to be assembled into
               a skeleton.
                   "18512"


                   1. Cats--Anatomy.  [1. Cats--Anatomy.]  I.
               Series.  II. Series: Elementary science study.
```

Example 84: Dig

This is an example of a simulation game in booklet form. Players are given directions for making the other game materials needed.

While *AACR 2* uses the British spelling "artefact" in referring to man-made items, libraries in the United States use American spellings in notes.

Notes are based on rules 10.7B11, 10.7B17.

Game booklets

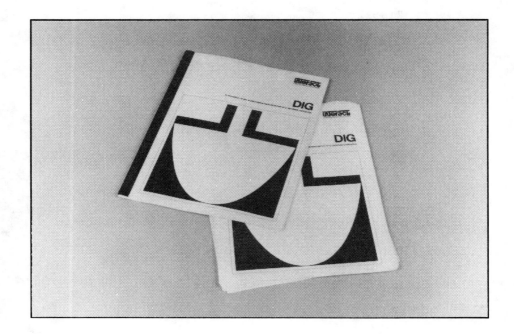

Example 84: Dig

From teacher's guide

SIMULATIONS AND THE "NEW" SOCIAL STUDIES

In America today social studies teaching is in ferment. No longer satisfied with classroom teaching dominated by textbooks, teachers are examining course content and teaching method in the light of concepts such as the following: inductive or inquiry learning; discovery of a discipline's structure; involvement through interaction and value conflicts; learning rather than teaching. One method incorporating all of these ideas is to apply game theory to classroom instruction by constructing simulations. The following educational simulation is one of several offered by INTERACT of Lakeside, California.

PURPOSE

In DIG your classroom will become an archeological lab, filled with the type of heated discussions and questioning interpretations that characterize the discipline of archeology. Unusual and exotic artifacts will be excavated by your students using the scientific techniques employed by professional archeologists. They will record their observations and measurements on the same forms used by many museums and universities. After the artifacts have been restored and analyzed, the "ancient" civilization responsible for the remains will "return" and allow the archeologists to discover the accuracy of their findings and interpretations. While most museums have cards that explain what archeologists *think* the artifacts mean, your museum display will have additional cards that explain *exactly* what the artifacts mean. Besides experiencing how it *feels* to be an archeologist, your students will acquire the following concepts, attitudes, and skills:

```
CC        Lipetzky, Jerry.
75           Dig [game] : a simulation of the archeological
          reconstruction of a vanished civilization / Jerry
930       Lipetzky. -- Lakeside, Calif. : Interact, c1969.
.10283       1 game (various pieces) ; bound in booklet (34
          p. ; 28 cm.) + 30 identical student guides.

             Teacher's guide has directions for making arti-
          facts and for the educational simulation and in-
          cludes pages to be reproduced to use in the simula-
          tion.
             Summary: Each of two teams creates a secret
          culture and makes artifacts which are excavated by
          the other team; a confrontation between teams
          reveals the accuracy of each reconstruction and
          analysis.

             1. Archaeology.  [1. Archeology. 2. Excavations
          (Archeology)]  I. Interact (Firm)  II. Title.
```

Example 85A: The Numbrella Tree (individual box)

These games are cataloged as a set and individually. For the individual cataloging, the title of the set is used as a series statement.

Rules for notes are 10.7B10, 10.7B17 (example 85A), 10.7B18 (example 85B).

Box of grade 2 games

Ends of box
Note tiny letter "A" below series name

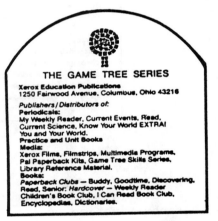

Box opened, showing one game board

Example 85A: The Numbrella Tree (individual box)

Teacher's guide

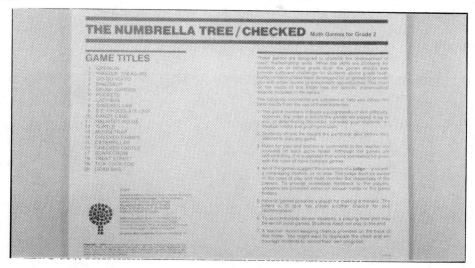

Example 85A: The Numbrella Tree (individual box)

```
QA        The Numbrella tree. A, Checked [game]. -- Columbus,
115           Ohio : Xerox Education Publications, c1978.
                 20 games : col. ; in box 23 x 29 x 8 cm. --
513           (Math skills games) (The game tree series)

           Game boards open to 28 x 44 cm. Set includes
        markers, cards, spinners, instructions.
           Summary: Designed to promote the development
        of basic mathematical skills in grade 2 stu-
        dents.

           1. Arithmetic.  [1. Arithmetic.]  I. Xerox
        Education Publications.  II. Series: Math skills
        games.  III. Series: The game tree series.
```

Example 85B: The Numbrella Tree (set)

```
QA        The Numbrella tree [game] : math skills games. --
115           Columbus, Ohio : Xerox Education Publications,
              c1978.
513           4 boxes of games : col. ; each box 23 x 29 x
           8 cm. -- (The game tree series)

           Contents: A. Checked (grade 2) -- B. Striped
        (grade 3) -- C. Polka-dot (grade 4) -- D. Plaid
        (grade 5).

           1. Arithmetic.  [1. Arithmetic.]  I. Xerox
        Education Publications.  II. Series: The game
        tree series.
```

Example 86: Jigsaw Puzzle Post Card

This item has a post card glued to the back of the plastic that covers the jigsaw puzzle; when the puzzle is unwrapped the postcard would be discarded, and the information about the picture would be lost.

Puzzle and post card

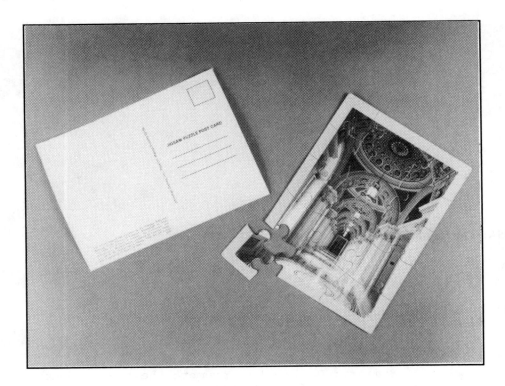

```
GV        Jigsaw puzzle post card [game]. -- Newton, Mass. :
1507         Whitehall Games, [1983]
.J5            1 jigsaw puzzle (15 pieces) : cardboard, col.
             ;  17 x 13 cm.
793.73
               Photograph by Anne Day of one of the
            corridors in the Thomas Jefferson Building of
            the Library of Congress.

               1. Jigsaw puzzles.  2. Library of Congress
            Thomas Jefferson Building.  [1. Puzzles.]  I.
            Day, Anne.  II. Whitehall Games, Inc.
```

Example 87: Minneapolis/St. Paul Scene

This is a game. The title has a slash in it, one of the prescribed marks of punctuation. The title must be recorded as shown with no space on either side of the slash, or the slash may be changed to a comma followed by a space. One needs to know how one's online catalog treats a slash—as a separator or a connector. If the slash joins the words on either side of it, the title becomes difficult to search and an added entry for the title without the slash would be needed.

This could be classed in F with Minnesota history or GV for games.

Game board, pieces and box

From the side of the box

City Scene Games

Each Scene Game is a unique interpretation of a specific city, highlighting streets, major businesses, and local personalities. Have fun and at the same time become educated while playing the Games about prominent American cities.

JOHN N. HANSEN CO. INC.   369 Adrian, Millbrae, CA 94030   (415) 697-7353
2861 La Cresta Ave., Anaheim, CA 92806   (714) 630-7000

Example 87: Minneapolis/St. Paul Scene

From the instruction sheet

```
    1 Playing Board
   28 Scene Cards (including 1 blank)
   24 Ownership Cards
    4 Debtor Cards
    4 Power Group Badges
   16 Connection Cards
    6 Tokens
    2 Dice
    1 Cardboard Card with Individual
      Markers
    5 Denominations/Money
```

THE OBJECT

The object of the game is to accumulate wealth. A player buys *Ownership Cards* representing various properties and businesses. A player may develop his acquisitions once he has made a deal with some of the *Power Groups* that control business in Minneapolis/St. Paul. The game ends when all the players are bankrupt except one, or at a predetermined time, or when a ball game is starting on TV.

```
F          Minneapolis/St. Paul scene [game]. -- Milbrae, CA :
614            John N. Hansen, c1981.
.M6               1 game (various pieces) : col. ; in box 27 x
               52 x 4 cm.
917
                  Summary: A game for two to four players in
               which the players try to accumulate wealth
               through buying and developing property, gaining
               power, and acquiring connections. All
               properties, etc., represent actual places and
               companies from Minneapolis and St. Paul,
               Minn. Game board is photo from space of the
               Twin Cities area.

                  1. Games.  2. Minneapolis (Minn.)  3. Saint
               Paul (Minn.)  [1. Board games. 2. Games.]  I.
               John N. Hansen Co., Inc.
```

Example 88: Froglegs Bean Bag

This is an example of a manufactured item with a distributor and a manufacturer. We do not know the name of the manufacturer, but we do know the country of manufacture.

The chief source of information for this item is the item itself with any accompanying material; there is a cloth tag sewn into a seam and a paper tag attached.

The note is based on rule 10.7B14.

Frog bean bag

Sewn on label

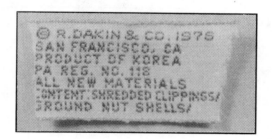

Attached label

DAKIN **Bean bags**

• *All new materials • Hand-crafted • Non-allergenic: Ground nutshell used in some items proven non-allergenic and completely safe by independent testing. TO CLEAN: We recommend using warm water, mild soap with sponge or cloth, cleaning as soiling occurs. When dry, brush to restore appearance of plush. Recommended for 3 years and up.*
My name is FROGLEGS BEAN BAG

```
GV        Froglegs bean bag [toy]. -- San Francisco :
1218         Distributed by R. Dakin, [197-] (Korea).
.B3            1 bean bag : fabric, green and white ; 27 cm.
           long. -- (Dakin bean bags)
688.72
                "Recommended for 3 years and up."

                1. Toys.  [1. Toys.]  I. Series.
```

Example 89: Frog Hand Puppet

The chief source of information for this item is the item itself with the attached paper tag. We assume a date of distribution, based on the date it was purchased. We use place and name of manufacturer (10.4D2, 10.4F2). Information on color and size of the puppets is included in the summary note because it is too complicated to describe briefly in the physical description area.

Frog hand puppet with Insect finger puppet

Tag on puppet

Example 89: Frog Hand Puppet

```
PN          [Frog hand puppet][toy]. -- [1979?](Austin, Tex.
1972            : Nancy Renfro Studios)
                2 puppets : fabric, col.
791.53
            Title supplied by cataloger.
            Summary: Yellow insect finger puppet (7 cm.
        long) attached by elastic to green and pink
        frog hand puppet (27 cm. wide); designed to be
        used with story or rhyme about a frog eating a
        fly.

            1. Puppets and puppet-plays.  [1. Puppets and
        puppet plays.]  I. Nancy Renfro Studios.
```

Example 90: Pac Man

This is a hand-held electronic game that contains a microcomputer chip. Because it is self-contained, it is cataloged by the rules in *AACR 2* chapter 10 rather than those in chapter 9.

Information that could have been given in several notes (10.7B1, 10.7B10, 10.7B14, 10.7B17) is combined into one note.

Box and game

```
GV          Tomytronic Pac Man [game]. -- Carson, CA : Tomy
1469.2          Corp., c1981 (Japan)
                    1 game : plastic, yellow and black ; 20 cm.
794.8           diam. x 6 cm. high in container 22 x 22 x 8
                cm.

                Electronic game with sound in which player
            controls movement of Pac Man as it eats bait,
            cherries, and monsters before the monsters eat
            it. Player can choose between amateur (slow) or
            professional (fast) versions.

                1. Electronic toys.  [1. Electronic toys.]
            I. Title: Pac Man.
```

Example 91: The Quest for the Rings

This was cataloged as a game because a set of materials is included in the package; the game cartridge is used to determine board moves. The computer software is not the dominant item, but only one of several items contained in the package, with no one item dominant.

Note the use of the systems requirement note, which is borrowed from the *AACR 2* chapter 9.

Rules for notes are, in order, 10.7B1, 9.7B1b, 10.7B6, 10.7B17.

Game package, board and parts

```
GV          The Quest for the rings [game]. -- [Los Angeles] :
1202            North American Philips Consumer Electronics,
.F35            c1981.
                1 computer chip cartridge, 1 game board, 6
793.932     game tokens, 1 keyboard overlay, 1 direction
            booklet ; in container 20 x 26 x 6 cm.

                Game for 2-5 players.
                System requirements: Odyssey2 videogame
            system; color TV.
                Software copyright by E. Averett.
                Summary: Players choose roles as wizard,
            warrior, changeling, or phantom and attempt to
            recover 10 rings of power. Players move through
            mazes on video screen (with sound and color) as
            they gather items hidden in the maze enabling
            them to move on the board.

                1. Video games.  [1. Video games.]  I.
            Averett, E.  II. North American Philips Consumer
            Electronics Corp.
```

Example 92: Cannon Ball

   This is a real manufactured object with no information provided. From its size and material we know the type of cannon ball it is; this type was used in the Civil War. We assume it was made in the United States during the Civil War. We do not know the name of the manufacturer, so use "s.n."

Cannon ball

```
E          [Cannon ball][realia]. -- ([United States : s.n.,
468.9          186-])
                  1 cannon ball : lead, gray ; 10 cm. in diam.
623.42

               Title supplied by cataloger.
               Summary: "12-pounder" cannon ball used in the
           Civil War.


               1. Ordnance.  2. United States--History--
           Civil War, 1861-1865.  [1. Ordnance. 2. United
           States--History--1861-1865, Civil War.]
```

Example 93: Forget-Me-Not Toothpick Holder

This is an item manufactured in small quantities; the only indication of manufacturer is the symbol on a paper sticker. The exact dimensions of the item, rather than rounded ones, are given because those dimensions are all that differentiate between the original and this reproduction.

We know where and by whom this was manufactured, and we know it was made sometime between 1965 and 1972. It was available for purchase in 1973, so this is used as date of distribution.

Rule numbers for notes are 10.7B1 combined with 10.7B10, 10.7B3, 10.7B11.

Toothpick holder

```
NK        [Forget-me-not toothpick holder] [realia]. --
9508         [1973] ([Cambridge, Ohio : Degenhart Crystal Art
              Glass, between 1965 and 1972])
748.8           1 toothpick holder : glass, bittersweet
             orange ; 6 cm. diam. x 6.3 cm. high.

                Reproduction of 1899 U.S. Glass Co. pattern
             Vermont; height slightly different from
             original.
                Title supplied by cataloger.
                Paper sticker inside with design, D in a
             heart.

                1. Toothpick holders.  I. Degenhart Crystal
             Art Glass (Firm)
```

Example 94: Cow Pull Toy

This hand-made toy is cataloged as shown. Because this toy is signed, we can use the name of the woman who made it in the statement of responsibility.

Rule numbers for notes are 10.7B1, 10.7B3, 10.7B10.

Cow pull toy

```
GV        Hardy, Margaret.
1218         [Cow pull toy][toy] / Margaret Hardy. -- 1982
.P8       (Trinway, Ohio)
             1 toy : wood, natural ; 26 x 34 x 16 cm.
688.72
             Wooden model of a cow mounted on wheeled base
          with string and handle for child to pull.
             Title supplied by cataloger.
             Signed and dated on bottom of base.

             1. Wooden toys.  [1. Toys.]  I. Title.
```

Example 95: Tree-of-Life Candleholder

The note describes the nature of the object rather than being a summary of the content.
Rules for notes are 10.7B1, 10.7B3, 10.7B10.

Tree-of-life candleholder

```
BL          [Tree-of-life candleholder] [art original] --
444             [1981?] (Mexico)
                    1 candleholder : clay, tan ; 26 cm. high.
745
.5933           Handmade sculpture of tree of life with two
                candle sockets and death's head at top, serpent
                in tree, Eve offering Adam apple near base.
                    Title supplied by cataloger.
                    Paper sticker under base: Made in Mexico.

                    1. Tree of life.  2. Folk art--Mexico.  [1.
                Folk art--Mexico.]
```

Example 96: Pot

This is an art object. Works by Maria have been appreciated by collectors for many years.
Rule numbers for notes are 10.7B1 combined with 10.7B6, 10.7B7, 10.7B10.

Pot

```
E          Martinez, Maria Montoya.
98              [Pot][art original] / Maria & Santana. --
.P8         [196-?]
                1 pot : clay, black ; 12 cm. diam. x 7 cm. high.
738.38
            Piece of pottery made by Maria, decorated by her
        son Santana, both of San Ildefonso Pueblo, N.M.
            Purchased in 1965 in Santa Fe, N. M.
            Signed in pencil on base.

            1. Pueblo Indians--Pottery.  [1. Pottery, In-
        dian. 2. Pueblo Indians--Art.]  I. Martinez,
        Santana.
```

Example 97: Nativity Set

If this set had a background, it could be called a diorama.

The name and address of the woman who made the set does not appear anywhere on the set; I got that information when I bought the set from her.

The first note combines information from 10.7B1, 10.7B6, 10.7B10.

Nativity set

```
N          Robbin, Betty.
8060           [Nativity set] [art original] -- [1982]
               12 figures : yarn, col. ; tallest 28 cm.
232.921
               Crocheted figures stuffed with batting; made by
           Betty Robbin, Columbus, Ohio.
               Title supplied by cataloger.

               1. Jesus Christ--Art.  [1. Jesus Christ--Nativ-
           ity.]
```

Chapter 9

MICROFORMS

AACR 2 Chapter 11

This chapter emphasizes the cataloging of those microforms that are all graphic materials. There are many sets of microforms available that are similar to sets of slides with captions; one of the examples, *Pottery Techniques*, is of this type. There are also many sets of microforms in which most or all the frames are graphic materials such as drawings or paintings or photographs or X-rays. The second example, *Architecture of Washington, D.C.*, is of this type. These materials are not reproductions of books; they are original publications in microform. All are cataloged by the rules given in *AACR 2* chapter 11.

Special Rules for Cataloging Microforms

In this section the special rules for cataloging microforms will be discussed. Parts of some of the rules are given; the user is referred to the rules themselves for complete text and examples.

Chief Source of Information

The chief source of information for a microform is the title frame(s). If there is no title frame on a microfiche, or if the information on that title frame is insufficient, the eye-readable information printed at the top of the microfiche is treated as the chief source of information. If that information includes a shortened title, and the accompanying materials or container provides a fuller form of the title, treat the accompanying materials or the container as the chief source of information.

Title and Statement of Responsibility Area

There are no special problems in this area. The GMD used for this material is "microform".

Publication, Distribution, Etc., Area

Information concerning the publisher and/or distributor of the microform is recorded here.

Physical Description Area

Extent of item

The number and name of the microform is given first. The plural of "microfiche" is "microfiches". The number of frames of a microfiche is added in parentheses if that number can be determined easily.

Other physical details

If a microform is negative, this is indicated.
If the microform contains or consists of illustrations, this is indicated.
If the microform is colored, this is indicated, but black and white is not indicated.

> *Examples:* `2 microfiches : all col. ill.`
> `1 microfiche : ill. (some col.)`

Dimensions

Dimensions are given in centimeters, height x width; for microfilm, only width is given. If microfiche is 10.5 x 14.8 cm, the standard dimensions, the dimensions are not given.

Accompanying material

This is recorded as in all other chapters.

Notes Area

Notes permitted in this chapter are:

11.7B1.	Nature, scope, or artistic or other form of an item
11.7B2.	Language
11.7B3.	Source of title proper
11.7B4.	Variations in title
11.7B5.	Parallel titles and other title information
11.7B6.	Statements of responsibility
11.7B7.	Edition and history
11.7B9.	Publication, distribution, etc.
11.7B10.	Physical description:
	Reduction ratio
	Reader
	Film
	Other physical details
11.7B11.	Accompanying material
11.7B12.	Series
11.7B13.	Dissertations
11.7B14.	Audience
11.7B16.	Other formats
11.7B17.	Summary
11.7B18.	Contents
11.7B19.	Numbers
11.7B20.	Copy being described, library's holdings, and restrictions on use
11.7B21.	"With" notes
11.7B22.	Notes relating to original

Explanation of notes

Each of the notes will be explained in the following section and examples of their use given.

11.7B1. Nature, scope, or artistic or other form of the item

To be used to name or explain the form of the item as necessary.

> *Example:* `X-rays of Egyptian mummies`

11.7B2. Language

To be used to name the language or languages of the item cataloged if not obvious from other information given.

> *Example:* `Abstracts in French, German, Italian, and English`

11.7B3. Source of title proper

To be used if the title proper is taken from other than the chief source of information.

> *Examples:* `Title from publisher's catalog`
> `Title supplied by cataloger`

11.7B4. Variations in title

To be used to note any title appearing on the item that differs significantly from the title proper.

> *Example:* `Title of fiche 2: Powered flights`

11.7B5. Parallel titles and other title information

To be used for parallel titles and important other title information not recorded in the title and statement of responsibility area.

> *Example:* `Subtitle on manual: A micropublication commemorating the`
> `seventy-fifth anniversary of the first flight by the Wright`
> `Brothers, December 17, 1903`

11.7B6. Statements of responsibility

To be used to record important information not recorded in the statement of responsibility area.

> *Example:* `Exhibition organized by Peter Thompson`

11.7B7. Edition and history

To be used for information about earlier editions or the history of the item being cataloged.

> *Example:* `Includes photographs of all works from the exhibition`
> `Grant Wood in America`

11.7B9. Publication, distribution, etc.

To be used for important information not recorded in the publication, distribution, etc., area.

11.7B10. Physical description

Reduction ratio. Give the reduction ratio if it is outside the 16×-30× range. Use one of the following terms:

> *low reduction* for less than 16×
> *high reduction* for 31×-60×
> *very high reduction* for 61×-90×
> *ultra high reduction* for over 90×; for these, give also the specific ratio
> *reduction ratio varies*

Reader. Give the name of the reader on which a microform is to be used if it can only be used on that reader.

Film. Give details of the nature of the film used, if desired.

Other physical details. Make notes on any other physical information considered important.

Comments: To be used for any important information not given in area 5, the physical description area.

> *Example:* `Microfiche in pockets in binder`

11.7B11. Accompanying material

To be used for any important information not given in the accompanying material part of area 5.

> *Example:* `Introductory material also on first frames of microfiche`

11.7B12. Series

To be used for any important information not recorded in the series area.

> *Example:* `Some material previously issued in series: American architec-`
> `ture`

11.7B13. Dissertations

To be used for the standard dissertation note when applicable.

> *Example:* `Thesis (Ph. D.)--University of Iowa, 1966`

11.7B14. Audience

To be used to record the intended audience of a work; use this note only if the information is stated on the item. Do not attempt to judge the audience for an item.

> *Example:* `For medical professionals only`

11.7B16. Other formats

To be used to list other formats in which the work is available. The Library of Congress lists all formats commercially available in this note.

> *Example:* `Issued also as slides (b&w, col.), and as photographic prints`

11.7B17. Summary

To be used for a brief objective summary of the content of the item.

> *Example:*   `Summary: Shows how to duplicate several Cherokee pots and`
> `bowls using techniques developed by Cherokee potters`

11.7B18. Contents

To be used for a formal or informal listing of the contents of the item.

> *Example:*   `Contents: The White House -- The Octagon -- Treasury`
> `Building -- General Post Office -- Washington Monument`

11.7B19. Numbers

To be used to list any important number appearing on the item other than those to be recorded in area 8.

> *Example:*   `"LC-USZ62-66609"`

11.7B20. Copy being described, library's holdings, and restrictions on use

To be used for any notes applicable only to the particular copy of the item being described. Also used for local library restrictions on the material being described, or for information of use only to patrons of the local library.

> *Examples:*   `Library copy lacks fiche 4`
> `Some photograph frames have been removed from microfilm`
> `reel`

11.7B21. "With" notes

To be used for "with" notes.

11.7B22. Notes relating to original

To be used for information on the original of a microform item.

> *Example:*   `Original negatives in collection of Prints and Photo-`
> `graphs Division, Library of Congress`

Example 98: Photography by the Wright Brothers

This example is an original publication in microform. The CIP copy shown on the verso of the title page is pre-*AACR* 2.

The size of the mircofiche is not given if 10.5 x 14.8 cm. (11 x 15 cm.)

Rules for notes are 11.7B1, 11.7B16.

Microfiches and guide

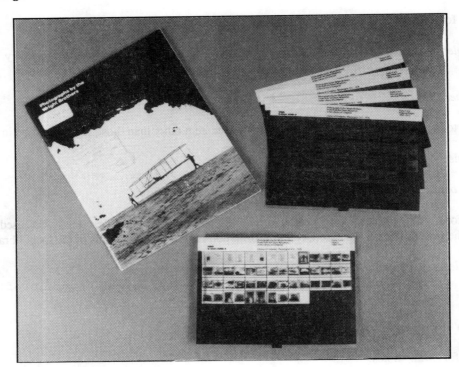

Example 98: Photography by the Wright Brothers

Microfiche

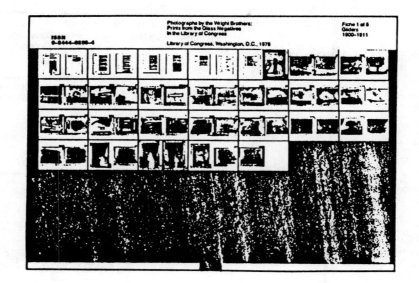

Example 98: Photography by the Wright Brothers

Title page and verso of title page of guide

LC 1.2: W 93

Photographs by the Wright Brothers

Prints from the Glass Negatives in the Library of Congress

A Micropublication Commemorating the Seventy-fifth Anniversary of the First Flight by the Wright Brothers, December 17, 1903

Library of Congress   Washington   1978

1D3   Orville Wright aloft, Kitty Hawk, Oct. 1911
LC–USZ62–66609

Library of Congress Cataloging in Publication Data

Wright, Wilbur, 1867–1912.
Photographs by the Wright Brothers.

Reproduced from the collection in the Prints and Photographs Division at the Library of Congress.

1. Aeronautics—United States—History—Pictorial works.   2. Wright, Wilbur, 1867–1912.·   3. Wright, Orville, 1871–1948.   I. Wright, Orville, 1871–1948, joint author.   II. United States.   Library of Congress.   Prints and Photographs Division.   III. Title. Microfiche TL521   629.13′0092′4   78–606137   ISBN 0–8444–0266–4

Cover

1B10   Starting Orville Wright in glider, Oct. 10, 1902. Wilbur Wright at left, Dan Tate at right. LC–USZ62–56227.

For sale by the Superintendent of Documents,
U.S. Government Printing Office, Washington, D.C. 20402
Stock Number 030–014–00003–1

☆ U.S. GOVERNMENT PRINTING OFFICE : 1978 O—275–332

Example 98: Photography by the Wright Brothers

```
TL        Wright, Wilbur, 1867-1912.
521          Photographs by the Wright Brothers [microform] :
          prints from the glass negatives in the Library
629       of Congress. -- Washington, D.C. : Library of
.130092   Congress ; For sale by the Supt. of Docs., U.S.
          G.P.O., 1978.
             5 microfiches : all ill. + 1 guide (20 p. : ill.
          ; 19 cm.)

             "A micropublication commemorating the seventy-
          fifth anniversary of the first flight by the Wright
          Brothers, December 17, 1903"--Cover of guide.
             Prints of each negative are available from the
          Library of Congress.
             ISBN 0-8444-0266-4.

             1. Aeronautics--United States--History.  2.
          Wright, Wilbur, 1867-1912.  3. Wright, Orville,
          1871-1948.  [1. Airplanes--History.]  I. Wright,
          Orville, 1871-1948.  II. Title.
```

Example 99: Pottery Techniques

This is an original publication in microform. It contains the same material as a set of slides would; it can be viewed in a microfiche reader or projected with a microfiche projector. The reduction ratio is 24×, so nothing about reduction ratio is specified.

I used "all col. ill." in the physical description area; nothing in *AACR 2* chapter 11 anticipated this type of microfiche, as rule 11.5C2 specified "ill." and "all ill."; 11.5C3 specifies "col." for a colored microform without illustrations, or "col. & ill." for a colored microform with illustrations, or "col. ill." for a microform on which only the illustrations are colored.

The University of Chicago Press has quite a few titles in this text/fiche series.

The information about the photographer appears on the title frame, which is the chief source of information. It does not appear on the eye-readable information at the top of the fiche.

First of four sheets of microfiche

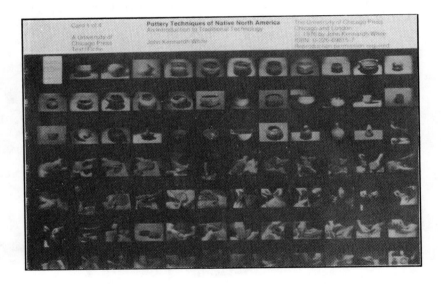

Eye-readable date at top of microfiche

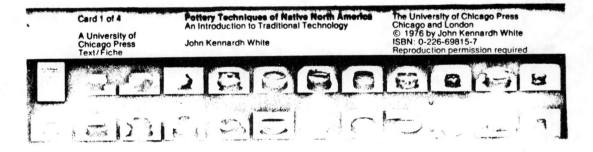

Example 99: Pottery Techniques

```
E              White, John Kennardh.
98                  Pottery techniques of native North America
.P8            [microform] : an introduction to traditional
               technology / John Kennardh White ; photographs by
738            Stewart J. MacLeod. -- Chicago : University of
.14089975      Chicago Press, c1976.
                    4 microfiches (336 fr.) : all col. ill + 1
               manual (52 p. : ill. ; 21 cm.). -- (A University of
               Chicago Press text/fiche)

                  Summary: Shows how to duplicate several Cherokee
               pots and bowls using techniques developed by Chero-
               kee potters. Shows many examples of pottery made by
               Indians in the southeast United States.
                  ISBN 0-226-69815-7.

                  1. Cherokee Indians--Pottery.  2. Indians of
               North America--Pottery.  3. Pottery craft.  [1.
               Pottery, Indian--Technique. 2. Cherokee Indians
               --Art.]  I. MacLeod, Stewart J.  II. Title.  III.
               Series.
```

Example 100: The Architecture of Washington, D.C.

This example shows a microform that is described by a bibliographic open entry. It is not a serial. The titles are original publications in microform. The pictures are also available from the publisher in other forms; the note is made giving that information.

This material has both a publisher and a distributor, both of whom are named, the distributor with an explanatory word inserted in square brackets.

Rules for notes are, in order, 11.7B11, 11.7B16, 11.7B17, 11.7B18.

Fiche 1 of ten, The White House

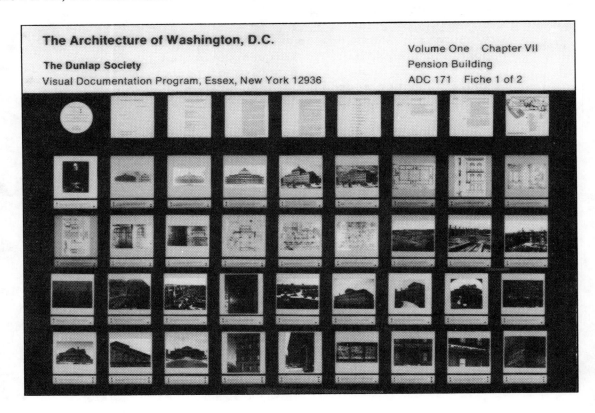

Cover of Volume 1

Example 100: The Architecture of Washington, D.C.

Volume 1 open to show contents

Frame of The White House, reproduced by permission of the Dunlap Society

Example 100: The Architecture of Washington, D.C.

```
NA          The Architecture of Washington, D.C. [microform] /
735            Bates Lowry, editor. -- Washington, D.C. :
.W5            Dunlap Society ; Essex, N.Y. : Visual
               Documentation Program [distributor], c1976-
720.9753         microfiches : ill. +    p. of
               introductory material.

                  Introductory material also on first frames of
               microfiche.
                  Also available as slides (b&w or col.) or
               photographic prints.
                  Summary: For each building includes all known
               early drawings, prints, and photographs of the
               setting, interior, and exterior, as well as
               selected construction drawings and photographs.
                  Contents: v. 1. The White House (10 micro-
               fiches). The Octagon (2 microfiches). Treasury
               Building (4 microfiches). General Post Office (2
               microfiches). Washington Monument (3 micro-
               fiches). State, War, and Navy Building (5 micro-
               fiches). Pension Building (2 microfiches). Union
               Station (4 microfiches). Lincoln Memorial (4
               microfiches). Supreme Court Building (4 micro-
               fiches) -- v. 2. The United States Capitol (21
               microfiches). Patent Office Building (4 micro-
               fiches). Smithsonian Institution Building (4
               microfiches). Library of Congress (5 micro-
               fiches). Pan American Union Building (4 micro-
               fiches). The Federal Triangle (8 microfiches).
               Jefferson Memorial (2 microfiches).
                  ISBN 0-89481-001-4 (v. 1)


                  1. Architecture--Washington (D.C.)--History.
               2. Washington (D.C).--Buildings, structures,
               etc. [1. Washington, D.C.--Historic buildings.]
               I. Lowry, Bates, 1923-     II. Dunlap Society.
```

Chapter 10

AUDIOVISUAL SERIALS

AACR 2 Chapter 12

This chapter covers the cataloging of audiovisual serials. Serials are cataloged by the rules of *AACR 2* chapter 12 in conjunction with the rules in the chapter for the type of material to which the serial belongs. Audiovisual serials use the rules of chapter 12 together with the appropriate rules of the chapters that cover their types of media. Serials can be found on many types of audiovisual material. *SoftDisk Magazette*, *Microzine*, and *SoftSide DV Magazine* are serials on computer disks. *VideoJournal* is a serial on videocassette. *Getting It All Together* and *Young Fashion Forecast* are filmstrip serials. There are many serials on sound cassettes for doctors; *Pediatrics* and *Audiology* are only two of these. There are online serials such as *The Online Hotline* and *The Online Chronicle*. Serials are now available as computer files on CD-ROM, including *Pediatrics* and *American Family Physician*. *Verbum Interactive* is a multimedia serial on CD-ROM, with interactive columns and articles.

Special Rules for Cataloging Audiovisual Serials

In this section the special rules for cataloging audiovisual serials will be discussed. Parts of some of the rules are given; the user is referred to the rules themselves for complete text and examples.

Chief Source of Information

The basis for the description is the title page or title page substitute of the first issue of the serial. If the first issue is not available, we base our description on the first issue we have. The chief source of information for a printed serial is the title page; for an audiovisual serial we would use as chief source of information that title page substitute specified in the appropriate chapter. For a serial sound recording, the chief source of information would be the disc label(s) of the first issue.

The Library of Congress catalogs serials at augmented level one; other title information is omitted.

Title and Statement of Responsibility Area

There are lengthy rule interpretations concerning titles of serials as well as concerning all other aspects of serials. Refer to these (*Cataloging Service Bulletin* 11-) if there is any doubt as to what information belongs in which area of the bibliographic record.

For an audiovisual serial, the appropriate GMD is used.

Numeric and/or Alphabetic, Chronological, or Other Designation Area

In the rules below, use standard abbreviations and numerals in place of words (see *AACR 2* Appendixes B and C). This area is omitted if the description is based on other than the first issue.

12.3B1. Give the numeric and/or alphabetic designation of the first issue of a serial as given in that issue....

12.3C1. If the first issue of a serial is identified by a chronological designation, give it in the terms used in the item....

12.3F1. In describing a completed serial, give the designation of the first issue followed by the designation of the last issue.

Publication, Distribution, Etc., Area

The information given in this area, as in the other areas, reflects the information given in the first issue of the serial.

12.4F1. ... Give the date of publication even if it coincides, wholly or in part, with the date given as the chronological coverage.

Physical Description Area

12.5B1. For a serial that is still in progress, give the relevant specific material designation preceded by three spaces....

Other parts of the physical description area are recorded as directed in the appropriate chapter.

Notes Area

The following notes are permitted in this chapter:

12.7B1.   Frequency
12.7B2.   Language
12.7B3.   Source of title proper
12.7B4.   Variations in title
12.7B5.   Parallel titles and other title information
12.7B6.   Statements of responsibility
12.7B7.   Relationships with other serials
12.7B8.   Numbering and chronological designation
12.7B9.   Publication, distribution, etc.
12.7B10. Physical description
12.7B11. Accompanying material
12.7B12. Series
12.7B14. Audience
12.7B16. Other formats
12.7B17. Indexes
12.7B18. Contents
12.7B19. Numbers
12.7B20. Copy being described, library's holdings, and restrictions on use
12.7B21. "Issued with" notes
12.7B22. Item described

Explanation of notes

Each of the notes will be explained in the following section and examples of their use given. There is no summary note listed for this chapter. When we need one for audiovisual material, we "borrow" it from the chapter for the physical form of the material.

12.7B1. Frequency

To be used to give the frequency of the serial.

>   *Example:*   `Weekly during the school year`

12.7B2. Language

To be used to name the language or languages of the item cataloged if not obvious from other information given.

>   *Example:*   `Text in English and French`

12.7B3. Source of title proper

To be used if the title proper is taken from other than the chief source of information.

>   *Examples:*   `Title from container`
>   `Title supplied by cataloger`

12.7B4. Variations in title

To be used to note any title appearing on the item that differs significantly from the title proper.

>   *Example:*   `Title on container: News lesson`
>   (*Title proper:* News program)

12.7B5. Parallel titles and other title information

To be used for parallel titles and important other title information not recorded in the title and statement of responsibility area.

>   *Example:*   `Subtitle on index: An audio journal for professionals`

12.7B6. Statements of responsibility

To be used to record important information not recorded in the statement of responsibility area.

>   *Example:*   `Editors: Larry J. Bradford, Frederick N. Martin`

12.7B7. Relationships with other serials

To be used to note the relationship between the serial being described and any serial it continues or is continued by, or with which it has some relationship.

>   *Example:*   `Continued by: Audiology (published in hard copy)`

12.7B8. Numbering and chronological designation

To be used for notes on complex or irregular numbering, etc., not already specified.

>   *Example:*   `Vol. 1, no. 3, numbered vol. 2, no. 3`

12.7B9. Publication, distribution, etc.

To be used for important information not recorded in the publication, distribution, etc. area.

  Example: `Publisher varies`

12.7B10. Physical description

To be used for any important information not given in area 5, the physical description area.

  Example: `Some issues on sound cassette, others on sound tape reel`

12.7B11. Accompanying material

To be used for any important information not given in the accompanying material part of area 5.

  Examples: `Guide in braille`
  `Occasionally supplemented by posters`

12.7B12. Series

To be used for series information related to the original of a reproduction.

  Example: `Some issues also part of: Math skills series`

12.7B14. Audience

To be used to record the intended audience of a work; use this note only if the information is stated on the item. Do not attempt to judge the audience for an item.

  Example: `Intended for health professionals working with the hear-`
  `ing-impaired`

12.7B16. Other formats

To be used to list other formats in which the work is available. The Library of Congress lists all formats commercially available in this note.

  Example: `Some numbers issued also on sound tape reels`

12.7B17. Indexes

To be used for notes on separately published indexes, and on cumulative indexes.

  Example: `Printed index issued for each volume`

12.7B18. Contents

To be used for details of inserts, special items with their own titles, and serials within the serial being cataloged.

  Example: `Poster included with first number of each semester`

12.7B19. Numbers

To be used to list any important number appearing on the item other than those to be recorded in area 8.

12.7B20. Copy being described, library's holdings, and restrictions on use

To be used for any notes applicable only to the particular copy of the item being described. Also used for local library restrictions on the material being described, or for information of use only to patrons of the local library.

> *Example:*   `Restricted for library use only`

12.7B21. "Issued with" notes

To be used for a note listing other serials issued with the one being cataloged.

12.7B22. Item described

To be used if the description is not based on the first issue.

> *Example:*   `Description based on: Aug. 1982`

Example 101: News Program

This is a serial filmstrip that is cataloged from the first issue.
Rules for notes are 12.7B1, 12.7B4, 8.7B17.

Box of filmstrips

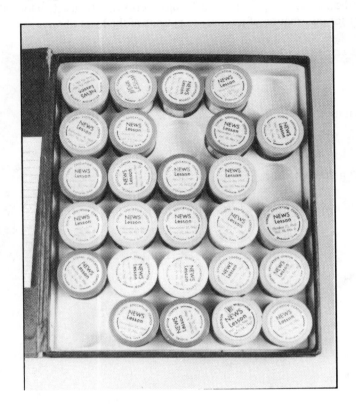

```
D          News program [filmstrip]. -- Vol. 1, no. 1 (Sept.
421            7, 1950)-    . -- Dubuque, Iowa : Visual
               Education Center, 1950-
909.82805         filmstrips : b&w ; 35 mm. +
           teacher's guides +    semester quizzes.

               Weekly during the school year.
               Title on container: News lesson.
               Summary: Pictures from the news of the week
           are presented with discussion questions.

               1. History--Study and teaching (Elementary).
           [1. Current events--Periodicals.]  [2. Histori-
           ography--Periodicals.]  I. Visual Education
           Center.  II. Title: News lesson.
```

Example 102: Pediatrics

This is an example of a sound cassette serial with varying frequency and format. A printed table of contents comes for each issue, and indexes are issued semi-annually. Notice the combination of description and notes from the serials chapter, and description and notes from the sound recording chapter.

Library of Congress/CONSER practice is not to guess at anything. If not cataloging from the first issue, area 3 is omitted and no date is included in area 4. A "description based on" note is used when cataloging from anything other than the first issue.

Rules for notes are 12.7B23 (moved to first position), 12.7B1, 12.7B10, 12.7B17.

Sound cassette

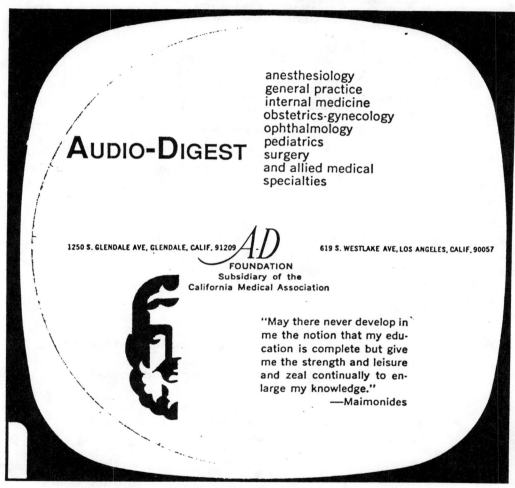

```
RJ        Pediatrics [sound recording]. -- Glendale, Calif. :
1             Audio-Digest Foundation,
                  sound cassettes : analog +    guides.
618
.920005       Description based on: Vol. 12, no. 1.
              Frequency varies: 24 or 48 nos. per volume.
              Some numbers on sound tape reels.
              Index issued for each volume.

                  1. Pediatrics--Periodicals.  [1. Children--
              Diseases--Periodicals.]  I. Audio-Digest Founda-
              tion.
```

Example 103: Audiology

This example is included to show a closed entry; the title actually continues its title and volume numbering, but the change in format calls for a new bibliographic record and the closing of this one.

Rules for notes are 12.7B1, 12.7B7, 12.7B10.

Sound cassette

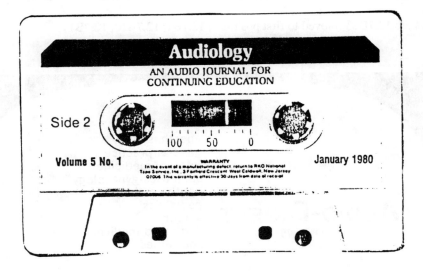

```
RF          Audiology [sound recording] : an audio journal for
290             continuing education. -- Vol. 1, no. 1 (Jan.
                1976)-v. 7, no. 12 (Dec. 1981). -- New York :
617.8005     Grune & Stratton, 1976-1981.
                7 v. (84 sound cassettes) : analog + 84
             printed guides.

                Monthly.
                Continued by: Audiology (published in hard
             copy.)
                Each volume in a binder; printed contents
             list issued annually.

                1. Audiology--Periodicals.  [1. Hearing--
             Periodicals.)  I. Grune & Stratton.
```

Example 104: Softdisk Magazette

This serial is issued on computer disks. Rules for notes are 12.7B1, 9.7B1b, 12.7B23 and 9.7B3, 9.7B7.

Disk label

SOFTDISK MAGAZETTE

3811 ST. VINCENT

SHREVEPORT LOUISIANA 71108

DOS 3.3   APPLESOFT

Month and year appear when the disk is run.

```
QA          Softdisk magazette [computer file]. -- Shreveport,
75.5           La. : Softdisk Magazette
               computer disks : sd., col. ; 5 1/4 in.
005.105
            Monthly.
            System requirements: Apple II or higher.
            Description based on: Aug. 1982; title from
            disk label.
            Began publication Sept. 1981.

            1. Programming (Electronic computers)--
            Periodicals.  [1. Programming (Electronic com-
            puters)--Periodicals.]
```

Example 105: Congressional Masterfile

This is not really a serial as the quarterly disk replaces the previous disk rather than supplements it, but we treat it as a serial rather than recataloging it each quarter.

The version number changes periodically.

Rules for notes are 9.7B1a, 12.7B1, 9.7B1b, 9.7B3, 12.7B8, and 12.7B23.

Installation diskette

CONGRESSIONAL
MASTERFILE 2
CIS/INDEX ON CD-ROM ■ 1970 TO PRESENT

Installation Diskette

Version 1.06 - May 1991

This diskette contains QA Gateway™ installation programs. Copyright 1991 by Quantum Access, Inc. Authorized for use only with CD-ROM products of Congressional Information Service.

Example 105: Congressional Masterfile

Compact disk

From the disk case

Example 105: Congressional Masterfile

Compact disk

From the disk case

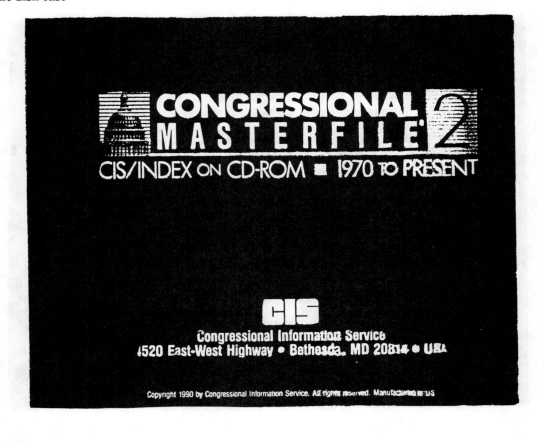

Example 105: Congressional Masterfile

```
Z           Congressional masterfile 2 [computer file] 1970-
1223           . -- Bethesda, MD : Congressional Information
.A2            Service, 1989-
                    computer disks ; 4 3/4 in. + 1 computer
328.73         disk (3 1/2 in.) + 1 user's manual.
```

"CIS/index to congressional publications and
legislative histories."
Quarterly.
System requirements: IBM PC or compatible;
hard disk drive; 640K; CD-ROM drive with Microsoft extensions.
Title from disk label.
First CD-ROM covers 1970-1982; second disk,
1983-   , replaced quarterly.
Description based on: 1970-1982, 1983-Mar.
1991.

1. United States. Congress--Committees--
Indexes. 2. Legislative hearings--United
States--Indexes. 3. United States--Politics and
government--Indexes. 4. United States--Govern-
ment publications--Indexes. I. Congressional
Information Service. II. Title: Congressional
masterfile two.

Chapter 11

KITS AND OTHER PROBLEMS

Kit. 1. An item containing two or more categories of material, no one of which is identifiable as the predominant constituent of the item; also designated "multimedia item". 2. A single-medium package of textual material. (*AACR 2*, p. 619)

Use *kit* for any item containing more than one type of material if the relative predominance of components is not easily determinable and for a single-medium package of textual material. (*AACR 2*, p. 20, footnote 2 (4)).

Kit. A collection of articles forming part of the equipment of a soldier, and carried in a valise or knapsack ... A number of things or persons viewed as a whole; a set, lot, collection. (*Oxford English Dictionary*, Oxford: Clarendon Press, 1933, v. 5, p. 716).

The definition of kit has changed over the years. Earlier school/library usage called any package containing more than one type of material a kit. Determination of predominant component was a later concept. There is still little agreement among catalogers as to what is, or is not, a kit. Some packages contain so many items that they clearly fall into the above definitions. Other packages are borderline.

A package containing a filmstrip with narrated sound on a sound cassette or disc, and a guide or script, is not a kit because the filmstrip is considered to be predominant, with the other materials accompanying the filmstrip. A package containing a filmstrip and a sound recording that is not narration and is not used simultaneously with the filmstrip would be a kit, as the package contains more than one type of material and no one type is dominant. The *Reading Habit Custom Pack*, containing 211 discussion cards for children's favorite books, 24 creative activity cards, and two cut-apart card games, would be a kit.

The *OED* definition given above is helpful. "A number of things ... viewed as a whole" is a useful definition when examining materials such as the reading materials mentioned above.

Rule 1.10 in *AACR 2* is the only rule for the cataloging of kits. However, the word "kit" is never mentioned. The rule is confusing, because it begins by saying it applies "to items that are made up of two or more components, two or more of which belong to distinct material types (e.g., a sound recording and a printed text)" (p. 56). This has led some to believe that anything with two or more components is a kit.

The rule continues, "If an item has one predominant component, describe it in terms of that component and give details of the subsidiary component(s) as accompanying material following the physical description or in a note." At this point, rule 1.10 should refer the cataloger to the appropriate chapter for describing the predominant component, for example to chapter 8 for a filmstrip.

Other problems

Some examples in this chapter are not kits, but are problems that do not fall neatly or easily into one of the other chapters.

Chief Source of Information

The chief source of information for a kit is the whole item; information for cataloging may be taken from anywhere on the item. Usually there will be a container that will have information useful for cataloging.

Physical Description Area

There are three methods given in 1.10C2 for physical description. We are told in the rules to apply whichever is appropriate.

1.10C2a. Give the extent of each part or group of parts belonging to each distinct class of material as the first element of the physical description (do this if no further physical description of each item is desired). *Optionally*, if the parts are in a container, name the container and give its dimensions.

Example: 8 filmstrips, 4 sound discs, 18 charts and posters, 34
        identical elementary booklets, 1 secondary booklet, 1
        teacher's guide ; in box 34 x 34 x 34 cm.

1.10C2b. Give a separate physical description for each part or group of parts belonging to each distinct class of material (do this if a further physical description of each item is desired). Give each physical description on a separate line....

Examples: 8 filmstrips : col. ; 35 mm. 4 sound discs : analog, 33
        1/3 rpm ; 12 in.
          8 charts : b&w ; 28 x 22 cm.
          10 posters : col. ; 36 x 24 cm.
          34 identical elementary booklets (32 p. each) : ill. ; 28
        cm.
          1 teacher's guide (32 p.) : ill. ; 28 cm.
          All in container 34 x 34 x 34 cm.

1.10C2c. For items with a large number of heterogeneous materials, give a general term as the extent. Give the number of such pieces unless it cannot be ascertained [easily]....

Examples: various pieces
          28 various pieces ; in box 34 x 34 x 34 cm.

The Library of Congress has said it will not use rule 1.10C2b.

Notes Area

See comments on notes in the general chapter.

1.7A5. ... When appropriate, combine two or more notes to make one note.

Types of notes:

   1.7B1.   Nature, scope, or artistic form
   1.7B2.   Language of the item and/or translation or adaptation
   1.7B3.   Source of title proper
   1.7B4.   Variations in title
   1.7B5.   Parallel titles and other title information
   1.7B6.   Statements of responsibility
   1.7B7.   Edition and history
   1.7B9.   Publication, distribution, etc.
   1.7B10. Physical description
   1.7B11. Accompanying material and supplements

1.7B12. Series
1.7B13. Dissertations
1.7B14. Audience
1.7B15. Reference to published descriptions
1.7B16. Other formats
1.7B17. Summary
1.7B18. Contents
1.7B19. Numbers borne by the item
1.7B20. Copy being described, library's holdings, and restrictions on use
1.7B21. "With" notes
1.7B22. Combined notes relating to the original

Explanation of notes

Each of the notes will be explained in the following section and examples of their use given.

1.7B1. Nature, scope, or artistic form

To be used to name or explain the form of the item as necessary.

> *Example:* `A supplemental teaching unit`

1.7B2. Language of the item and/or translation or adaptation

To be used to name the language or languages of the item cataloged if not obvious from other information given.

> *Examples:* `Text in German`
> `Posters in German and Swedish`

1.7B3. Source of title proper

To be used if the title proper is taken from other than the chief source of information.

> *Example:* `Title supplied by cataloger`

1.7B4. Variations in title

To be used to note any title appearing on the item that differs significantly from the title proper.

> *Example:* `Title on cassette: Step by step 2`
> (*Title proper:* Step by step two.)

1.7B5. Parallel titles and other title information

To be used for parallel titles and important other title information not recorded in the title and statement of responsibility area.

> *Example:* `Subtitle from guide: A supplemental teaching unit from the`
> `records of the National Archives`

1.7B6. Statements of responsibility

To be used to record important information not recorded in the statement of responsibility area.

> *Example:*   `Project designer, John Victor ; programmers, Stephen`
> `Chmielewski, Kathleen Fortmeier`

1.7B7. Edition and history

To be used for information about earlier editions, or the history of the item being cataloged.

> *Example:*   `Continuation of: New step by step`

1.7B9. Publication, distribution, etc.

To be used for important information not recorded in the publication, distribution, etc., area.

1.7B10. Physical description

To be used for any important information not given in area 5, the physical description area.

> *Example:*   `HO scale`

1.7B11. Accompanying material and supplements

To be used for any important information not given in the accompanying material part of area 5.

> *Example:*   `Teacher's guide includes bibliography, exercises,`
> `worksheets, glossary, time line`

1.7B12. Series

To be used for any important information not recorded in the series area.

> *Example:*   `Filmstrips previously issued as part of series: Minne-`
> `sota, its land and people`

1.7B13. Dissertations

To be used for the standard dissertation note when applicable.

> *Example:*   `Thesis (Ed. Sp.)--St. Cloud State University, 1980`

1.7B14. Audience

To be used to record the intended audience of a work; use this note only if the information is stated on the item. Do not attempt to judge the audience for an item.

> *Example:*   `For ages 8 years and up`

1.7B15. Reference to published descriptions

To be used to refer to published descriptions of the material.

1.7B16. Other formats

To be used to list other formats in which the work is available. The Library of Congress lists all formats commercially available in this note.

Example: `Issued also with intermediate-level guides`

1.7B17. Summary

To be used for a brief objective summary of the content of the item.

Example: `Summary: Introduces young people to the field of archae-`
`ology through stories of discoveries made by children,`
`stories of youngsters who were influential in ancient times,`
`and stories recreating childhood experiences from other`
`times and cultures`

1.7B18. Contents

To be used for a formal or informal listing of the contents of the item.

Example: `Contents: America moves toward war -- Women and the war`
`effort -- Uncle Sam needs you -- Reactions to the call --`
`When Johnny comes marching home`

1.7B19. Numbers borne by the item

To be used to list any important number appearing on the item other than those to be recorded in area 8.

Example: `"Y 2259-2"`

1.7B20. Copy being described, library's holdings, and restrictions on use

To be used for any notes applicable only to the particular copy of the item being described. Also used for local library restrictions on the material being described, or for information of use only to patrons of the local library.

Example: `Color fading on library copy`

1.7B21. "With" notes

To be used for "with" notes.

Kit Problems

Office practice sets and accounting practice sets can be considered kits, as they would fall under the definition of "lab kits." A package containing all the materials (workbooks, charts, quizzes, etc.) that would be used in a year of fifth-grade social studies would be a kit. These kits are designed to be used up by a class.

A set of material (transparencies, activity cards, models, games, etc.) purchased bound together in book form but designed to be taken apart for use could be cataloged as a kit. There should be a note on the bibliographic record for such an item indicating the item was purchased in book form.

Example 106: Immigrant Experience

A brief form of this bibliographic record is included in chapter 2 of this manual as an example of level one cataloging.

This package of media clearly has no dominant component. It contains narrated filmstrips, but also contains a significant amount of other material.

Rules for notes are 1.7B11, 1.7B17.

Some of the kit contents

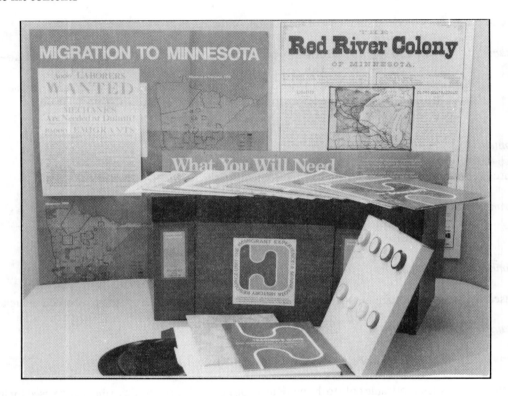

Container

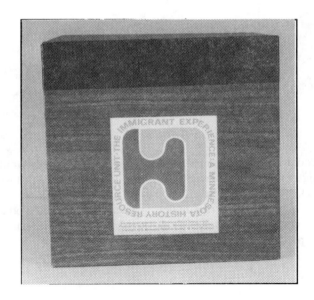

Example 106: Immigrant Experience

From the container label

The Immigrant Experience: A Minnesota History Resource Unit
Produced by the Education Division, Minnesota Historical Society,
© Copyright 1979, Minnesota Historical Society. St. Paul, Minnesota

Container, showing 3 boxes, each with container label

```
F          The Immigrant experience [kit] : a Minnesota
606            history resource unit / produced by the
               Education Division, Minnesota Historical
325.776        Society. -- St. Paul, Minn. : The Society,
               c1979.
                  8 filmstrips, 4 sound discs, 10 biography
               banners, 1 intermediate booklet, 30 identical
               copies of secondary booklet, 1 teacher's guide,
               1 set of resource materials ; in box 34 x 34 x
               34 cm.

                  Resource materials include reproductions of
               tickets, posters, ship manifests, blueprint of
               Ellis Island, maps, census schedules, birth,
               death, and marriage certificates, and time line;
               teacher's guide includes scripts of sound film-
               strips.
                  Summary: Designed to present intermediate and
               secondary students with a historical account of
               the migration and immigration of people to
               Minnesota, with particular emphasis on the
               nineteenth and twentieth centuries.

                  1. Minnesota--Emigration and immigration.  2.
               Minnesota--History--1858-      [1. Immigration
               and emigration. 2. Minnesota--History. 3. United
               States--Immigration and emigration.]  I. Minne-
               sota Historical Society. Education Division.
```

Example 107: World War I

This is an example of an assortment of paper material that is a kit.

The chief source of information is the container. The publisher information is given in a different form in each location it is used, but the form found on the container, the chief source, is used in area 4 of the bibliographic record.

Rules for notes are 1.7B1, 1.7B11, 1.7B18.

An ISBN for the package is given on the guide, and is used in area 8.

Kit cover and some contents

Information on box cover

> # NATIONAL ARCHIVES
> ## and
> ## SirS, Inc., Publishers
> ## P.O. Box 2507, Boca Raton, Florida 33432

Example 107: World War I

```
D          World War I [kit] : the home front. -- Boca Raton,
570            Fl. : National Archives and SirS, [1982?]
.A35           4 posters, 1 chart, 12 reproductions of
           photographs, 2 news sheets, 28 reproductions of
973.913    documents, 1 teacher's guide ; in box 37 x 23 x
           2 cm.

               "A supplemental teaching unit from the
           records of the National Archives"--Teacher's
           guide.
               Teacher's guide includes bibliography, exer-
           cises, worksheets, glossary, time line.
               Contents: America moves toward war -- Women
           and the war effort -- Uncle Sam needs you --
           Reactions to the call -- When Johnny comes
           marching home.
               ISBN 0-89777-015-3.

               1. World War, 1914-1918--United States.  2.
           United States--History--1913-1921.  [1. World
           War, 1914-1918--United States.]  I. Social
           Issues Resources Series, Inc.  II. National
           Archives Trust Fund Board.
```

Example 108: Secrets From the Past

This item could be considered a book with accompanying material, but I see it as a kit. The poster is significant, as is the activity booklet. More notes could be used to bring out the contents of the activity book and of the duplicating masters. There is no box for this; the items came shrink-wrapped together.

Rules for notes are 1.7B6, 1.7B10, 1.7B17, 1.7B18.

Contents of package

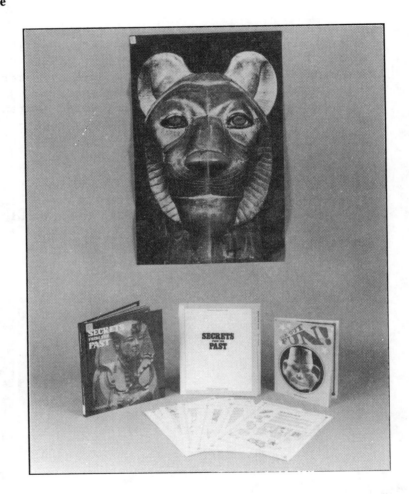

Example 108: Secrets From the Past

```
CC          Secrets from the past [kit]. -- Washington, D.C. :
100              National Geographic Society, c1979.
                 1 book, 1 poster, 2 games, 8 duplicating
930.1        masters, 1 activity booklet.

                 Text of book (104 p.) by Gene S. Stuart.
                 Gameboards on back of poster.
                 Summary: Introduces young people to the field
             of archaeology through stories of discoveries
             made by children, stories of youngsters who were
             influential in ancient times, and stories recre-
             ating childhood experiences from other times and
             cultures.
                 Games: Senet -- Snakes and ladders.

                 1. Archaeology.  [1. Archeology.]  I. Stuart,
             Gene S. Secrets from the past. 1979.  II. Senet.
             1979.  III. Snakes and ladders. 1979.  IV.
             National Geographic Society (U.S.)
```

Example 109: Step by Step Two

This is a kit because it contains more than one type of medium and neither the sound cassettes nor the computer disk is predominant; they must be used together. The sound cassettes do not narrate the disk; they lead the user through lessons contained on the disk. There are two copies of the computer disk.

The system requirement note is from *AACR 2* chapter 9.

Chief source of information for this kit is the container.

Rules for notes are 9.7B1b, 9.7B3, 1.7B6, 1.7B7, 1.7B10, 1.7B17.

Containers and cassettes

Information from title page of workbook

Project Designer:	JOHN VICTOR
Programmers:	STEPHEN CHMIELEWSKI
	KATHLEEN FORTMEIER
Editor:	LYN SANDOW
Graphic Design:	HOWARD PETLACK

Example 109: Step by Step Two

Cassette label

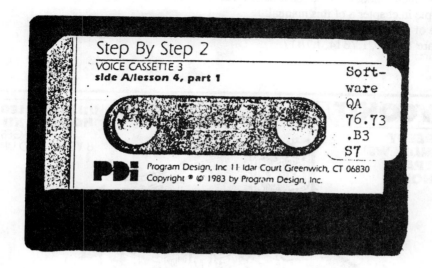

QA
76.73
.B3

005.262
B

Step by step two [kit] : an intermediate course in
    BASIC programming. -- Greenwich, CT : Program
    Design, c1983.
       4 sound cassettes, 2 computer disks, 1
    workbook ; in container 30 x 26 x 5 cm.

      System requirements: Apple II computer.
      Title on cassette: Step by step 2.
      Project designer, John Victor ; programmers,
Stephen Chmielewski, Kathleen Fortmeier.
      Continuation of: New step by step.
      One disk is back-up.
      Summary: Student uses computer while sound
cassettes guide student through each of five
lessons.

      1. BASIC (Computer program language). [1.
Programming languages (Electronic computers)--
Problems, exercises, etc. 2. BASIC (Computer
programming language)--Problems, exercises,
etc.] I. Victor, John. II. Chmielewski,
Stephen. III. Fortmeier, Kathleen. IV. Program
Design, Inc. V. Title: Step by step 2.

Example 110: Speedy Andrew's Repair Shop (kit)

This is a kit from which a model is to be constructed. The finished model, designed to be used with HO scale model railroads, is an example in chapter 8 of this manual.

The chief source of information for this kit is the box cover.

Rules for notes are 1.7B10, 1.7B14, 1.7B17.

Kit box cover

```
TL         Speedy Andrew's repair shop [kit]. -- Moorestown,
153            N.J. : Tyco Industries, c1977 (West Germany :
               Pola)
629.286          76 pieces ; in box 17 x 32 x 4 cm. --
               (Tycokit)

               HO scale.
               "For ages 8 years and up."
               Summary: To be assembled into plastic model
           of automobile repair shop of the 1920's.

               1. Automobiles--Service stations.  [1. Auto-
           mobiles--Service stations--Models.]  I. Tyco
           Industries.
```

Example 111: The Real Mother Goose Piano Book

Here's an item that is somewhat challenging to catalog. It is a book of songs, with music. It has a tiny electronic "piano" with numbered keys; the music is similarly numbered. The piano is glued into the book in such a way that the user can turn the pages of the music and play on the piano. What do we call this? If the piano were ignored, the item would be a songbook, and would be cataloged as a score. So we will catalog it as a songbook with attached "keyboard."

It is a collection of Mother Goose songs, so needs to have a uniform title main entry for Mother Goose.

The note uses rules 5.7B1, 5.7B10.

Book cover

```
M        Mother Goose.
1992        The real Mother Goose piano book [music] /
         illustrated by Blanche Fisher Wright. -- New York :
398.8    Checkerboard Press, [1987?]
            [18] p. of music : col. ill. ; 29 cm. + 13-key
         electronic piano.

            Nine nursery rhymes with piano accompaniment
         numbered for attached electronic keyboard.

            1. Children's songs.  2. Nursery rhymes.  I.
         Wright, Blanche Fisher.  II. Checkerboard Press.
         III. Title.
```

Example 112: The Malinsay Massacre

Here's another cataloging problem. It's made like a scrapbook, fastened together with a red ribbon drawn through three holes. The contents include facsimiles of typed and handwritten letters, telegrams, newspaper clippings, photographs, maps, and other items, together with a typed narrative of the crime. The solution to the crime is contained in a sealed section at the back of the book. From the back cover: "The third murder mystery dossier ... the complete file of the actual evidence including letters, maps, press reports, and photographs." The item is a reprint of a 1938 publication, in the same format.

I decided that, because it is bound as a book and intended to be used in that form, that it should be cataloged as a book.

The notes are based on rule numbers 2.7B1 combined with 2.7B10, 2.7B3, 2.7B10, 1.7B22.

Cover of book

Example 112: The Malinsay Massacre

Book open to show contents

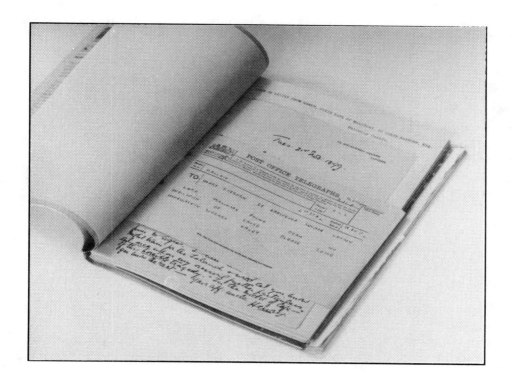

```
PR        Wheatley, Dennis, 1897-1977.
6045         The Malinsay massacre / Dennis Wheatley presents
.H127     a third murder mystery planned by J.G. Links. --
          New York, N.Y. : Rutledge Press, [1982?]
823.912      [105] leaves : ill. ; 27 cm.

             Murder mystery with solution in sealed section
          at back of book.
             Cover title.
             Contains "the complete file of the actual evi-
          dence including letters, maps, press reports, and
          photographs"--Book jacket.
             Reprint. Originally published: London : Rutledge
          Press, 1938.

             1. Detective and mystery stories, English.  II.
          Links, J. G. (Joseph Gluckstein), 1904-  III.
          Title.
```

Appendix A

HOW CATALOGING RULES ARE CHANGED

The procedure for changing cataloging rules is complicated and takes several years.

The Joint Steering Committee for Revision of AACR [JSC] is made up of representatives of the five "authors" of *AACR 2* (the American Library Association, The British Library, The Canadian Committee on Cataloguing, the Library Association, and the Library of Congress) plus the two editors of *AACR 2*. The Canadian Committee on Cataloguing representative is appointed by that Committee which includes representatives from the Canadian Library Association, the National Library of Canada, and the Association pour l'advancement des sciences et des techniques de la documentation. In 1981 a member was added to represent the National Library of Australia and the Library Association of Australia (JSC Press Release, 23 Mar. 1983).

Anyone may request a change to a cataloging rule through the appropriate cataloging committee; for those of us in the United States, the committee is the Committee on Cataloging: Description and Access (CC:DA), Cataloging and Classification Section, Association for Library Collections & Technical Services, American Library Association.

When CC:DA receives a request for change, the request goes on the agenda of the next semiannual meeting. At that meeting, the topic is discussed, and the request may be approved, amended and approved, referred to a task force for further study, sent back to the originator for more information, or rejected. If CC:DA approves the request, it prepares a document for the next annual JSC meeting requesting the change.

When CC:DA requests JSC to make a change, JSC examines the request, and can choose to approve it, revise it, send it back for more information, refer it on to the other countries for further consideration, or reject it. A new or modified proposal will be referred back to the national constituents for their consideration if even one member so requests. Formal votes are seldom taken, because decisions are usually reached by consensus.

For complicated or controversial proposals, the request may go back and forth more than once, with changes negotiated at every step.

Appendix B

AUDIOVISUAL CATALOGING AT THE LIBRARY OF CONGRESS

The Library of Congress attempts to catalog all motion pictures, videorecordings, filmstrips, sets of transparencies, and slide sets released in the United States or Canada which have educational or instructional value. At present, the kits cataloged are limited to those items added to the collections of the Library of Congress. Data needed for the catalog entries are supplied mainly by producers, manufacturers, film libraries, or distributing agencies. The National Audiovisual Center provides information for United States government materials. In most cases cataloging is done from the information thus provided, without actual viewing of the material itself.

Beginning September 1951 cards for motion pictures and filmstrips were printed from data supplied by producing or distributing agencies; from 1951 through April 1957, cards were also printed for virtually all the motion pictures and filmstrips registered for copyright during that period. From May 1957 through 1971, cards in addition to the cards printed from data, were printed for those copyrighted films that were added to the collections of the Library of Congress. Beginning in 1972 cards have been printed almost entirely from data.

The Library of Congress began issuing printed cards for motion pictures and filmstrips in September 1951. The cards printed in 1951 and 1952 were included in the issues of the *Library of Congress Author Catalog* during 1951 and 1952 and are represented in a special quinquennial cumulation of the *Library of Congress Author Catalog, 1948-1952.* The cards which represented films issued after January 1, 1945, were also included in the 1951 and 1952 issues of the *Library of Congress Subject Catalog* and in the quinquennial cumulation of the *Library of Congress Catalog--Books: Subjects, 1950-1954.*

The LC catalogs in book form were reorganized in 1953 and *Films* became a separate catalog that year. In 1954 the title was changed to *Motion Pictures and Filmstrips* to designate more precisely the kinds of material the catalog then embraced. From 1951 to 1972 the entries in this catalog were produced from printed Library of Congress catalog cards. In early 1972 the Library began to include film cataloging records in the MARC data base. Later in the year, sets of transparencies and slides were added to the materials cataloged, and in 1973 the title of the bibliography was changed to *Films and Other Materials for Projection* to reflect the expanded coverage. In 1979 videorecordings and kits were added to the materials cataloged and the title was changed to its present form to once more reflect the expanded coverage (*Audiovisual Materials.* Washington, D.C.: Library of Congress. 1980. Foreword).

The last book catalog in this series was the 1982 annual volume of *Audiovisual Materials.* Since that time the audiovisual cataloging of the Library of Congress has been included in the microfiche publication, *National Union Catalog: Audiovisual Materials.* In 1984 this publication cumulated the retrospective records of the entire LC MARC Films file--all records cataloged since 1972. It provides access by title, corporate and personal name, subject, and series title to over 65,000 titles.

Because the Library of Congress cataloged most audiovisual material from data sheets, we do find some LC bibliographic records that have incorrect titles or other information. Sometimes this happened because the producer changed the title or information in question after the data sheet was submitted; sometimes it was because the person filling in the data sheet for the producer was unaware of the requirements of cataloging. Because the catalogers at the Library of Congress usually did not have the physical item to examine, they could not make corrections to the data.

Many of us depended on Library of Congress cataloging of audiovisual materials and music before the bibliographic utilities permitted input of bibliographic records for these materials. We learned how to catalog by studying their examples. We appreciate the rule interpretations they provided, as these LCRI's, developed for the guidance of Library of Congress catalogers, served as guidance for all of us and aided in the standardization of cataloging of audiovisual materials.

As this third edition is written, it has been announced the data sheet program will be discontinued and the Audiovisual Section disbanded.

Appendix C

BIBLIOGRAPHIC ACCESS TO NON-PRINT MATERIALS: A CHRONOLOGY

Edited by
Suzanne Massoneau

Expanded by
Nancy B. Olson

(Originally published as an appendix to *Problems In Bibliographic Access To Non-print Materials*, Project Media Base, final report (1979). Reprinted with the permission of the National Commission on Libraries and Information Science.)

The chronology which follows highlights events in the development of bibliographic and networking activities that are pertinent to the control of audiovisual materials. Any chronology of a topic is necessarily the skeleton of its history, and a disjointed one at that. Due to the limitations of the format it is difficult to show the interaction of events to produce a particular result, and it is equally difficult to single out or emphasize the most important events. Further, when several paths lead to a climax of some sort, it is hard to identify the events belonging to the particular paths. There is an almost inevitable result that trends become tangled and conclusions which should be obvious become obscured. In addition to these problems, there is the risk that some obscure event may be given attention, while another event of great importance is omitted.

This chronology could have begun with prehistoric cave paintings, traced the development of the alphabet, the invention of printing, the background of modern cataloging theory, and the invention of computers and the accessory technology. However, even a cursory search of the most obvious events and publications revealed a volume of material that would be impractical to attempt to cover. Suggestions were sought from the authors and the members of the Task Advisory Committee, state-of-the-art studies were reviewed, and from these sources the most frequently mentioned or apparently significant events were selected. In the interest of primary relevance, however, the remote background events were excluded and only those seeming to have direct or eventual bearing on the development of a national network system for audiovisual materials were included.

Despite the attempt to include only the most significant events, the reason for inclusion of some may seem obscure. Usually such inclusions were necessary as background and support for later events of unquestioned importance. Brief explanatory comments were added to some entries in order to either justify their inclusion or clarify their significance. In some cases the exact beginning dates were difficult to determine, therefore errors of one or two years are possible.

The selection of publications to be included from extensive bibliographies was particularly difficult and may have resulted in serious omissions. Numerous locally produced catalog codes and commercially supported selection aids were omitted intentionally. For those publications which have been through several editions and revisions, no attempt was made to include every issue, and while works are not cited in standard bibliographic form, sufficient information was included to provide accurate identification. Sources of information and quotations are not documented, but whenever possible statements were taken from committee reports and/or the publication being cited (From Introduction to 1979 chronology).

The chronology has been expanded and brought up to date. Publications about audiovisual material and about cataloging audiovisual material have been included, as have developments in *AACR 2* to include all types of material.

Frequently Used Abbreviations and Acronyms

AACR	*Anglo-American Cataloging Rules*
AACR 2	*Anglo-American Cataloguing Rules*, second edition
AECT	Association for Educational Communications and Technology
ALA	American Library Association
CLR	Council on Library Resources
ISBD	International Standard Bibliographic Description
ISBD(NBM)	International Standard Bibliographic Description: Non-Book Materials
LC	Library of Congress
MARBI	ALA Committee on Representation in Machine-Readable Form of Bibliographic Information
MARC	Machine-readable cataloging
NELINET	New England Library Network
NICEM	National Information Center for Educational Media
OCLC	OCLC Online Computer Library Center, Inc.
OLAC	Online Audiovisual Catalogers, Inc. (formerly OnLine Audiovisual Catalogers)
USOE	United States Office of Education.

1901   Library of Congress initiated sale of catalog cards for books, thus promoting the distribution of standardized bibliographic information.

1918   American Library Association Education Committee adopted a committee report of the North Central Association of Secondary Schools and Colleges specifying provision for lantern slides, Victrola records, etc., in high school libraries.

1923   National Education Association of the United States established the Department of Visual Instruction, predecessor of its Department of Audiovisual Instruction, later the Association for Educational Communications and Technology.

1924   ALA Committee on Relationships Between Libraries and Moving Pictures was established by the ALA Council. This was the first of a long succession of ALA committees to concern itself with various aspects of access, use, distribution, production, and evaluation of audiovisual media. Films remained the principal focus for many years.

1934   ALA Visual Methods Committee recommended to the ALA Committee on National Planning that regional centers for visual aids be established and attached to existing libraries. The Committee on National Planning did not follow this recommendation, but did conclude that "libraries should assume responsibility for the preservation and use of visual materials and mechanical substitutes for the printed page."

1936   Publication of *Educational Film Catalog* by the H.W. Wilson Company began, continuing to 1962. Title changed to *Educational Film Guide* in 1945.

1940   Joint Committee on Educational Films and Libraries was formed with representatives from the American Film Center, Association of School Film Librarians, Motion Picture Project of the American Council on Education, and ALA.

1940   ALA Visual Methods Committee and Library Radio Broadcasting Committee merged to form the ALA Audiovisual Committee. One function was "to further the establishment of national and regional clearinghouses for such materials."

1943   Educational Film Library Association was formed as a clearinghouse for information about 16mm film utilization, selection, evaluation, production, and distribution.

1945   LC organized a Motion Picture Project which developed a questionnaire to determine the bibliographic control needs of the producers and users of films.

1946   U.S. Copyright Office drafted rules for cataloging films which were applied to motion pictures and filmstrips registered for copyright. The result was the *Catalog of Copyright Entries: Motion Pictures and Filmstrips.*

1948   LC published the *Final Report on the Rules for Descriptive Cataloging in the Library of Congress*, prepared by the ALA Committee on Descriptive Cataloging. It concluded that rather than "attempting to draw up one body of rules which can be applied to all types of materials ... simplified rules for special materials should be included in the code."

1949   LC Descriptive Cataloging Division published *Rules for Descriptive Cataloging in the Library of Congress.* Rules for special materials, except maps, were not included as they had not yet been developed. Rules completed in following years were issued as supplements to this publication.

1950   ALA's *Booklist* began inclusion of films and filmstrips with full bibliographic information. This was subsequently suspended, then revived as interest increased. During 1969 and 1970 full coverage of audiovisual forms was permanently established.

1951   LC Film Cataloging Committee drafted cataloging rules for motion pictures and filmstrips based on those rules developed by the Copyright Office in 1946.

1951   Eastman House and the Film Council of America sponsored an International Film Cataloging Conference. LC was urged to issue catalog cards for new films being registered for copyright and to publish the rules used by the Copyright Office. Film companies agreed to send information about their films to the Library on data sheets in order to speed up cataloging.

1951   LC began issuing printed catalog cards for motion pictures and filmstrips (later expanded to include other materials for projection). From 1951 through April 1957, cards were printed for materials registered for copyright; thereafter only materials added to the collection or for which data forms were received from producing or distribution agencies were included.

1952-65   LC published successive editions of supplements to its *Rules for Descriptive Cataloging in the Library of Congress* under the following subtitles: *Motion Pictures and Filmstrips, Phonorecords, Pictures, Designs and Other Two-Dimensional Representations.*

1953   UNESCO sponsored meetings in the United Kingdom and Washington, D.C., to promote international standards for film cataloging. The conference in Washington recommended that the rules of LC and the British Film Institute form the basis for world-wide standards for descriptive cataloging. The UNESCO Secretariat was to study the recommendations and attempt to develop internationally acceptable standards.

1953   LC began issuing printed catalog cards for phonorecords.

1953   *Library of Congress Author Catalog, 1948-52* included music and phonorecords, and data for motion pictures and filmstrips cataloged in 1951-52 were included in a separate volume. Works cataloged since 1952 have been included in separate publications.

1953   Cards for music and recordings published semiannually in *Library of Congress Catalogs: Music and Phonorecords.*

1954   *The Library of Congress Catalogs: Films* becomes *The Library of Congress Catalogs: Motion Pictures and Filmstrips.* Both published quarterly.

1955   Eunice Keen issued a revised edition of her *Manual for Use in the Cataloging and Classification of Audio-Visual Materials for a High School Library*, updating the preliminary edition of 1949. This early attempt to systematize cataloging of audiovisual materials was begun under the guidance of Jesse Shera.

1956   Council on Library Resources was founded "to aid in the solution of library problems; to conduct research in, develop and demonstrate new techniques and methods and to disseminate through any means the results therof." Since its origin CLR has provided full or partial funding for many projects relating to access to library materials, with emphasis on computer applications and cooperative efforts.

1957   ALA Special Committee on the Bibliographic Control of Audiovisual Materials reported the results of its survey, emphasizing the need for standardized cataloging rules, better coverage by LC cataloging, better subject headings for audiovisual materials, and research on how catalog users approach audiovisual materials in the catalog. One respondent suggested that "it would be helpful if the producer put the information needed for cataloging on the label on the film container."

1958   ALA published *Code for Cataloging Music and Phonorecords*, which was prepared by the Joint Committee on Music Cataloging of the Music Library Association and the ALA Division of Cataloging and Classification.

1959   Margaret I. Rufsvold and Carolyn Guss conducted a study "to determine a feasible method of establishing bibliographic control of education audiovisual materials and their educational utility." A national catalog of audiovisual materials was proposed, resulting in the *Educational Media Index* in 1964.

1960   Educational Media Council was formed in recognition of the need for coordinated efforts among professional, governmental, and industrial organizations in the educational media field.

1961   Cataloging experts meeting at the International Conference on Cataloging Principles agreed on a "Statement of Principle," upon which the first and second editions of the Anglo-American Cataloging Rules were based. The word "book" in the statement was interpreted to "include other library materials having similar characteristics."

1962   University of Southern California began an automated cataloging project using a computer to generate catalogs for educational film libraries. This led to development of the National Information Center for Educational Media.

1963   Project MAC (Machine-Aided Cognition, Man and Computer, Multiple-Access Computers) was organized at Massachusetts Institute of Technology for the development of computer systems for direct and economical access through the Compatible Time-Sharing System. The essential idea was the use of the computer as a public utility, capable of benefiting a wide range of consumers.

1963   LC published *Automation and the Library of Congress*, a survey sponsored by CLR. It concluded that "automation of bibliographic processing, catalog searching, and document retrieval is technically feasible in large research libraries," and recommended funding "devoted to securing system specifications for the automation of the internal operations of the Library of Congress and the functions it performs for other libraries."

1964   Educational Media Council's *Educational Media Index* was published by McGraw-Hill. This fourteen volume work was planned as a complete resource guide for all media, but was not continued after the first edition.

1964-67   Recognition of need for cooperation and for computer-based regional technical processes by New England state university librarians led to CLR funding of a pilot project under the sponsorship of the New England Board of Higher Education, and the formation of the New England Library Information Network. Establishment of other regional networks throughout the country followed.

1965   CLR published *The Recording of Library of Congress Bibliographic Data in Machine Form*, by Lawrence F. Buckland, a study of the feasibility of converting bibliographic data on LC cards to machine-readable form for the purpose of printing bibliographic products by computer, and distribution of bibliographic data to other libraries.

1966-68   The MARC Pilot Project was initiated at LC. Working from the preliminary findings of the Buckland report, it was designed to demonstrate the feasibility and utility of making LC cataloging data available to other libraries in machine-readable form. CLR provided funding.

1966   NICEM began to build a comprehensive data base of bibliographic information for nonprint materials.

1967   NICEM and LC began cooperative use of data sheets obtained from producers, media centers, and others to catalog motion pictures and filmstrips.

1967   Work began at Stanford University on the development of an on-line interactive technical services support system using a time-sharing computer. Subsequently the system became operational as BALOTS (Bibliographic Automation of Large Operations using a Time-sharing System), now RLIN.

1967   National Technical Information Service issued *The Identification of Data Elements in Bibliographic Records*, by Ann T. Curran, et al. The purpose was to supply background information to the Subcommittee on Machine Input Records (SC-2) of the American National Standards Institute Committee Z-39, which would help them "in determining which data elements should be tagged (identified) in machine readable records." This was to lead to development of standards for the identification, representation, and recording of information by the Subcommittee.

1967   Ohio College Library Center (OCLC) was chartered by the State of Ohio and eventually developed into an interactive on-line bibliographic network utilizing MARC records from LC and user input. In 1977 the name was changed to OCLC, Inc., with changes in governance to include all users of the system. The name was later changed to OCLC Online Computer Library Center, Inc.

1967   ALA published the *Anglo-American Cataloging Rules*, North American Text, with Part III devoted to the specific rules for cataloging the principal forms of audiovisual materials. General rules for books and book-like materials were extended to audiovisual materials, unless "specifically contravened or modified."

1968   LC began publishing guides (updated by addenda and periodically revised) called *MARC Formats* for *Books, Maps, Music, Serials, Manuscripts*, and *Films*. The latter covered motion pictures, filmstrips, and other pictorial media intended for projection.

1968   Association of College and Research Libraries Audiovisual Committee issued *Guidelines for Audiovisual Services in Academic Libraries*.

1968   Audio-Visual Associates established MEDIAFILE, which is a data base of records in machine-readable form utilized for the publication of several media indexes, including *The International Index to Multi-Media Information*. On-line searching of the data base is possible.

1968   *Standards for Cataloging, Coding, and Scheduling Educational Media* published by Department of Audiovisual Instruction, National Educational Association (DAVI). This was the first edition of the publication that later became the AECT *Standards*.

1969   National Audiovisual Center was created to make audiovisual materials produced by the United States government available for public use and to serve as the central clearinghouse for all federal audiovisual materials.

1969   RECON (Retrospective Conversion) Pilot Project was initiated at LC to study the feasibility of conversion of LC bibliographic records to machine-readable form. Development and implementation of the format recognition process was an important achievement of the Project. Retrospective conversion of LC bibliographic records did not result.

1969   Project Intrex (Information Transfer Experiments) at Massachusetts Institute of Technology was developed to apply the technology for on-line interactive bibliographic systems and resource sharing through networking.

1969-70   A three-week institute sponsored by USOE held on Systems and Standards for the Bibliographic Control of Media. Two additional meetings held prior to ALA in Chicago and AECT in Detroit in 1970. Papers of the Conferences were edited by Pearce Grove and Evelyn Clement, and published by ALA in 1972 under the title *Bibliographic Control of Nonprint Media*.

1970   National Commission on Libraries and Information Science (NCLIS) was established by the U.S. Congress to advise the Congress and the President on national library policy. It was to "give first priority in its planning effort to providing new and improved services that will be helpful to all libraries in the country and their users, at every level of society."

1970   ALA and USOE sponsored the Conference on Interlibrary Communications and Information Networks to examine every aspect of library networking and make recommendations for a plan of action and future implementation. The Conference called on NCLIS to "devise as a matter of priority a comprehensive plan to facilitate the coordinated development of the nation's libraries, information centers, and other knowledge resources." Proceedings were published by ALA in 1971.

1970   Federal Communications Commission took a position regarding common carrier competition that permitted development of customized private line services and the capacity to interconnect to form a computer-based national network.

1970   R.R. Bowker began publishing significant guides and resource indexes in the audiovisual field, including *Audiovisual Market Place, Educational Media Year Book*, and the *Consortium of University Centers-Bowker Educational Film Locator*. Bowker's Bibliographic Information Publishing System (BIPS) was developed to form the basis for their computer-based publishing.

1970   *Developing Multi-Media Libraries*, by Warren B. Hicks and Alma M. Tillin, published by Bowker.

1970   Canadian Library Association published *Non-Book Materials, the Organization of Integrated Collections*, preliminary ed., by Jean Riddle, Shirley Lewis, and Janet Madconald. This preliminary edition was recommended by the Canadian Library Association Council and the ALA/RTSD/CCS Executive Committee "as an interim guide for the cataloguing of nonbook materials with the proviso that a permanent ALA/CLA committee be established to work on any necessary revision for the final edition and its supplements". In summer 1972 NBM was formally adopted by the Australian School Library Association "for use in all schools throughout Australia."

1971   *Standards for Cataloging Nonprint Materials*, revised edition, by the Cataloging Committee of AECT (William J. Quinly, Katharine Clugston, Alma Tillin, Ford Lemler, Robert E. Hayes, and Carolyn I. Whitenack), published by AECT. This was revised from the 1968 DAVI Standards.

1971   American National Standards Institute published the *American National Standard Format for Bibliographic Information Interchange on Magnetic Tape* (ANSI Z39.2) which described "a generalized structure which can be used to transmit, between systems, records describing all forms of materials capable of bibliographic descriptions as well as related records such as authority records for authors and subject headings."

1971   *Non-book Materials: Their Bibliographic Control, a Proposed Computer System for Cataloguing of Audiovisual Materials in the United Kingdom*, by Leslie A. Gilbert and Jan W. Wright was published by the National Council for Educational Technology (U.K.).

1971   Joint Advisory Committee on Non-Book Materials was established to advise the authors of *Nonbook Materials: The Organization of Integrated Collections* on the content and format of the first edition. Representatives were from ALA, CLA, AECT, Educational Media Association of Canada, and Canadian Association of Music Librarians. The function of the Committee was subsequently broadened to provide a forum for discussion on nonprint isues on the international level. It continues to advise the authors on revisions of the above-mentioned book.

1971   Consortium of University Film Centers (CUFC), a cooperative organization of universities maintaining 16mm film rental libraries, was established. The Data Bank Committee worked toward raising the standards and systematizing the development and utilization of film cataloging information, resulting in the publication of the *Consortium of University Film Centers-Bowker Educational Film Locator* in 1977.

1972   *Standards for Cataloging Nonprint Materials*, third edition, by the Information Science Committee of AECT (William J. Quinly, Katharine Clugston, Alma Tillin, Ford Lemler, and Robert E. Hayes), published by Association for Educational Communications and Technology.

1972   *Organizing Nonprint Materials, A Guide for Librarians,* by Jay E. Daily, published by Dekker.

1972   Following three years of computer-based cataloging services through Inforonics (based on MARC tapes), and a six-month test project at Dartmouth College, NELINET signed an agreement for on-line cataloging through OCLC. Other regional networks subsequently contracted for services from OCLC.

1972   LC began inputting records for motion pictures, filmstrips, slide sets, and sets of transparencies in the MARC system. LC began distribution of machine-readable catalog records for these materials through its MARC Distribution Service. MARC records were used in preparing the first computer-produced catalog in LC entitled *Films and Other Materials for Projection*.

1973   Katharine Clugston retired as head of the Audiovisual Section at LC and was succeeded by Vivian Schrader.

1973   Canadian Library Association published *Nonbook Materials: the Organization of Integrated Collections*, 1st ed., by Jean Riddle Weihs, Shirley Lewis, and Janet MacDonald. This work was particularly designed to facilitate the development of "omnimedia" catalogs.

1973   National Council for Educational Technology and Library Association published *Non-book Materials Cataloguing Rules*, prepared by the Library Association's Media Cataloguing Rules Committee.

1973   *Library of Congress Catalogs: Music and Phonorecords* expanded to include reports from other libraries. Title becomes *Library of Congress Catalogs: Music, Books on Music, and Sound Recordings*. Published semiannually.

1973   *Library of Congress Catalogs: Motion Pictures and Filmstrips* became *Library of Congress Catalogs: Films and Other Materials for Projection*. Both published quarterly.

1974   "Nonprint Media Guidelines," developed by a task force funded by Baker & Taylor Company, were published in *Southeastern Librarian* under the title "Nonprint Media Cataloging, Classification, and Designation: Recommended Standards." Media designations and codes were adopted with slight modifications in AECT's *Standards for Cataloging Nonprint Materials* (1976).

1974   Cooperative MARC (COMARC) pilot project was initiated to test the feasibility of augmenting LC's monograph MARC output with machine-readable records created by other libraries from printed LC cataloging copy. While the desirability of including non-print media records in the program was recognized, the project was terminated before this could become reality.

1974   Council for Computerized Library Networks (CCLN) was established to coordinate and determine network policy through which national and international computerized library networks could be built and administered.

1974   Joint Steering Committee for the Revision of AACR was formed to guide revision of the Rules and coordinate ideas of the committees representing the authors. Expansion and improvement of the rules for audiovisual media were among the goals of the revision.

1974   International Federation of Library Associations published the *International Standard Bibliographic Description for Monographic Publications (ISBD(M))*. This was followed by preparation of a general ISBD and ISBDs for nonbook materials, maps, and serials.

1974   ALA published a revision of *AACR* chapter 6, *Separately Published Monographs* in order to "incorporate the provisions of the *International Standard Bibliographic Description (Monographs)* into the text in regular cataloging rule form."

1975   *Nonprint Media in Academic Libraries*, edited by Pearce S. Grove, published by ALA as no. 34 in the *ACRL Publications in Librarianship.*

1975   ALA published a revision of *AACR* chapter 12, *Audiovisual Media and Special Instructional Materials*, improving the rules for motion pictures and filmstrips, adding rules for media not previously covered, and incorporating rules for slides and transparencies from chapter 15. Lacking a specific ISBD for audiovisual media, the authors "patterned the rules whenever possible after the standard for monographs."

1975   LC issued Addendum Number 5 to *Films: A MARC Format*, expanding coverage for the other audiovisual media incorporated in the revision of *AACR* chapter 12.

1975   NCLIS issued *Toward a National Program for Library and Information Services: Goals for Action* mandating equal opportunity of access to our knowledge resources, including audio and visual materials.

1975   ALA Audiovisual Committee, descendent of the ALA Committee on Relationships Between Libraries and Motion Pictures (1924) voted to abolish itself as audiovisual interests had become dispersed among numerous ALA committees and a central coordinating unit was no longer workable.

1975   Planning began to extend BALOTS into a multi-library network, and all modules planned for Stanford University became operational.

1975   UNESCO issued a report by C.P. Ravilious of his worldwide survey of bibliographic treatment of audiovisual materials: *A Survey of Existing Systems and Current Proposals for the Cataloguing and Description of Nonbook Materials Collected by Libraries.*

1976   AECT published *Standards for Cataloging Nonprint Materials*, 4th ed., by Alma Tillin and William Quinly.

1976   NCLIS and AECT sponsored PROJECT: MEDIA BASE "to develop goals, objectives and functional specifications for the bibliographic control of non-print media."

1976   ALA published a revision of *AACR* chapter 14, *Sound Recordings*. These rules did not include any ISBD provisions.

1976   *Films Format: A Description of Fixed Field, Variable Fields, Indicators and Subfield Codes* was issued by OCLC, and inputting of materials covered by *AACR* chapter 12 became possible.

1976   Office of the Special Assistant for Network Development was established at LC (name changed to Network Development Office in 1977) "to insure that the Library of Congress meet its responsibilities in regard to library bibliographic networking and to coordinate the planning activities leading toward the development of the library bibliographic component of the National Library and Information Service Network, in cooperation with other network-related organizations."

1976   Network Advisory Group was established by LC "to explore the requirements and the possibilities for increased cooperation among the components of the evolving system." The Group was also to advise the Librarian of Congress on LC's role in national networking. The name of the Group was changed to Library of Congress Network Advisory Committee in 1977.

1976   AVLINE (Audio Visuals On-Line), a data base maintained by the National Library of Medicine containing references to audiovisual instructional materials in the health sciences, became operational.

1976   International Standard Book Number (ISBN) International Panel agreed at the request of AECT and the Consortium of University Film Centers that national agencies were authorized to supply numbers for nonbook materials and agreed to inform the International Organisation for Standardization of these applications to nonbook materials.

1976   LC implemented the rules in *AACR Chapter 12 Revised*, for those nonprint materials within the scope of its cataloging program.

1976   ERIC Clearinghouse on Information Resources published *Nonprint Media Information Networking: Status and Potentials*, the papers from a conference, edited by James W. Brown. Conference participants considered the feasibility and desirability of developing a system "capable of obtaining, storing, and selectively retrieving dependable qualitative (as well as technical or purely descriptive) data about specific nonprint media items."

1976   NICEM and the Library of Congress revised data sheets used in cooperative cataloging to reflect revisions in rules in *AACR* chapter 12.

1976   NCLIS and the Institute for Computer Sciences and Technology of the National Bureau of Standards established and operated a task group to address the general problem of providing for the nationwide automated interchange of information among existing and planned library and information science networks.

1977   Library of Congress issued the preliminary edition of *Toward a National Library and Information Service Network: The Library Bibliographic Component*, prepared by the Library of Congress Network Advisory Group.

1977   Network Technical Architecture Group was created, upon recommendation of the Network Advisory Group (LC), to design a national library network for bidirectional interlinking of bibliographic utilities for information sharing.

1977   Quarterly issues of the National Library of Medicine's *Current Catalog* began inclusion of items cataloged for the AVLINE data base, consisting of three parts: name section, subject section, and procurement section. Annual cumulations will be published separately from the *Current Catalog*.

1977   LC Network Advisory Committee (replacing the Network Advisory Group) was "established by the Librarian of Congress to advise him on various issues concerning the Library's role in the evolving national library and information service network proposed by the National Commission on Libraries and Information science in its program document."

1977   Executive Board of the Resources and Technical Services Division of ALA approved the publication of the second edition of *AACR*. This edition includes detailed rules for the cataloging of nonprint materials, and will be implemented by LC in 1980. It incorporates the internationally approved ISBDs.

1977   National Film Board of Canada published *A Plan for an Information/Distribution System for Canadian Audiovisual Products*, describing a comprehensive computer-based system to encourage and facilitate use of audiovisual materials.

1977   *ISBD(NBM): International Standard Bibliographic Description for Non-Book Materials* published by IFLA. A working group was recommended in 1973, was constituted in 1975, and prepared four drafts during 1976.

1977   *Managing Multimedia Libraries*, by Warren B. Hicks and Alma M. Tillin, published by Bowker.

1978   *A Style Manual for Citing Microform and Nonprint Media*, by Eugene B. Fleischer, published by ALA.

1978   *Anglo-American Cataloguing Rules*, second edition, published. Includes Chapter 6 "Sound Recordings," Chapter 7 "Motion Pictures and Videorecordings," Chapter 8 "Graphic Materials," Chapter 9 "Machine-Readable Data Files," and Chapter 10 "Three-Dimensional Artefacts and Realia." To be implemented at LC January 1, 1980.

1979   *Library of Congress Catalogs: Films and Other Materials for Projection* became *Library of Congress Catalogs: Audiovisual Materials* as videorecordings and kits were added to the materials cataloged. Both catalogs published quarterly.

1979   *Problems in Bibliographic Access to Non-Print Materials: Project Media Base: Final Report*, published by National Commission on Libraries and Information Science. This report recommended the use of established standards, such as the *Anglo-American Cataloguing Rules* and the MARC communications format, be promoted in the audiovisual community.

1979   The White House Conference on Library and Information Services was held, following a series of 58 state, territorial, and topical conferences. Audiovisual materials were considered to be normal library materials in these discussions.

1979   *Nonbook Materials, the Organization of Integrated Collections*, second edition, by Jean Weihs with Shirley Lewis and Janet Macdonald, published by Canadian Library Association.

1980   Vivian Schrader retires as head of the Audiovisual Section at LC.

1980   OnLine Audiovisual Catalogers organized in New York City during ALA. Open to all AV catalogers. Quarterly newsletter begins publication in 1981.

1980   *Cataloguing Audiovisual Materials: A Manual Based on the Anglo-American Cataloguing Rules II*, by Eugene Fleischer and Helen Goodman, published by Neal-Schuman.

1980   Nancy B. Olson, AV cataloger, wins Esther J. Piercy Award.

1981   *AACR 2* implemented at LC on January 1, after delay of one year.

1981   *Cataloging of Audiovisual Materials, A Manual Based on AACR 2*, by Nancy B. Olson, published by Minnesota Scholarly Press. Includes appendix with bibliographic records coded and tagged for OCLC input.

1981   Richard Thaxter appointed head of the Audiovisual Section at LC.

1981   Special Material Cataloging Division formed at LC from the former Audiovisual, Manuscript, and Music Sections of the Descriptive Cataloging Division. The rare book catalogers are also in the new division, whose chief is David A. Smith.

1981   *A Manual of AACR 2 Examples for Motion Pictures and Videorecordings*, by Jean Aichele and Nancy B. Olson, published for the Minnesota AACR 2 Trainers by Soldier Creek Press.

1981   *A Manual of AACR 2 Examples for Music and Sound Recordings of Music*, by Wesley Simonton, Nancy B. Olson, Phillip Mannie, published for the Minnesota AACR 2 Trainers by Soldier Creek Press.

1982   Nancy B. Olson, AV cataloger at Mankato State University, appointed Visiting Distinguished Scholar at OCLC to study problems of AV cataloging. She organizes a series of meetings on problems of cataloging microcomputer software.

1982   MARC format for machine-readable data files approved by MARBI and LC; to be implemented by OCLC as soon as published by LC, permitting cataloging of microcomputer software on OCLC.

1982   *Nonprint Cataloging for Multimedia Collections, A Guide Based on AACR 2*, by JoAnn V. Rogers, published by Libraries Unlimited.

1982   *Cataloging Machine-Readable Data Files: An Interpretive Manual*, by Sue A. Dodd, published by ALA.

1982   *Library of Congresss Catalogs: Audiovisual Materials* ceases; to be replaced in 1983 by microfiche publication *National Union Catalog: Audiovisual Materials*, to be published quarterly.

1982   *Graphic Materials: Rules for Describing Original Items and Historical Collections*, compiled by Elisabeth W. Betz, published by LC.

1983-1988 Problems of cataloging microcomputer software studied by various people, committees, and task forces in the United States, Canada, Australia, and Great Britain. These discussions result in the publication of interim *Guidelines* (1984), a draft revision of AACR 2 chapter 9 (1987), and a revised chapter 9 in the 1988 revision of AACR 2.

1983   Carolyn O. Frost produces *Cataloging Nonbook Materials: Problems in Theory and Practice*, published by Libraries Unlimited. Compares *AACR 2* (1978) and *Nonbook Materials* (1979).

1983   *A Manual of AACR 2 Examples for Microcomputer Software and Videogames*, by Nancy B. Olson, published for the Minnesota AACR 2 Trainers by Soldier Creek Press.

1984   Resources and Technical Services Division of ALA sponsors series of Regional Institutes on Nonbook Materials, to be held 1984-1986 in six locations.

1984   *Accessible Storage of Nonbook Materials*, by Jean Weihs, illustrated by Cameron Riddle, published by Oryx Press.

1984   *Guidelines for Using AACR 2 Chapter 9 for Cataloging Microcomputer Software* published by ALA as a result of intensive work by ALA Task Force on the Descriptive Cataloging of Microcomputer Software.

1984   *Access to Media: A Guide to Integrating and Computerizing Catalogs*, by Sheila S. Intner, published by Neal-Schuman Publishers.

1984   LC publishes *Archival Moving Image Materials: A Cataloging Manual*, compiled by Wendy White-Hensen.

1984-1989 Jean Weihs, Canadian AV cataloger, serves as chair of JSC.

1985   The second edition of Nancy B. Olson's *Cataloging of Audiovisual Materials* is published by Minnesota Scholarly Press.

1985   ALA publishes *Cataloging Microcomputer Files* by Sue A. Dodd and Ann M. Sandberg-Fox.

1986   "Standards for College Libraries, 1986," approved by ACRL, includes statement that the collections "shall comprise all types of recorded information, including ... audiovisual materials, sound recordings, materials used with computers, graphics, and three-dimensional materials."

1986   Jean Weihs receives Margaret Mann Citation from ALA "in recognition of her pioneering efforts to standardize the bibliographic control of nonbook materials and to promote the philosophy of integrated collections."

1986   *Cataloging Special Materials: Critiques and Innovations*, edited by Sanford Berman, published by Oryx Press.

1986   *Guidelines on Subject Access to Microcomputer Software* published by ALA.

1986   *Descriptive Terms for Graphic Materials*, compiled and edited by Helena Zinkham and Elisabeth Betz Parker, published by LC.

1987   Sheila Intner and Richard Smiraglia edit *Policy and Practice in Bibliographic Control of Nonbook Media*, published by ALA, based on the RTSD regional institutes of 1984-1986.

1987   *Nonbook Media: Collection Management and User Services*, published by ALA.

1987   The draft revision of *AACR 2* chapter 9, *Computer Files*, published by ALA after extensive series of meetings and discussion.

1987   *LC Thesaurus for Graphic Materials: Topical Terms for Subject Access*, compiled by Elisabeth Betz Parker, published by LC.

1988   *Anglo-American Cataloguing Rules*, second edition, 1988 revision, published. Includes extensive revison of chapter 9 (Computer Files), and reconciles a number of inconsistencies among the audiovisual chapters.

1988   *Music Subject Headings*, compiled from LCSH by Perry Bratcher and Jennifer Smith, published by Soldier Creek Press.

1988   *Cataloging Sound Recordings, A Manual with Examples*, by Deanne Holzberlein, published by Haworth Press.

1988   OCLC publishes Nancy B. Olson's *Audiovisual Material Glossary*.

1988-1990 Verna Urbanski appointed chair of CC:DA, the first AV cataloger to serve in that position.

1988   *Cataloging Microcomputer Software*, by Nancy B. Olson, published by Libraries Unlimited. Includes history of the development of cataloging rules for this material, 100 examples.

1988   *Moving Image Materials: Genre Terms*, compiled by Martha M. Yee, published by LC. Updates are published in the *Cataloging Service Bulletin*.

1989   *Nonbook Materials: The Organization of Integrated Collections*, third edition, by Jean Weihs with assistance from Shirley Lewis, published by Canadian Library Association.

1989   Carolyn O. Frost prepares *Media Access and Organization: A Cataloging and Reference Sources Guide for Nonbook Materials*, published by Libraries Unlimited. An interesting combination of information, with annotated listings of useful sources.

1990   Announcement made at OLAC conference that the Audiovisual Section is to be disbanded at Library of Congress in 1991.

1990   *Guidelines on Subject Access to Individual Works of Fiction, Drama, Etc.* published by ALA.

1990-1991 Discussions at OLAC meetings about cataloging interactive media lead to invitational meeting at ALA in Atlanta on this topic. Discussions continue in OLAC meetings and newsletter and at various ALA meetings.

INDEX

Examples have been indexed only in those cases where a particular aspect of cataloging has been discussed in the introduction to the example.